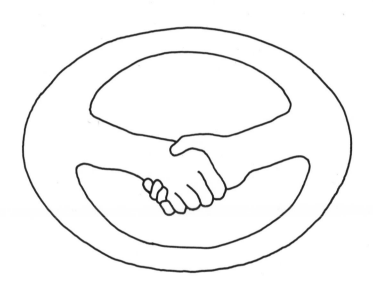

WE OWN IT

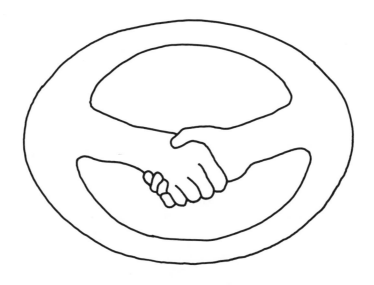

Starting & Managing
Coops
Collectives
& Employee-Owned
Ventures

Peter Jan Honingsberg

Bernard Kamoroff

& Jim Beatty

Bell Springs Publishing, Laytonville, California

Published by
Bell Springs Publishing
P.O. Box 640
Laytonville, California 95454

FIRST EDITION

May, 1982
Printed in the United States of America
Library of Congress Catalog Number 82-70528
ISBN 0-917510-02-X (cloth)
0-917510-03-8 (paper)

An Important Note. Please Read.

We have done our best to give you useful and accurate information about cooperatives, corporations, partnerships and other legal business structures and about state and federal tax laws. But please be aware that laws and procedures are constantly changing and are subject to differing interpretations. Cooperative law in particular is less well defined than conventional business law and less understood even by government agencies and the courts.

You have the responsibility to check all information you read in *We Own It* before relying on it. The information given is not intended to substitute for legal advice and cannot be considered as making it unnecessary to obtain such advice. In all situations involving federal, state or local law, obtain specific information from the appropriate government agency or from a competent person.

Neither Bell Springs Publishing nor the authors make any guarantees concerning the information in this book or the use to which it is put.

Bell Springs Publishing is committed to keeping *We Own It* up to date. If this is an older edition of the book, do not rely on the information without checking it in a newer edition.

TABLE OF CONTENTS

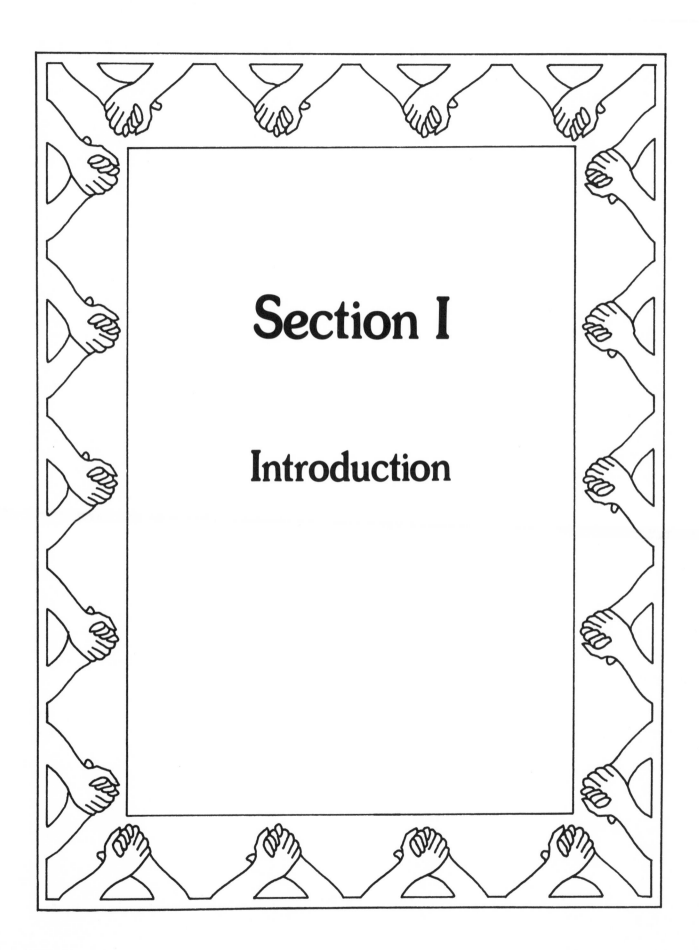

Section I

Introduction

People rarely succeed at anything unless they have fun doing it.

Introduction

All across the country there are some 50,000 cooperatives serving over 40 million households. Among the most visible serving consumers are food and other retail cooperatives, housing cooperatives and child care centers. Serving the agricultural community are a wide range of farm supply, production and marketing cooperatives. There are also hundreds of worker owned and operated businesses in the United States employing thousands of employee-owners.

Some of the largest businesses in the country and some of the smallest are coops and employee owned ventures. Sunkist, Ocean Spray and Land O'Lakes are giant farm coops. Yellow Cab Company is a cooperative owned by the cab drivers and dispatchers. Sunset Scavenger, the company which hauls garbage for the city of San Francisco, is employee owned. So is Little Professor Book Centers, a chain of over 100 stores.

Possibly the largest consumer cooperative in the United States, with 300,000 members, is Recreational Equipment Incorporated (REI). It is a forty year old organization based in Seattle with other locations in Anchorage, Portland, Berkeley, Los Angeles and Minneapolis. REI has established an enviable record of producing and retailing quality recreation equipment especially for mountaineering. REI outfitted the first American team to successfully climb Mt. Everest.

Probably the most activist consumer coop in the U.S., and one of the largest, is the Consumers Cooperative of Berkeley known to everybody in the San Francisco Bay Area as "the Coop". The Coop operates supermarkets, pharmacies, hardware and camping stores; it has a membership of more than 100,000. One of the Coop's stores has the largest per-capita volume of any supermarket outlet west of the Mississippi.

One of the largest worker cooperatives in the country is International Group Plans (IGP), located in Washington D.C. Founded in 1964, the 300 member worker-owned insurance company is best known for its innovations in group insurance plans and experiments in workplace democracy.

Group Health of St. Paul is one of the most unique cooperatives in the midwest. Convinced that they could successfully apply the cooperative format to the practice of medicine, a group of farm coop and union leaders researched and implemented the plan. Today Group Health of St. Paul serves its nearly 200,000 members through a number of locations in the Twin City region. Group Health was one of the first Health Maintenance Organizations (HMO's) to adopt a pre-paid health plan and to develop a program philosophy based upon preventative health care service. This has had a measurable effect upon the reduction of health problems and the need for hospital care. Although there are only a few cooperative health plans in the country all have achieved notable accomplishments in the health care field.

The Solar Center located in San Francisco is a worker cooperative which designs and installs solar heating. In just a few years it has become the largest solar installer of existing multi-family residences in the Bay Area. The Solar Center is unique in that it is organized both as an Employee Stock Ownership Plan (ESOP) and as a worker owned and controlled cooperative. Founded in the mid 1970's the Solar Center employs over twenty workers and is one of the most successful worker cooperatives of the recent wave.

The pioneering spirit of rugged individualism and tough one-upmanship is still alive in the world of small business. But a different spirit, one of cooperation, of sharing, of working with and being open to people is also alive, and it's growing. As the cooperative spirit grows, so does the need to find ways to channel this energy, ways to turn an ideal into a reality.

Cooperatives, collectives and worker owned businesses can provide the framework, the guidelines, the ways and means for people who want to work, shop and live cooperatively. We've written this book to provide the framework, the guidelines and the ways and means to start and successfully operate these cooperative ventures.

All coops are economic enterprises. You may not want to call your coop a business but it's a business none the less. What's more, the coops most likely to succeed are the ones who do acknowledge the fact that they are businesses, who set up a formal business structure, who educate themselves on the laws, the management procedures and the operating methods used by successful businesses.

Cooperative law, unfortunately, is often more complex than conventional small business law. Coop law is not as well defined, partly because it is not used as much as conventional business law. Coops are chartered by the states, not by the federal government. Some states have excellent coop laws, some have very restrictive laws. Coops are sometimes subject to laws specifically written for coops, sometimes to conventional business laws, and sometimes to both.

Some of our goals in writing this book are to provide you with basic legal information common to all coops; to list the many legal alternatives available to you and explain the benefits and drawbacks of each; and to describe, in regular English, the federal and state laws you may have to deal with. The clearest explanations in the world, however, cannot simplify complex laws. You will still need the help of a competent accountant or attorney in organizing and setting up your business.

A cooperative is a social organization as much as it is an economic one. Coops are, first and last, people — people who can work together, who can understand and respect one another, who can agree on common needs and goals and how they're to be accomplished. It is the people who will make or break any business, and it is this "working together" which will require the most work of all.

As "ideal" as coops are supposed to be, the people in the coops are no more ideal than you or me. They have egos, they have idiocyncracies, they have very minor differences of opinion which *always*, six months later, are suddenly chasms threatening the very existence of the coop. So this is a special warning to you facts-and-figures people, to you well-organized all-business people: the balance sheet, the cash flow, the beautiful new storefront, the perfected accounting system are all for nothing, a waste of time and money and energy, if the people aren't cooperating, aren't totally in tune with each other, aren't totally honest (with themselves mostly).

There are no hard and fast rules where people are concerned. Still, there are certain ways for people to organize, to operate a business together, and to deal with their day to day needs and problems, ways which work better than others. Part of the purpose of this book is to tell you the lessons other coops have learned, the mistakes they have made, the problems they've encountered and how they've solved them.

All three of us have several years' experience working with cooperatives and with small business in general. The information and ideas we present come out of our experience and also out of months of research, out of questioning each other over and over again, and out of the amazing cooperation we've received from so many helpful people.

We hope this book reflects the energy and love that went into it.

Christopher Hale is a clothes designer who started his own one-man business and as it grew, hired others and eventually turned the venture into a collective. Neither he nor his co-workers had any experience. They improvised, tried out different ideas and learned as they worked:

What happened to me is probably something that could happen to a lot of people who start our as an individual artist, craftsperson or artist. They have something successful and people want it. They're faced with hours and hours of repeating the design. It's boring to do all that, and there are a lot of people looking for work. So I started getting involved with people.

Initially the people worked *for* me but I found that it was difficult to get people consistently involved. They'd place more demands on me than I'd place on them. They could never understand why they were getting a particular amount of money and the garment was selling for four times that. Where was all that money going? They thought I was making a lot of money when I wasn't.

The reason for making it a collective was to share the responsibility of making a business happen and hopefully to broaden the base and to make the quality of each person's work improve because their incentive was improved. And it's true; that really happened.

There were a lot of problems in the transition. People talked about wanting to make it a collective but had a lot of difficulty facing the responsibility, financially and management wise. A lot of them didn't want it. They liked it much better when they could just work for somebody and get paid. And yet they didn't like being in that position either. It was a real twist. I was the person interested in setting it up as a collective, so I was doing all the setting up. The real making-it-happen wasn't happening from the group. It was hard to find people who matched my energy. One person, Sherry, who worked with me the longest, consistently did match my energy. As soon as I could, I was turning things over to her but we both were being swamped. When both of us started yelling, "Hey, this is too much, you're all taking advantage of us, each person has to be involved in these different things," then they started to act more like owners. But the number of workers dropped, which was good because we had too many people.

Each person gradually fit into the part of the job they liked to do best. Decisions were made collectively. Sometimes in the transition that was a little difficult because I found some of the ideas and opinions of the members not as educated, in terms of experience, as mine. They might want to do something or go in a direction that I knew wouldn't work very well. But the internal harmony of the people working together is extremely important, and we've discovered that the collective was the only way to give ourselves that internal harmony. And it's amazing to see people who had no previous experience working together and having a business.

Another thing about being a collective: When you get tired the business still happens because the other people are there making it happen. If you need to withdraw, to build your house or to go on vacation or whatever you need to do, everybody holds up for each other. I used to be worried. I had accounts. If I stopped doing the work for an account, if I went away — business thrives on consistency. If you can't always be there you have to depend on other people. In a collective, there can always be one lax person, there can always be one person on the outside corner recuperating, getting ready to plunge in again. It's also been an incredible way to know my neighbors, people who live in my community. To work with somebody, you really get to know them. People have a family feeling about the collective, being together.

People outside the collective are interested in what we make but a lot of times they're also interested in who we are. There's a certain magic behind the word collective. There's a certain pride in it. There's a real beauty in being able to open people's eyes to this kind of working together.

The History of Cooperation

One of the first known cooperatives in the world was the Philadelphia Contributorship, a mutual insurance company founded in 1752 by none other than Benjamin Franklin. From the 1750's through the 1830's, there were singular and mostly isolated attempts at cooperatives. It was in 1844, on a cold December night in the small industrial town of Rochdale, England that the modern cooperative movement actually began. It was started by 28 weavers in a small store with only five items to choose from. However, those weavers had commitment, a plan, a philosophy and a need to provide quality goods at a low price.

From the weaver's small store on Toad Lane was born an idea now serving hundreds of millions of people in almost every nation. The weavers drew up the Rochdale "Principles of Cooperation" which have been amended over time and are now known worldwide as the Principles of the International Cooperative Alliance. We reprint these Principles in the following chapter.

The Rochdale pioneers original store on Toad Lane, Rochdale, England, December 21, 1844. From a pen and ink drawing by C.W. Chapman.

European Directions

It was not long after the Rochdale weavers' pioneering effort that consumer cooperatives sprang up all over Europe. By the 1930's, consumer coops operated some of the largest retail businesses in most of the north European countries.

In the period since World War II the role of cooperatives in European economies has undergone a major transformation. Consumer cooperation has continued to move steadily ahead in the Scandinavian nations to a point where it has captured over one third of the retail trade. Cooperative housing is now also an important part of the cooperative movement in Scandinavia. In Germany consumer cooperatives are on the decline in retail trade but on the rise in housing. In Holland the entire consumer cooperative movement in retail trade has ended but other forms of cooperation still thrive among the farm communities. In Great Britian consumer cooperatives have watched their share of retail trade diminish from a high of 15% of total retail trade to today's 7%. While their share is now somewhat stable they are no longer "the Giant on High Street". In the other European countries the retail consumer cooperatives have generally declined. Consumer cooperatives did not adapt to the post-war economy and did not enter new fields of retailing when the boom occured. Whether consumer coops will survive throughout Europe, or maintain their presence in only a few select economies, is yet to be seen.

The sector of cooperative activity which has been most impressive in the post-war period has been worker cooperatives. However, their growth is only apparent in France, Italy and Spain. These three countries have a long history of worker cooperatives along with their consumer cooperative movements. In other northern European countries the powerful Social-Democratic Parties and Labour Movements forcefully opposed worker cooperatives and stunted their development.

Today in France, Italy and Spain, thousands of worker cooperatives employ nearly 200,000 worker-members. In Italy coops now control 5% of national trade, in France they are the fastest growing type of business, and in Spain they are the leader in national productivity.

The most impressive example of a worker cooperative is Mondragon, begun in the 1950's in the Basque region of Spain. From one small business Mondragon has developed into an intergrated system of nearly one hundred firms, employing nearly 20,000 worker-members in high growth and high technology industries. Each worker-member has to invest $4,000 in the cooperative and that investment is returned to the worker on retirement. Mondragon now has its own bank with nearly one billion dollars in deposits, its own year round training school, cooperative housing, and 100,000 members in its consumer cooperative retail stores. Because of its success "the Mondragon experiment" (as it's known worldwide) is under study by numerous governments, trade unions and social scientists. It is proof that under certain conditions worker cooperatives can flourish and constitute an important part of the economy.

The success of worker cooperatives in the southern half of Europe is beginning to have effect upon the north. In Britain where there were only 50 worker cooperatives in 1974 there are now 500. To assist this growth both the Labour and Conservative Party Governments have financed the creation of a Cooperative Development Agency which has made worker cooperatives its first priority. The European Parliament is also now considering supportive legislation for worker-owned firms. Clearly worker cooperatives are a dynamic agenda item of a Europe grappling with rising unemployment, high inflation and industrial conflict.

Consumer Cooperatives in the United States

The first consumer coop in the United States was a buying club started in 1844 by John Kaulback, a tailor living in Boston. He convinced the members of his labor union to undertake joint buying of their household supplies and to distribute them at the weekly union meetings. The first purchases were a case of soap and half a case of tea. The coop grew. In 1845, a store was open. By 1847, twelve "divisions" had been formed; they called themselves the New England Protective Union. By 1852 there were 403 divisions throughout all of New England and the Protective Union had become a forceful factor in both the retail and wholesale marketplace. Unfortunately the Protective Union was later destroyed by internal dissention,

organizational weakness, unsound business pracitices, deteriorating economic conditions and the Civil War.

The first major growth of consumer cooperation took place in the 1870's. Farmers through the Grange Movement and workers through the Knights of Labor organized cooperatives as part of their member services. During this era many of the cooperatives adopted the rules and principles of the Rochdale method of cooperation from England. The growing presence of British and other European cooperators in the labor movements in the U.S. led to a greater and more effective dissemination of cooperative ideas, practices and philosophy.

Until the 1930's cooperative activity in the United States was for the most part led by the different streams of immigrants. The most prominent coops were Italian and Jewish ones in the East. Central Europeans initiated cooperatives in Ohio and Illinois. Scandinavians led cooperatives in New England, the upper Midwest and the Northwest. In particular the cooperatives of Minnesota, Wisconsin and upper Michigan built an efficient and integrated retail and wholesale system. By 1930 most of this wave of cooperation had come to an end. Without the zeal of the needy immigrant, who looked upon the cooperative as part of the old country, the organizations diminished. In the midwest, struggles between communist and non-communist Finns dramatically ended the growth of the cooperative movement in that area of the country.

Just as the initial immigrant-based cooperative movement faded, coops got a new lease on life. In the late 1920's and early 1930's, cooperatives suddenly became an "American idea" as Hoover and Roosevelt struggled to conquer the nation's depression. Hoover's themes of individualism, voluntarism, and decentralization pointed to cooperation as a valuable path to ending the nation's and especially the farmer's plight. A cooperative marketing plan adopted by the Coolidge Administration was further refined when Hoover took office in 1928. Not only did Hoover strongly support farm cooperatives, he became the first President to sign credit union legislation into law. In his book *American Individualism* Hoover wrote, "Cooperation in its current economic sense represents the initiative of self-interest blended with a sense of service."

When Roosevelt took office in 1933 he further developed the potential of farm cooperatives and cooperative forms of financing. His greatest contribution to cooperative development was the creation of the Rural Electrification Administration (REA) in 1935. The corresponding growth of rural electric cooperatives provided, for the first time, electric power to rural communities — "the day the lights came on."

A number of other programs under the Roosevelt Administration addressed cooperatives, though none were quite as successful as the REA and farm coop programs. Never before had a government been more sympathetic to the philosophy and aims of the consumer cooperative movement.

Consumer cooperatives didn't actually receive direct aid from the Roosevelt Administration but they did benefit from the friendly climate of the New Deal. Due to the government's interest and the growing "American" nature of cooperative development, more and more coops were being started in all areas of economic activity. Many of the consumer cooperatives present today have their origins in what is considered the Golden Age of American Cooperation.

With the onset of the Second World War interest in social and economic change was curtailed in favor of the war effort. Because the war economy brought the Depression to an end there was less interest in the development of cooperatives. After the war the staid, thrifty cooperative movement was bypassed by the boom economy. By the 1950's the thousand or so consumer cooperatives remaining in the U.S. were located in the Midwest or in college towns; coops had disappeared completely from most of mainstream America. To many in the consumer cooperative movement it appeared that their aspirations had come to an end and that cooperatives were to be a utopian legacy rather than a thriving economic sector.

Unexpectedly, an era of abundance — the 1960's — spurred the next wave of cooperative activity. Out of a decade of dissent, of civil rights marches and anti-war demonstrations came a generation of Americans who looked to a new economic order to share the nation's wealth equitably. Once again thousands of cooperatives sprang up across the country as symbols of economic democracy and local control. Most often they symbolized rebellion against technocracy, hierarchy and "business as usual." All too frequently the cooperatives closed as ephemerally as they opened. Few made it past the first couple of years. Still, many did survive. Today some of these coops, ten and fifteen years old, are stable thriving businesses. The rebellion has

given way to other needs. Or as one aging rock and roll star put it, "I'm not only part of the establishment, I am the establishment."

Worker Cooperatives in the United States

In 1791, only 25 years after the signing of the Declaration of Independence, a group of Philadelphia carpenters gathered in Independence Hall and formed the first worker cooperative in the United States. Despite this early start, there was no large scale interest in worker cooperatives until the 1870's and 1880's. The largest wave of activity was stimulated by the Knights of Labor, the leading national labor organization of the period. Close to 200 cooperatives were started by the Knights of Labor, mostly in the industrialized regions of the country. There were also many other worker cooperatives started independently of the labor movement as a way of creating jobs and obtaining higher wages and better working conditions.

After 1886, the power of the Knights of Labor declined. Class-conscious unionism replaced the more utopian goals of the past, and worker cooperation waned. The number of worker cooperatives declined considerably and by 1925 only 39 such enterprises were found in the United States. Although many kinds of worker cooperatives were formed during the Depression, their existence was normally only a short one and filled temporary aims such as make-work schemes or community development.

The next wave of worker cooperatives came in the 1940's. The impetus for this new interest actually dates back to 1921 with the founding of Olympic Veneer Company in the State of Washington. Given the radical and Scandinavian traditions of Washington State it was a likely place for cooperative development. It was twenty years before another plywood company started as a cooperative but in the years following World War II another 21 were formed. By 1964 there were 24 worker-owned plywood companies in operation.

Not until the 1960's and 1970's was there to be much more interest in worker cooperatives. Like the consumer cooperatives of this era, the focus was more a rebellious social and cultural statement than an economic necessity. The period was rich in workplace experimentation, job sharing and job rotation; dealing with racism and sexism; getting rid of bosses, time clocks, work schedules and all forms of hierarchy; criticizing and foregoing most forms of technology; and boosting "dropping out" and decentralization. Although the philisophical strains were identified closely with anarchism, for the most part the movement was a middle class rebellion against the norms of society and in search of freedom without responsibility. Although it was Woodstock in the workplace, it did clarify that workplace alienation was very much a concern to a generation about to take its first job. Of all the issues that arose during the 1960's, the quality of working life has retained the most potent force.

The 1980s

In today's unstable economic climate there is once again a growing interest in cooperatives, both worker and consumer. Since the industrial revolution, people have turned to cooperatives in times of extended economic hardship. In a nation searching for answers to the future, cooperatives should certainly play a role. The key seems to be commitment and the competency required for success. The social and cultural concerns about the workplace must blend with economic concerns. Coops which can attain both economic and non-economic goals will succeed. They will in fact be a model for the new world where corporation can be a strong, viable force.

Copyright Jane Scherr

Principles of the
International Cooperative Alliance

The original Rochdale "Principles of Cooperation" have been amended over the years but remain today basically the same as when they were established in 1844. The 1966 Congress of the International Cooperative Alliance approved this wording of the six Cooperative Principles.

1. Membership of a cooperative society should be voluntary and without artificial restriction or any social, political, racial or religious discrimination, to all persons who can make use of its services and are willing to accept the responsibilities of membership.

2. Cooperative societies are democratic organizations. Their affairs should be administered by persons elected or appointed in a manner agreed by the members and accountable to them. Members of primary societies should enjoy equal rights of voting (one member, one vote) and participation in decisions affecting their societies. In other than primary societies the administration should be conducted on a democratic basis in a suitable form.

3. Share capital should only receive a strictly limited rate of interest.

4. The economic results arising out of the operations of a society belong to the members of that society and should be distributed in such a manner as would avoid one member gaining at the expense of others. This may be done by decision of the members as follows: (a) by provision for development of the business of cooperative; (b) by provision of common services; or, (c) by distribution among members in proportion to their transactions with the society.

5. All cooperative societies should make provision for the education of their members, officers, and employees and of the general public in the principles and techniques of cooperation, both economic and democratic.

6. All cooperative organizations, in order to best serve the interest of their members and their communities, should actively cooperate in every practical way with other cooperatives at local, national, and international levels.

Terminology

"Cooperative" (and its abbreviation "coop" which some people spell "co-op") has different meanings to different people. A cooperative is an organization owned and controlled democratically by its members. A cooperative can be a business such as a retail store; it can be a sharing of talent such as a group of dancers; it can be most anything the people of the coop want it to be. A coop can be set up to serve its members only, such as a food buying club, or it can serve the entire community.

Some cooperatives see their main function as providing needed goods or services to the community (or to themselves) at the lowest possible prices with no desire to make a profit. Some coops are set up by the workers for the purpose of providing those workers with a decent living. And, again, some coops combine these goals.

Cooperatives are variously known as "consumer" coops, "producer" coops or "worker" coops. Each of these three is a different type of operation (though worker coops are sometimes considered producer coops) often with different federal and state laws and regulations. Within these three basic categories are sub-categories. All these distinctions are explained in detail in this book.

Throughout the book we use the words "coop", "cooperative", "business", "organization", "enterprise", and "venture" interchangably. When we use these words we are referring to all types of cooperatives. Where we refer specifically to, say, "consumer coop", we are talking about consumer coops only.

A "collective" is another name for a worker cooperative. We use these two terms interchangably but we prefer "worker coop" or just "coop" over collective, for an important reason: Sometimes state and federal laws address consumer coops and producer coops but make no mention of worker coops. Worker coops may need to define themselves as producer coops to take advantage of some particular law. Some people in the government and in the coop movement itself would like to separate worker coops out of the cooperative movement — a destructive and narrow mentality. Since "coop" is often as much a state of mind as it is some legal designation, by calling your collective a coop you help educate others; and you help yourself, hopefully, because you might be able to squeeze into the legal definition of a coop and benefit from coop legislation. Still, a lot of people love the word "collective"; to them it has much more meaning and feeling that "worker cooperative". By all means, call your venture whatever you like. If you do call yourselves a coop or cooperative, however, make sure your state law allows you to use these words in your legal business name; many states restrict the use of the term. We don't know of any state which restricts the use of the word "collective".

Most coops are organized legally as either corporations or partnerships. Both "corporation" and "partnership" have very specific legal meanings and are discussed in detail in the book. When we use the words "corporation" or "partnership" we are referring to specifically defined legal terms.

We use the words "owner" and "member" interchangably and sometimes even refer to "owner/member". Members of coops do in fact own their coops, whether they realize it or not. "Member", however, is a broader term, and to some people it connotes more of a community spirit than "owner", which to some has a capitalistic flavor. It all may seem a little silly to you, but words can have a lot of power. People are easily confused and sometimes irritated when they misunderstand a word. More important than simple semantics, however, is the law. Sometimes state law will refer to "members" and "memberships". If your cooperative is organized under a law which refers to the coop's owners as "members" or which talks about issuing "memberships" (instead of corporate stock) you should stay with the state's terminology. If the law says you're a member, you're a member.

"Profit" is a loaded word. We discuss profit — both the word and the real thing — in the book. When we use the word "profit" in the text, we are usually referring to the excess of income over expenses (income-expenses=profit). We define income and expense in the bookkeeping section. When we use the word "profit" in a narrow legal or tax sense, we define it in context. Many coops, by legal definition, do not make a profit — even when they make one. They have a "surplus" or a "net margin" or a "savings". Distribution of the surplus or savings is, in some cases, referred to as "patronage refunds". These terms are defined and discussed in the text.

"Capital" is a business word with several definitions but usually it means money. "Starting capital" is the money you have or are trying to raise to get the coop started. "Working capital" is

money available for regular day to day business expenses such as stocking your store, paying wages, rent, utilities, etc. "Equity capital" is money provided by the members (the owners) as opposed to loans to the business (which are called "loans").

There are all kinds of taxes (don't you know it!): income, sales, payroll, property, inventory, excise, franchise, gross profit, estimated, unemployment, self employment, social security, excess retained earnings, capital gains, windfall profits, federal, state, county and local taxes. Throughout the book we try to specify which taxes we are referring to, but when we refer simply to "taxes" we are usually talking about income taxes.

The word "employee" has a specific legal meaning. An employee is an individual earning a wage or a salary working for another individual (other than himself), or working for an unincorporated business (a sole proprietorship or a partnership) owned by someone else, or working for a corporation or an incorporated coop no matter who owns it. An "owner-employee" or a "member-employee" (the same thing) is employed by the incorporated coop which the employee owns.

There is an important legal distinction for owner-employees which hinges on whether the cooperative is incorporated or not. We discuss it later in the book but briefly, a corporation (many coops are corporations) can hire its members as employees. A sole proprietorship or a partnership (many coops are partnerships) cannot hire its owners as employees; the owners can work for the business and can even draw a salary, but legally they are not employees. When we use the word "employee" we use it in the legal sense.

"Worker" is a more general term and means anyone who works for the coop. When we use "worker" we are referring to member-employees, employees who are not members, working members who are not employees, volunteers and anyone else who is working there.

The world of business has its own vocabulary. Business words usually have very specific meanings. Sometimes a word used in regular non-business conversation has an entirely different meaning in business. We have made a concerted effort to define every business word we use. When you discuss business with accountants, lawyers, bankers and other business people, it is important for you to understand the words being used. Don't be embarrassed to ask for definitions. Here are a few to start you off:

Inventory: goods for sale, your store's stock, your repair shop's parts, the raw materials used to manufacture a product, the product thus manufactured. Inventory is also a verb, as in "taking inventory", and refers to the act of counting and valuing the goods on hand (the inventory) at a given point in time.

Overhead: a general term which refers to the day to day expenses of a business not directly related to the product or service you are selling. Overhead is the rent, utilities, permits and licenses, stationery, vehicle expenses and all the miscellaneous little stuff. Employee wages are not usually considered overhead. Inventory is not overhead. Equipment, furniture, tools, etc. are not overhead.

Assets: a broad term of referring to everything the coop owns. Money, accounts receivable (money owed by the customers), inventory, equipment and the like. "Current" or "liquid" assets are those in cash or easily converted to cash; "fixed" or "capital" assets are the machinery, equipment, tools, furniture, fixtures and vehicles owned by the business.

Liabilities: a broad term referring to all the debts of the coop, usually loans and accounts payable (money you owe your suppliers).

Net Worth: assets-liabilities=net worth.

Credit: this word has several meanings. In double-entry bookkeeping, "credit" is a type of bookkeeping entry. "Credit" is also what you extend to your customers who don't pay cash when they make a purchase and what your suppliers extend to you when they give you 30 days to pay a bill. "Credit" also describes others' opinions of your standing with the bank ("the coop is a good credit risk") and with your suppliers ("the coop has good credit; they pay their bills on time"). When someone "credits your account", they usually mean they are posting a payment you've made and reducing the amount you owe. And, of course, when you do a good job, you should get "credit" for it. Enough, don't you think?

One More Word Before We Start

We suggest you read this entire book carefully at least once before you start drawing conclusions and making decisions. Much of the information is interrelated. For example, many of the issues covered in the consumer coop chapter also apply to producer and worker coops, and vice versa; many items covered in the corporation chapters apply to partnerships. You should get an overview of the whole subject before getting down to details.

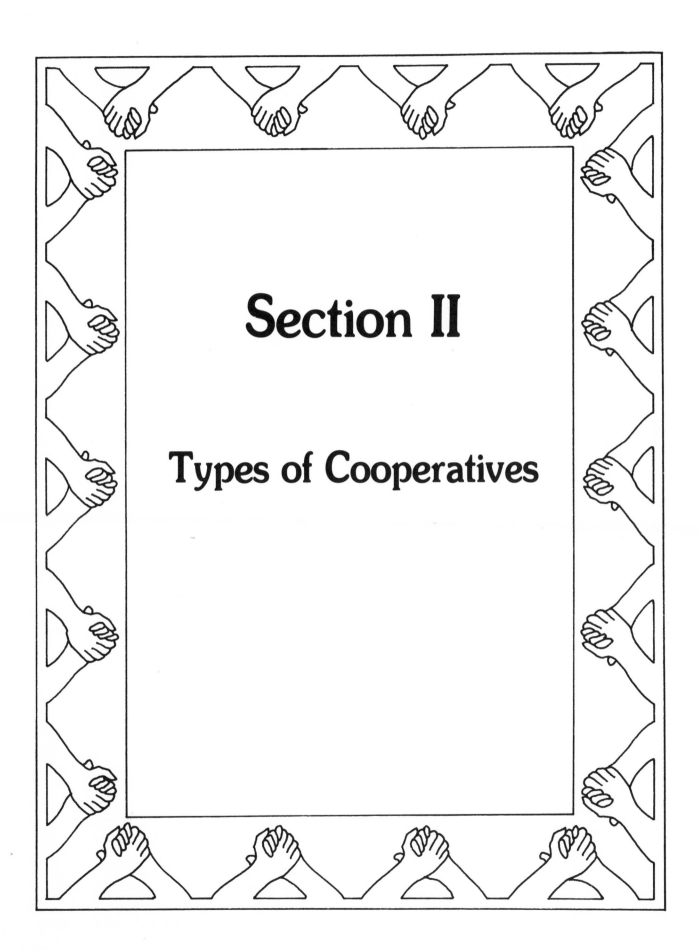

Section II

Types of Cooperatives

Cooperation touches no man's fortune, seeks no plunder. It enters into no secret associations, it needs no trade unions to protect its interest. It contemplates no violence, it envys no dignity, it accepts no gifts nor asks any favor. It keeps no terms with the idle and it will break no faith with the industrious.
— George Jacob Holyoake, 1875

TYPES OF COOPERATIVES

There are three basic types of cooperatives: consumer, producer and worker. Within these three categories are numerous subcategories. Some people consider producer and worker coops to be one category. We find the differences and distinctions significant enough to deal with them separately.

"Old Wave" is a term given to older, established coops, particularly those begun in the 1930's. Generally, the coops which started in the depression years grew up on the notion that coops needed to become large businesses in order to compete in the marketplace and demonstrate the value of a cooperative economy. They strived to increase their membership and patronage as much as possible. Old Wave coops are very much economic entities; "professionalism" is the key word.

Some cooperatives which began in the 1960's and 1970's — out of the civil rights and Viet Nam era — are described as "New Wave" coops. New Wave coops have different concerns than the Old Wave. They stress the social aspects of cooperation. They are committed to a looser, more personal, less hierarchical working situation. Political and community involvement are also important concerns. In food coops, there is an emphasis on natural foods. Many New Wave coops work on the premise that "small is beautiful". They often limit their membership, and some will not sell to non-members.

Several new and fast growing coops have gone a step further and refer to themselves as "Third Wave". Third Wave coops are in a sense a blend of Old Wave and New Wave. Many began as New Wave coops but have grown substantially in a short period of time and they find that they must now adopt some Old Wave approaches to maintain equilibrium. They find they have to establish some sort of managerial or professional level of worker, hire employees and sell to non-members.

Consumer Cooperatives

A consumer cooperative is set up to provide goods and services to its members, and possibly to non-members as well, at fair prices. Consumer coops are also concerned with raising people's consciousness about consumer and cooperative issues. Consumer coops are often active in the community.

Food Buying Clubs

Many consumer cooperatives begin as food buying clubs or "pre-order" coops. Community people gather together each week with their orders for cheese, grains, vegetables and the like. A few volunteers collate the orders and create a master list. Sometimes several local groups combine their lists to increase their purchasing power with the wholesalers. The wholesalers might be neighborhood shops which agree to sell at a very low markup, farmers markets or conventional wholesalers. The bulk purchases are then broken down into individual orders and distributed to the members. A small markup is added to each member's cost to cover expenses such as gas and spillage and possibly for reserves. If the buying club is run efficiently, members can save 15% to 30% of what they would pay for the same food at a regular store.

Small Coop Stores

A successful food buying club often decides to expand into a storefront business. The savings at coop stores is usually less than through buying clubs because of the higher overhead. But the coop store reaches farther out to the community and often provides a greater selection of products and more convenient shopping hours. Storefront consumer cooperatives may decide to sell to members only or to the general public as well.

Small food coop stores were the heart of the burgeoning New Wave cooperative movement of the seventies. A recurring name would be "People's Food Store". Some became very successful and grew rapidly. The Arcata, California Food Cooperative took over an empty Safeway store. The Homestead Exchange in Ukiah, California not only moved to larger quarters but expanded into doing its own trucking to buy directly from the farmer and other suppliers. Several coops joined with other coops in inter-city or regional agreements to share shipping and warehousing. Together, the coops own the trucks and warehouse. In effect, the cooperatives are creating a new coop to which they all belong. A coop whose members are other coops is called a federation.

Consumer coops, of course, can and do provide a lot more than just food. Most any product can be sold cooperatively. One unusual example is the Appropriate Home Energy Cooperative in Ottowa, Ontario. It provides heating oil to its members each winter at a 10% to 15% savings. This cooperative has been so successful that many other people are interested in forming similar heating fuel coops.

Services may also be provided cooperatively. Housing cooperatives, credit unions, cooperative health and legal services, funeral societies, childcare cooperatives and cooperative auto repair shops are types of consumer service coops. Housing coops are unique among consumer cooperatives; we devote an entire separate chapter to them. Several groups which call themselves service cooperatives such as certain health and medical plans, mutual insurance companies and mutual savings and loans are not really coops as we define them. They are not controlled by the members. The only cooperative feature is that they return savings to the member-stockholders.

Consumer Coop Income

If a consumer coop makes any money above its expenses, the money is called a "net savings" (some people also call it a "surplus" or "net margin"). "Savings" rather than "profits" is the proper term for consumer coop income. Since members own the business and are interested in lowering the cost of the product and providing other services like consumer education, rather than in making as much money as possible for the company and its investors, the cooperative is not interested in profits. It is interested in savings for its members.

Many consumer coops return all or part of their savings to members in the form of "patronage refunds" (sometimes called "patronage distributions" or "patronage dividends"). Patronage refunds are distributed in proportion to the amount of business the member did with the coop. Nonmembers do not share in the refunds. The coop may choose to keep some of the savings, in reserve for equipment, expansion and emergencies.

The taxability of patronage refunds is discussed in the chapter "Special Federal Tax Considerations — Sub Chapter T".

Member Discount Coops

Some coops do not wish to deal with the extensive bookkeeping and delayed refunds inherent in a patronage refund coop. Rather than wait until the close of the year to return savings, "member discount" coops will give members substantial discounts on their purchases immediately. Nonmembers, when permitted to make purchases, do not get discounts. This immediate discount policy obviously can lead to financial problems, however, if not enough money is left over to cover basic overhead such as rent, utilities, etc. People who operate member discount coops have to be knowledgeable about their store's operation and experienced enough to gauge their financial needs.

Direct Charge Coops — Cooperative Depots

In the 1970's, several groups decided to create a variation on the traditional consumer cooperative. Since coops often need more capital then the usual member's small minimum fee, the direct charge coop (also known as "D.C." or "depot") was created to require a specific investment and weekly charge. The weekly charge or dues would be used to offset part or all of the operating costs. In other types of coops, operating costs are usually covered by higher markups. The shelf price in D.C. coops is, accordingly, lower. Some direct charge coops require a minimum investment of at least $100, possibly payable in installments. Some coops return the initial investment when a member leaves and some don't. The weekly charge is often $2 to $5. Some coops charge each adult, some charge children as well, some have family rates. Regardless of the charge, membership is usually by household. Thus a family of three dues-paying adults only holds one membership. The smaller D.C. coops often expect members to work a certain number of hours each week in lieu of or in addition to paying the dues. Larger stores usually find it too unwieldy to require members to work. In most direct charge coops, only members are permitted to make purchases at the store. Where non-members may also purchase, the members are usually given an additional discount. Direct charge cooperatives have the advantage of a strong com-

mitment and a sound economic base which builds each week from the beginning. Because of the weekly dues, there's an obvious incentive to make all your purchases at the coop (though sometimes the dues are a deterrant to a small purchaser-member, such as an elderly person who may not be able to make up the fees in savings and purchases).

The Nanaimo Cooperative in British Columbia laid the tracks for the successful direct charge coop. It began as a credit union and heating coop and opened its direct charge store in 1971. It has expanded to include garden equipment and appliances. Its sales are around $25 million a year. The Nanaimo Coop has been so successful that a couple of other markets in town have been forced to close down. Several direct charge coops in California including Isle Vista, Briarpatch and Cooportunity followed Nanaimo's lead, though none has grown very large. The Wheatsville Food Coop in Austin, Texas began in 1976 as a direct charge coop, with a $50 investment requirement, a direct charge of $6 per month and a work requirement of three hours per month or $2 per hour. However, in 1979, as the store became highly successful, it abandoned the capital requirement and cut back the direct charge, replacing them with higher markups and patronage refunds. It did so because the recordkeeping had become unwieldy — a problem that besets many coops which don't take the accounting and bookkeeping aspect seriously from the start.

The Good Day Market in Portland, Maine, is a consumer coop operated by volunteers. Douglas Uraneck wrote us about the market and the problems it had with bookkeeping and taxes:

The coop was started with a gift from OEO of three coolers for the purpose of having a meat buying cooperative in the poor district of Portland. The project fell through when the leadership dissipated due to unforseen circumstances. The coolers took on a life of their own. A cooler-in-a-truck was taken over by Parks and Recreation for hauling tools. Two found their way into the hands of the people who started the Good Day Market.

The market was very poor in the beginning — and still is — so to raise money they had a paying membership. For $25 you could belong to the coop and receive a discount of 20% off the mark-up, which was 40%, for one year. This money was used to build up inventory. There was a working membership which received no money. Workers earned a 30% discount off the mark-up.

I appeared at the end of one year in response to an appeal for a little help with year-end taxes. My background is three semesters of accounting and a religious interest in charity, coops and economics-in-the-battle-with-greed. I was fascinated and horrified by the problems. The concept of growth was not understood, nor profits nor any of the basic concepts of double-entry bookkeeping. A daily receipts tally was kept as well as a cash disbursement check book. But we had no data or feel for how much the discount was worth. Were we gaining or losing? Was it fair or just? Who really was footing the bill for the store? It was all very loose and sort of a quagmire at the end of the year.

The bookkeeper who came in once a year to do the taxes did not really help the store understand what was going on. The store was supposed to ·be non-profit, there was never much in the bank, everyone was unpaid, chronic problems with pricing, etc — yet every year taxes were due. Whence our profits? Obviously from the mark-up. It also turns out that the paid-in membership has to be seen as a sale, not as equity. But the donated labor is the real source. If we had to pay for this typical store expense, we would have no profits to tax. In fact, we'd probably go broke.

Housing Cooperatives

A housing cooperative is a group of people organized for the purpose of owning, building or rehabilitating housing for its members and possibly for other people. The coop itself is a corporation which owns the housing in which the resident-members live. Each resident owns one share or membership in the corporation. Like other types of coops, housing coops are democratically managed: one member, one vote. Members usually elect a board of directors who manage the cooperatively owned housing.

A housing coop is actually a form of consumer coop. Depending on how you view it, the coop is providing a service (housing) or a product (a home) to its members.

Housing coops are often eligible for 100% financing. A coop can purchase housing without raising significant capital from its members. The corporation holds one mortgage for the entire coop, collects the rents, makes the mortgage payments, pays the property taxes, pays the bills, does the bookkeeping and maintains the buildings. The corporation is responsible for major repairs, insurance, replacement of worn out equipment and upkeep of common grounds and facilities. Sometimes the corporation hires professional managers and sometimes the members manage the operation themselves. Members are not personally liable for the coop's mortgage.

Federal law and most state laws allow members of housing coops to deduct their share of the mortgage interest and property taxes on their personal tax returns.

Some housing coop bylaws specify that when a member moves out, the member's share is repurchased by the corporation for the same amount the member originally paid or possibly for a slightly greater amount to compensate for inflation. This kind of set up is often referred to as a "limited equity coop". The members do not benefit from any increase in the market value of the real estate. In essence, the member is renting housing from the cooperative (except, of course, no landlord can jack up the rent or evict a tenant at will). The member's original "down payment"—the membership fee—is much like a cleaning or security deposit, refunded when the member moves out. This limited equity system creates housing which is affordable by low-income families and keeps it that way. There is no incentive for speculators to buy memberships, hoping to resell and make a large profit. To further discourage speculation and profit, the bylaws of many housing coops require that all members be residents of the coop. This way, people are not allowed to buy an inexpensive membership and then sublease the housing to others at high rents.

Some housing coops allow departing members to sell a membership for whatever it will fetch on the open market. Such coops are called "market rate" or "full equity" coops. As the cost of housing escalates, so does the cost of a membership. Few coops survive under such an arrangement. The value of a membership increases until only wealthy people can afford shares. Speculators buy up memberships in hopes of reselling them at a handsome profit. The drive to make a killing in the housing market destroys the principles and ideals which coops stand for.

Allowing memberships to sell at market value can have disastrous results for the entire coop if prices climb significantly. People, desperate for housing, buy in at prices they can't realistically afford; they are unable to make the steep monthly payments; the other members of the coop are unable to cover the payments; the entire coop faces foreclosure and loss of its housing. A limited equity coop will prevent this scenario.

Housing coops are most successful when a few specific procedures are followed:

1. The board of directors keeps members informed of all its actions. A system of regular communications through meetings, newsletters, bulletin boards, etc. is set up and maintained.

2. The coop maintains adequate cash reserves for emergencies, for replacements and for repairs. Reserves reduce the possibility of members having to pay unexpected additional fees.

3. The board has the right to approve new member-residents. Boards often run credit checks on prospective members. Boards often meet with prospective members to explain the rights and responsibilities of coop membership.

4. Sub-leasing is restricted to a short term or else not allowed at all. Where allowed, the bylaws specify the maximum time and how much rent may be charged.

Producer Cooperatives

Producer cooperatives are organized by people who individually produce a product and then band together to market their products collectively. Sometimes a producers coop will own the workspace and the equipment used by its members. Sometimes a coop will only be a marketing outlet for its members. The latter type is known as a "marketing coop". Any product can be marketed through a producer coop. In some cases, the coop purchases the products from the members and then resells them. In other cases, the coop merely acts as an agent, selling the product for the members.

The main distinction of a producer coop is that its members work independently and separately to produce their products. Each member earns money only from the sale of his or her own products.

Any surplus (profits) realized by a producer coop is returned to the members in proportion to the amount of business each member has done with the coop. The member whose products sell the most would collect the largest share of the surplus. The returned surplus is very similar to the patronage refunds distributed by consumer coops. The IRS calls it "per unit retain allocations". To keep things simple (and to keep the sentences from getting unnecessarily long) we will refer to the returned surplus as patronage refunds. The taxability of these refunds is discussed in the chapter "Special Federal Tax Considerations — Sub Chapter T".

Farmer Coops

The first producer coops were farmer coops (agricultural coops). Even today, most producer coops are agricultural. Two of the largest are Ocean Spray and Sunkist. One of the smallest is La Cooperativa Colonia Mexicana Unida, which farms 200 acres of state reclamation land in Yolo County in central California. It is one of the few coops which grows crops in all four seasons. Most agricultural coops specialize in one or two crops, thereby restricting most of their members to seasonal work. Cooperativa Colonia keeps fifteen families with 28 adults employed all year.

Farmer coops (and the farmers themselves) are blessed with many tax breaks not available to most other types of cooperatives. Under Section 521 and Section 501(c) of the Internal Revenue Code, farmer coops can be non-profit tax exempt corporations. All states allow farmer coops to incorporate under the state cooperative corporation laws.

Purchasing or Supply Cooperatives

Coops have also been organized to provide a producer coop with the supplies it needs. The producer coop may set up the supply or purchasing coop itself or deal with an already existing one. The buying process for supplies is similar to that of a consumer coop, the differences being that the goods bought are for the production process rather that for consumption by individuals.

An arts and crafts coop which is both a producer and purchasing cooperative would work like this: The members individually produce their arts and crafts work and market it through their coop. The cooperative purchases suplies and materials (like clay, tools and glazes) in bulk and sells these to the members individually, similar to the way a consumer cooperative would operate. At the end of the year, two separate systems would be set up to return any income or surplus earned during the year by the coop. One system would distribute the surplus from sales of supplies to each member in proportion to the member's purchases from the cooperative. The other would distribute the surplus from sales of the arts and crafts (after each member has collected the agreed payment for each item sold through the coop) to each member in proportion to the business the member did with the coop in providing arts and crafts items for sale.

The precise difference between the various producer coops is often separated by too fine a line. Definitions vary and distinctions blur. Most states, in fact, do not distinguish at all between producer, marketing, purchasing, supply and worker coops (worker coops are discussed below). All these categories, for purposes of state law, can usually be included under the more general term "producer".

Worker Cooperatives — Collectives

Worker cooperatives are owned and managed by their workers. Worker coops are usually some type of a business, selling a product or providing a service to the public. Worker coops exist primarily to provide employment to their member-employees.

Many worker coops call themselves collectives. Because the term "worker cooperative" is used more frequently in coop literature and because the word "cooperative" has certain legal distinctions important to worker coops (discussed previously in the "Terminology" chapter) we've decided to use the term "worker coop" throughout the book. There is no difference between a worker coop and a collective.

Some worker coops maintain strict requirements that every worker be an owner and that each owner be working. Some worker coops have a policy of "once an owner, always an owner" even if the owner no longer works there. Some coops hire non-member employees to do some of the (usually more unpleasant) work. Some worker coops rotate jobs and give equal pay and equal say to every member; other coops are structured in a more hierarchical manner much like a conventional business. Regardless of how the coop is structured, democratic management — one member, one vote — is the guiding line.

Worker coops usually pay most of their earnings to their member-employees in the form of wages. Any surplus can be retained by the coop or distributed to the workers in proportion to their wages earned or work contributed, similar in concept to patronae refunds. The taxability of the surplus and the distributions depends on how the coop is legally structured and whether it taked advantage of the Sub Chapter T tax laws. Legal structure and taxation are discussed in subsequent chapters.

Worker coops are different from producer coops in that all the facilities, materials, supplies, equipment, etc. are equally owned collectively by the members. The goods and services are seen as being provided by the coop, not by individual members. Still, as we indicated in our discussion of producer coops, worker coops are often considered a special kind of producer coop. Many state and federal laws distinguished only between consumer and producer coops; in such cases, worker coops should consider themselves producer coops.

Recently, an ideological stance has been taken by some people in their definition of cooperatives. They argue that worker coops are not really true coops. Worker coops do not have unlimited open membership — the coop is necessarily restricted by the number of workers it can efficiently employ — and worker coops are "profit making".

This arguement is narrow and, in our opinion, incorrect. Many producer and marketing coops limit their memberships. Producer and consumer coops both make "profits" although they are called "savings" or "surplus". As long as the profit is not being made on the back of someone else's labor, a worker coop is as much a cooperative as any other. Worker coops also maintain all the basic characteristics of a cooperatively run venture with control in the hands of the member-workers.

Another argument we've heard voiced against worker coops is that even if some worker coops do qualify as producer coops, sales and service type coops which "produce" nothing couldn't possibly qualify. But again this begs the question of what is a worker coop. Sales and service worker coops besides providing ("producing") important services also adopt the basic cooperative principles. They should be treated no differently than any other coop.

Though most worker cooperatives begin when people organize together to form the cooperative, there have been several instances especially within the past decade where employees of an existing company take over ownership. Employees become owners when the company is about to close down its plant, usually because it is losing money or not making the "necessary" percentage of profits. The union and sometimes the community offers to work out an agreement to keep the plant going and the workers employed. The agreement usually provides for the employes to either purchase the plant directly or purchase controlling stock of the company. Since the workers do not need to make the high profit margin previously required by the company, the business can usually survive and in fact often becomes a successful "cooperative" venture.

These employee owned companies are sometimes called worker cooperatives but often they differ substantially from cooperatives as we define them. Neither democratic management nor one member, one vote is adhered to. This situation is discussed at length in the chapter "Employee Stock Ownership Plans".

The Solar Center in San Francisco has been a worker cooperative ever since it was started in 1976. The company designs and installs solar hot water systems. This interview with Peter Barnes, an original member of the collective, first appeared in In Business magazine:

We had two primary objectives: to help make solar energy a reality in the San Francisco Bay Area, and to demonstrate that an employee owned business could compete successfully with conventional businesses. These somewhat idealistic motives — rather than the expectation of making a quick buck — are what spurred us into action and sustained us through many hard months.

One of our first problems was how to organize the business legally and financially in such a way that we could maintain employee ownership and yet raise capital from outside sources. We explored the idea of a limited partnership with wealthy outsiders as limited partners and ourselves as the general partner. The idea was that the outsiders could write off our expected early losses on their income taxes. But we finally decided to incorporate, mainly for reasons of limiting liability.

We became a close corporation — a corporation with 10 or fewer stockholders — and elected to be a Sub Chapter S corporation for federal tax purposes.

Each of the founders purchased or pledged to purchase $5,000 worth of common stock during the first year. We then sought to raise $50,000 more in outside capital.

Our initial plan was to sell stock — but always a minority share — to outside investors, and at one point we almost landed an eccentric oil millionaire. That deal — quite fortunately, in retrospect — fell through, and we began to re-think our capitalization strategy.

After participating in a course in financial development at the New School for Democratic Management, a San Francisco-based alternative business school, we decided to seek debt rather than equity investments, and to retain 100 percent employee stock ownership.

Contrary to standard business procedure, we launched the business before we had assurance that we would be able to raise the targeted amount of capital. We were anxious to get started and, being somewhat idealistic, assumed that we would find the necessary capital as we went along.

In fact, we did. Within a year, several individuals loaned us a total of $39,500, and one man guaranteed a bank line of credit of $30,000. All the loans were long-term and at below-market interest rates. The lenders, like us, were motivated more by a belief in solar energy than by a desire to make a high return on investment.

Peter Barnes, the Solar Center, San Francisco (a worker cooperative):

Besides wanting to succeed as a solar business, which would be hard enough, we also wanted to succeed as an employee-owned and democratically managed business.

Some of the ingredients of democratic management, at least as we've been practicing it, are the opportunity for all employees to become equal stock owners; equal pay for all employees with minor and temporary deviations based on need; collective decision-making, usually by consensus, at weekly staff meetings and periodic staff retreats; and clear-cut assignment of responsibilities, with accountability to the group.

Since the start up of the business, two of the original employee-owners have left, with their stock being returned to the corporation, and two new employees have become stockholders. Our present plan is for each new employee who chooses (and is chosen) to stay with the business after a six month trial period to purchase $2,500 in stock from the remaining founders, so that stock ownership will be equalized at $2,500. Typically, stock is purchased out of current salary, so it's really a form of sweat equity.

The equal pay policy has meant, among other things, that installers receive a fixed monthly salary rather than an hourly wage, and that sales persons receive the same monthly salary rather than commissions. This is not the normal way to run a contracting business, and its success depends largely on the motivation and commitment of the individual employees. Recently, we did switch one salesperson from salary to commission in an effort to improve his productivity.

Our experience with collective decision-making has been quite satisfying. A common distaste for excess verbiage and a high regard for efficiency have contributed to speedy and productive staff meetings. Because of the individuals involved, ego clashes have been minimal. We've developed constructive ways of criticizing each other and holding each other accountable. And we've become experts at supporting each other through difficult periods — as well as celebrating birthdays together, rafting rivers together, and in general becoming a kind of family while respecting each other's separate lives outside of the business.

Naturally, we occasionally ponder the reasons for our success thus far, given the high mortality rate of small businesses and especially businesses in new industries where the markets are small and difficult to penetrate. The main factors seem to be these:

1. Hard work;

2. Moderate pay (about $800 per month till now);

3. Careful husbanding of capital (we've learned to get by with low inventory and used trucks);

4. Friendly investors;

5. Satisfied customers (of course we worked hard to satisfy them);

6. The idealism that got us into the business in the first place;

7. The togetherness that comes from shared ownership, equal pay, collective decision-making, and mutual concern for everyone's growth and job satisfaction.

As the elected business manager of the corporation, I can testify to the supreme importance of the last-mentioned factor. Neither I nor anyone else at The Solar Center could have pulled it off as a traditional owner-boss. We would not have had the confidence, the energy, the staying power, or the wisdom that comes from collectivity — nor would we have had half the fun.

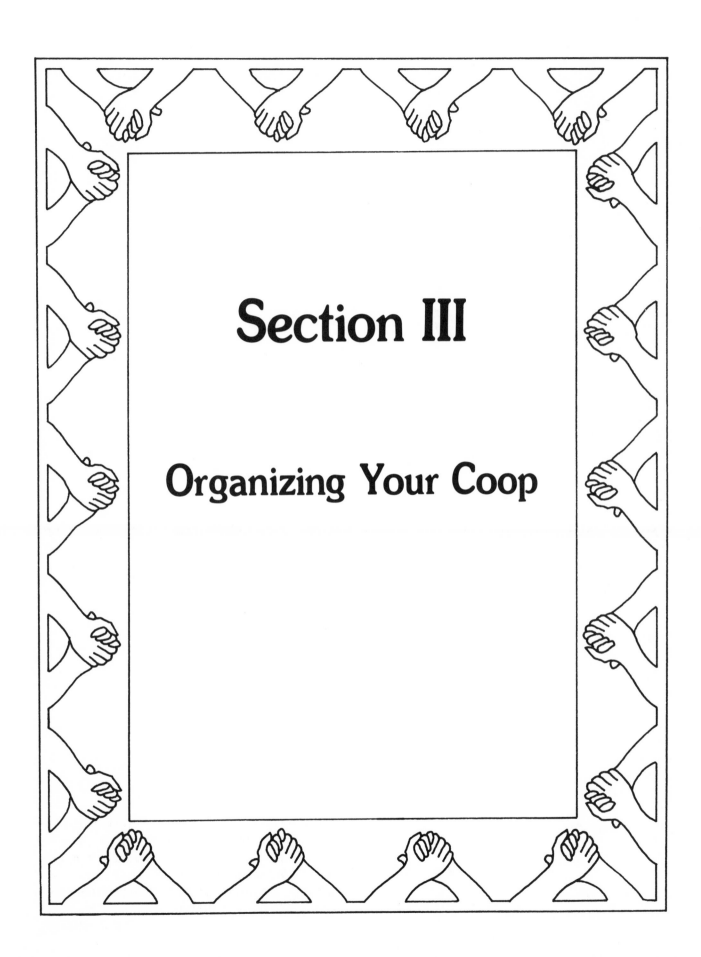

Section III

Organizing Your Coop

Disconnect from the monopolies. Use land and plant your own vegetables — cooperative farming. Form your own cooperative consumer action groups. And make sure you get a slice of TV time locally, because without that you can't quickly disseminate good ideas.
— Ralph Nader

ORGANIZING YOUR COOPERATIVE

One of the first things you will need to consider in setting up your cooperative is how to organize the business. Almost all coops are legally organized as either partnerships or some type of corporation. No matter how you set up the business, you can manage your internal affairs cooperatively; but the legal form under which you are set up will make a difference in the taxes you may have to pay, in the legal liability of the members and in certain activities you may be allowed to conduct. Knowing all this before you begin can save you lots of money and headaches. This chapter will outline the types of legal business structures your cooperative can form. We suggest that you review all the possibilities and discuss them with an attorney or an accountant.

Sole Proprietorship

This is the simplest form of business relationship. One person or a married couple owns the business. As owner, you cannot hire yourself as an employee. Your profits are your wages and are taxed as such. You can, of course, hire others as employees, but the owner alone is personally and fully liable for all debts and lawsuits against the business.

In most situations, a sole proprietorship does not lend itself to a cooperatively owned and managed busines. But there have been times when people began a business as a sole proprietorship just to get it going, intending all along to make it into a cooperative. They did so because neither the landlord nor the bank would negotiate with a cooperative. One person agreed to take full responsibility. Once the business got on its feet, the cooperative incorporated. The landlord and the bank had no problem then in dealing with the corporation.

Occasionally you'll find the situation where someone sets up a sole proprietorship for his or her own profit but after awhile decides to liberalize the business and give everyone equal pay and a voice in the decision making. The owner says that the business is now run "cooperatively". But this is not a cooperative. The owner is still the only person legally responsible. Moreover, because of the owner's original investment and risk-taking, the owner is likely to claim a larger share of the profits. If the owner really intends to make it a cooperative, he should sell out to the employees.

We have seen examples of people working together who think of themselves as a cooperative yet who structure their business as several sole proprietorships. We know a group of artists, each with a different yet related skill, who rent a studio together. They call themselves Design Associates. Sometimes they all participate in a project and sometimes they get separate work. Whichever artist performs the work earns the pay. The artists are individually responsible for their portion of the rent and utilities; they purchase their own supplies; they keep separate books and file separate tax returns. It's certainly not a coop in the formal sense of the word, but it's a coop just the same.

An even better example is the Country Mouse, a second-hand store selling clothes mostly, in Garberville, California. It's owners consider it a collective.

There are five owners and the store is open five days a week. Each owner tends store one day. Couples count themselves as one owner. Each owner pays 1/5th the store rent, 1/5th the utilities, 1/5th the miscellaneous overhead expenses. The telephone is a pay phone so no one is stuck figuring out the bill.

The goods in the store are separately owned. Each owner acquires his and her own goods to sell and decides on a price. The price tag on each item in the store includes a code symbol which tells the person at the counter whose dress or coffee cup is being sold. All of the money from a sale goes to the owner whose goods sold. Once a week the owners get together and divide up the cash. No credit sales, no credit cards. Each owner files a separate tax return as a sole proprietor on a Schedule 1040-C. One accountant is hired to prepare all five returns.

For people who want to work together but are not fond of complicated and intertwined business/paperwork transactions, this is about as simple a system as you could devise. Obviously, such a system has limited application. Separate buying and separate ownership of inventory is not possible or practical in most businesses though it works well for this operation. The business would fold immediately without financial responsibility on the part of all five owners.

Many people will consider the extra effort of keeping track of five different people's sales — and the duplicated and inefficient efforts of five people shopping for the store each with limited funds — less than optimum, and they would be right. There are more efficient and more cost-effective ways to run a store. But this particular store probably never would have happened if it could not have been set up the way it was.

One potential legal problem with this kind of set up could occur if someone outside the group — a creditor or a supplier or a customer — is led to believe that he is dealing with a partnership and not with an individual. If a lawsuit was filed, a court might rule that the "associates" (or whatever they choose to call themselves) were presenting themselves to the world as a partnership, that the person filing the suit had every reason to believe he was dealing with a partnership, and that all the "partners" are individually responsible for a debt which rightly belonged to only one of them. If you carefully choose your associates and have a clear understanding amoung youselves how you are to operate, such a problem should be easily avoided.

Obviously, the legal structure of a business need not be some form of a coop for the people to consider themselves a collective or to work cooperatively. "Whatever works" is and always will be Number One consideration. The ideal, elaborate cooperative structure can easily collapse under the weight of complicated bookkeeping and tax laws. Always keep your real goals in mind. Any legal structure should be subordinate to these goals.

Partnership

Two or more people (other than husband and wife) are owners of the business. They may share equally or agree to some other division of the profits and losses. As a partner you can hire employees, borrow money, bind other partners and the partnership to contracts you make. Each partner is personally liable for all debts and lawsuits against the business, even though another partner contracts the debt. Thus, if the partnership cannot afford to pay a debt, the creditor can collect it from any partner's personal assets. Like a sole proprietor, a partner is considered an owner of the business; partners cannot hire themselves as employees.

The partnership itself pays no income tax. The profits of the business are divided among the partners according to whatever agreement the partners made, and each partner pays his and her individual taxes. Partners are taxed on all profits of the business whether or not the money is distributed to them.

A partnership need not be in writing. But if you've ever been in business, you will appreciate the need for a written agreement. People often have short memories and long needs.

Many cooperatives begin as partnerships. They are easy to set up: people just get together and do it. And if the business is structured so that each partner will own an equal share and have an equal vote, a partnership can fit right into the cooperative spirit. Partnerships, however, have legal limitations which hinder coop change and growth. Every time a new partner is added and every time a partner leaves, the partnership is technically dissolved. The coop may continue as before and to all appearances may be unchanged, but legally a business has ceased to exist and a new business has begun. The ledgers of the old partnership must be closed and new ledgers set up. Separate tax returns for the "old" coop and the "new" coop will have to be filed at tax time. It is more of a bookkeeping nuisance than anything else. But even with these problems, it is usually easier and less expensive to start a partnership than to start a corporation. A lot of worker coops in particular start out as partnerships. Then when it looks like things are going well and the coop will succeed, they switch over and become a corporation.

Setting Up a Partnership

Starting a partnership is simple. You agree to be partners and you commence operation. That is all you need to do to be legally recognized as a partnership. If you start a coop without formally agreeing to be partners (and without incorporating) the IRS and the courts will usually rule that you are operating as a partnership.

Some partnerships have had problems with the Department of Labor which enforces the minimum wage and overtime laws. In some cases, the Department has ruled that a member-partner who owns less than 20% interest may be considered an employee for purposes of the minimum wage and overtime law. The law specifically says, "Membership in a cooperative does not necessarily establish a partnership arrangement." There is no strict rule; cases are decided on an individual basis. The Department usually does not step in unless they receive a complaint. We feel that if your partnership agreement clearly states that members are partners, names the members and states how they are to be compensated, you should have no trouble with the Department of Labor.

The Partnership Agreement

A partnership agreement is an "understanding" between partners as to how the business will be conducted. Many partnership agreements are nothing more than a handshake and a "let's do it." Often such agreements turn out to be more of a "misunderstanding" than anything else. A written partnership agreement is not required by law but it is something no partnership should be without. It reduces the possibilities of misunderstanding and future problems.

The partnership agreement should be detailed and should cover everything the articles and bylaws of a corporation cover. It is a good idea to read the entire chapter "Incorporating Your Cooperative". Although a partnership does not have articles, bylaws or a board of directors, the issues addressed in setting up a corporation should also be included in a partnership agreement.

The partnership agreement is legally binding on all partners who sign it. It does not, however, need to be filed with any government agency.

The agreement should include:

1. Name of the partnership, names of the individual member-partners, term of the partnership (indefinite or for a set, limited time), date started.

2. The purpose of the coop: what is it being set up to do and what are its goals.

3. The basic cooperative principles should be included: democratic management and one member, one vote. The specifics should be spelled out. Do you want majority rule or consensus or some other arrangement? Will the coop have a hierarchical management structure with specific duties assigned to specific members or will all members have a say in all activities?

4. How much each partner will contribute — in cash, in property and in labor. There are no federal laws requiring partners to make equal or simultaneous contributions.

5. How and when partners are to be paid and how each partner will share in the profits and losses. Although partners are not employees, they may pay themselves a wage (called a "guaranteed payment"). The agreement should specify what wages, if any, are to be paid to the partners. Any profit in excess of wages can, at your option, be divided among the partners (equally or based on any other arrangement you may choose) or retained by the coop for its own use. All the profits, however, are taxable to the individual partners whether distributed to them or not. The partnership itself pays no income tax.

6. Admission of a new partner-member. This is usually done by unanimous agreement. Remember that a new partner legally terminates the old partnership. New ledgers must be set up and a new partnership agreement drafted, though it can be identical to this agreement. You should state in the agreement whether or not an incoming partner is personally responsible for the coop's existing debts. Some states have specific laws about assumption of prior partnership debts.

7. Departure of a partner — voluntarily, by expulsion or because of death or disability. Remember also that the departure of one partner legally ter-

minates the old partnership. One of the most important items in the agreement is how to value the departing partner's interest in the coop and how to compensate that partner. This is discussed in more detail below. Many states specifically forbid a partner to convey his or her interest in the partnership to another person or to a personal creditor without consent of the other partners, but you should include such a clause in the agreement anyway.

8. Amending the agreement. The agreement is such a basic and important document that you probably should require a unanimous vote of all partners to amend it.

9. What else is important to you? What else do you want to say about your coop and the people who will own and operate it with you? It is always better to work out every detail and every possibility you can foresee, now when everyone feels good about everyone else in the coop, than to wait until a problem develops.

Departing Partner-Members

The issues which must be dealt with are investment, equity in the coop, and worth or value of the business. Does the departing member merely get a refund of her investment, does she get her share of the business equity, or does she get her share of the "worth" of the business?

The "investment" is the actual money contributed to the venture by the members. The "equity" is the value of the business as it appears on the ledgers: the investment plus any undistributed profits (see the following chapter "Partners Capital Accounts"). The "worth" or "value" of the business is what it will fetch on the open market if it were sold as a going concern.

What happens to your collective when a departing member who is, say, a 10% owner demands 10% of the value of the business? Your venture may be quite successful, maybe someone might think it is worth $50,000; but you only have $180 in the bank account. What do you do? What you do is make sure you have covered the problem before it arises.

It is common for coops to specify that departing members receive a return of investment and no more. It is common for cooperative partnerships in particular to specify that departing partners get their equity in the business and no more. Some agreements, however, call for an appraisal of the market value of the going business and payments to the departing partner, often over an extended period of time, of that partner's share of the worth of the business. If you do not make the decision yourself at the start, some court of law, possibly under hostile circumstances, may decide for you later on.

Partners Capital Accounts

One aspect of bookkeeping which often gets overlooked or discussed all too briefly is the record of member-partners capital (equity in business). Small partnerships in particular seem to be the most lax in keeping track of members' equity. Our experience as tax accountants is that businesses which keep precise records of sales and expenses often fail to keep even rough records of partners' capital contributions and withdrawls. The result is a balance sheet out of balance and many hours trying to reconstruct the cash flow. What should be a fairly simple tax return becomes tedious, lengthy and expensive.

Another reason for keeping close track of members' capital (other than keeping your bookkeeper and tax accountant from getting ulcers is because actual ownership percentages will fluctuate as members contribute and withdraw different amounts of money at different times. The assets and liabilities of a coop owned equally by several people may not in fact be owned in equal proportions.

For example, let's take a very simple three owner worker coop legally structured as a partnership. Each of the three members contributed $10,000 to start the business and all three put equal time into the business. At the start of business, each 1/3 member owned 1/3 of the $30,000 capital. Now, let's say that member A is drawing $400 per month as a salary; members B and C don't need the money and have decided not to take any money out of the business for awhile. At the end of the first year, the business made a $15,000 profit (before deducting member A's draw). The capital account for the three members looks like this:

	Member A	Member B	Member C	Total
Start of business	$10,000	$10,000	$10,000	$30,000
Profit for year	5,000	5,000	5,000	15,000
Draw during year	(4,800)	0	0	(4,800)
End of 1st year	$10,200	$15,000	$15,000	$40,200

All three members are still equal partners but if the business were liquidated at the end of the first year, all three would not get equal shares from the liquidation.

Even if you don't set up a formal capital account ledger, at least keep a notebook or ledger sheet of contributions and withdrawls — the amounts and the dates. Just take a minute when you pull $20 out of the cash register or when you make change for a customer out of your pocket, and write it down.

Other Business Forms Not Likely to be Used by Cooperatives

Before we discuss corporations, we thought we would include a brief description of some of the lesser known legal structures. Your cooperative may wish to consider these forms but you are not likely to adopt any of them. In some instances, your state may not legally recognize the form. In other instances, as you will see, the form does not serve the purposes of the coop.

Limited Partnership

The kind of partnership described in the "Partnership" chapter is known as a "general" partnership. A "limited" partnership allows investors to become partners without assuming unlimited liability. Limited partners usually risk only their investment. There must always be at least one general partner who will assume full risk and responsibility.

Limited partners are basically just investors. They are severely restricted by law from participating in the management of the partnership. This kind of inequality among partners is certainly not in keeping with the way coops should function. All members in a coop should have a say in important matters. Hence, few coops will organize as limited partnerships. For people who merely want to invest in the coop, there are other more suitable ways.

Joint Venture

A joint venture is a partnership set up for a specific one-time limited purpose. A joint venture does not envision a long-term relationship. When the "venture" is completed, the business is dissolved. A common example of a joint venture occurs when people form a business to mine some land. They know that once the minerals run out or when it becomes too expensive to extract them, the venture will be dissolved. The same laws and legal responsibilities that apply to partners in a general partnership also apply in a joint venture.

Since most coops begin in the hope that they will continue for a long time, the joint venture form is too restrictive.

Association

Associations are unincorporated charitable, educational, scientific and civic organizations, social clubs and trade groups. Associations are not businesses. Associations are not intending to make profits. For example, a group of people in northern California who have organized to try to stop a nickel strip mine call themselves the Red Mountain Association. A buying club which deals only with its members (no sales to non-members) may structure itself as an association.

Associations are somewhat like partnerships but without a partnership agreement or a profit motive. Unlike partnerships, however, one member of an association cannot, in contracting with outsiders, bind the association or other members without first receiving specific authority from the members.

Many coops do organize as associations, sometimes intentionally sometimes "by default" because they have neither formally set up a partnership nor have they incorporated. We don't recommend that your coop organize as an association. There is often confusion and different IRS rulings about the legal and tax status of an association which can lead to unwanted complications for your coop. The IRS sometimes considers associations to be partnerships if their structure and operation resembles a partnership. But the IRS will treat an association as a corporation if the business has the characteristics of a corporation such as bylaws, directors and officers. Consequently, though you could organize as an association, you run into the problem of not knowing for sure how the state and federal government will define your coop for tax purposes.

Partnership Association

A partnership association is a quasi-partnership, quasi-corporation with some of the aspects of each. It has limited liability like a corporation, providing the word "limited" in its title. But unlike a corporation, a partnership association does not issue stock. People become partner-members just as they do in a partnership.

Only a very few states recognize partnership associations. You might want to check with your state's office of corporations or the secretary of state to see whether a partnership association form exists where you live. If it does, your coop might find this form of organization useful. We recommend that you speak to an attorney or an accountant to fully understand the benefits and drawbacks of partnership associations.

Business Trust/Massachusetts Trust

A business trust, or a Massachusetts Trust as it is also known, is organized when only property is involved. It is not limited to Massachusetts; every state permits it. Certain people, called trustees, have title to and manage the property. Other people, usually investors, hold certificates (similar to corporate stock) showing their interests in the property. The certificate owners have limited liability. A business trust allows the sale or transfer of a person's interest (sale of a partnership interest and, in some cases, sale of corporate stock require approval). A business trust is also not affected by the death of a member/certificate-holder.

Though it is not common for a coop to be set up as a business trust, housing coops may want to look into whether a business trust offers any advantages over the usual cooperative form. Check with an attorney.

Joint Stock Company

A joint stock company is similar to a business trust without a trustee. It is a for-profit business venture usually involving shared ownership of property. The company is governed by "articles of association" similar to a corporation's bylaws. Like a corporation, it has a board of directors, and owners hold shares or certificates. It is taxed as a corporation. Unlike a corporation, however, a joint stock company is not usually allowed limited liability, and so it has been out of fashion. If you can't get limited liability, there is no advantage in organizing as a joint stock company, especially since you will be paying taxes as though you were a corporation.

You are not guaranteed your choice of associates in a joint stock company. Shareholder-members cannot represent the company; the company is managed by officers and directors (though each member of the company is personally and individually liable for the company's debts just as in a partnership). For these reasons, a joint stock company is not a viable business form for a cooperative.

ESOP: Employee Stock Ownership Plan

Employee stock ownership plans have become recognized as successful ways to provide employee ownership of a corporation. ESOP's are used when employees want to take over an already existing company. ESOP's have been set up to salvage companies facing liquidation, to finance companies needing capital and to provide financing where a majority stockholder wants to sell out to the employees.

ESOP's are usually set up in relatively large already-existing companies where large amounts of money are necessary to buy the stock. They are not appropriate if you are beginning an employee-owned business from scratch. But if you are in a situation where employees are trying to buy out the employer, regardless of size, you should at least look into whether an ESOP would be feasable.

Here's how ESOP's work. A program is created, usually by the company (though outside community-interest organizations could also set it up) whereby a fund is started for the benefit of the employees. The fund is called an "employee trust" and it borrows money from a bank and/or from local and federal sources interested in keeping the business operating in the community. Often the company contributes to the loan or guarantees all or part of it. The employee trust uses the money to purchase company stock on behalf of the employees. The stock may be newly issued to provide additional capital to the company, or it may be a block of stock owned by one or more people who want to sell. The payments on the loan are made from the annual pre-tax net earnings of the company. Unlike repayments of conventional loans, these loan payments are tax deductible because the payments are made to what is considered to be an employee benefit or retirement plan.

Though an ESOP appears to be an attractive way to set up an employee owned company, ESOP-financed companies are often very different from worker cooperatives. In more than half of the existing ESOP's, owning shares of stock is not equated with control of the company. Management retains power over the voting stock. Employees usually receive stock in proportion to their length of service with the company and their job responsibilities; so the cooperative principle of one member, one vote is not adhered to even in those relatively few companies where employees can vote.

Experience has shown that employees participating in ESOP's do not want to make company decisions and take management responsibilitiy. In many companies, employees figure that "management" can do a better job. Unions as well as management personnel prefer to keep the distinction between employee and manager as clear as possible to perpetuate their existence. Nor do the employees wish to relinquish the rights they have obtained over the years. They don't want equal stock ownership; they want their ownership percentage to reflect their seniority or position in the company. Unlike people who come together to form a worker coop with the democratically-controlled collective spirit, employees in ESOP's often continue to think of themselves merely as employees trying to keep their jobs however they can. Educating them to the collective ideal can be a task.

A recent General Accounting Office report concluded that the managers of ESOP's, in general, use the assets of worker-owned companies to accumulate personal wealth while the employee-owners fared no better financially than they would under a more traditional operation. The G.A.O. said it found widespread abuse of the financial authority given to the managers who handle the accounting duties.

Worker Owners On Strike

"Welcome To South Bend Lathe, America's Largest 100 Percent Employee Owned Company." So reads the sign in front of the sprawling red brick factory in South Bend, Indiania. Below that sign is another sign, hand lettered and hand held: "South Bend Lathe Employee-Owners On Strike, Local 1722."

Richard Faverty/N.Y. Times

In 1975, 70 year old South Bend Lathe was threatened with liquidation because its performance was not up to the expectations of its owners, Amsted Industries Inc., a Chicago based conglomerate. The employees obtained $5 million in private loans, and the Economic Development Administration lent another $5 million to the city of South Bend which in turn lent it to an employees trust. The trust bought the company. Workers purchased stock in the company through the trust. South Bend Lathe became the first 100% employee owned company in the U.S. acquired by means of an Employee Stock Ownership Plan.

Little changed at the company. Professional managers still direct the operations as they always have. Worker participation is limited to one representative on the eight member board of directors. "The executives didn't pay one more penny for the company than the workers, yet we're excluded from important decisions," said one union member. By virtue of their higher income, the mamagers were assigned more stock as individuals than the hourly workers.

In 1980, some 290 members of United Steel Workers Local 1722 struck the plant they own. There are two versions of why the owner-emloyees are on strike.

One comes from president J. Richard Boulis, who was sitting in his air conditioned office inside the front gates of the factory. Mr. Boulis believes that the union wants to return to the traditional guarantees of retirement security through pensions. When South Bend Lathe became owned by the employees, they were told they would have to give up their pension fund, but their stock shares would provide more security in the long run, provided the company became profitable. Boulis says the dispute is a result of the workers' unwillingness "to think and act like owners".

The other version comes from the striking workers, sitting in the 90 degree August heat on the other side of the gate. They contend that the strike was called to determine who should run the company, the professional managers or the people who own a majority of the stock — the workers. "I was told that I was going to be the owner of the plant just as equally as Boulis or anybody else," said the president of the local. "But now he decides how the company invests its money, he decides how the profits are divided, he decides who will be fired and hired." The workers have found that their stock ownership means little at present.

The problem, according to Norman G. Kurland, a Washington lawyer and consultant who helped put the ESOP together, is that "the local union has never been provided with competent professional help to enable rank-and-file workers to understand and negotiate effectively with management on ESOP issues. Considering that management had continual access to top legal and other professionals, little wonder that the local union was at such a disadvantage from the beginning, leading to misunderstandings and frustrations among workers, much of which could have been avoided or worked out over time. Where South Bend Lathe went wrong, in my view, was in failing to provide workers with a continuing ownership-sharing education program and a structured two-way dialog for improving the ESOP after the employee buyout was completed. The workers still have voting power and can easily negotiate to improve the ESOP."

No Legal Structure At All

It is a fact of life that some coops, particularly small food coops, sometimes begin operation with absolutely no designated legal structure. They don't incorporate, they don't have a partnership agreement (written or vebal), they don't get business licenses and they don't file tax returns. Some of these coops go on for years operating "informally", their existence unknown to the IRS and state and local government agencies.

If your cooperative is only a small food buying club or something similar, with no paid employees, with no profits and with no sales to the general public, you are probably not breaking any serious laws by not becoming "official" and not filing papers and tax returns. But we couldn't say for sure that you are operating legally; and even if you are, we do not recommend that you operate in this manner anyway — it is fraught with danger to all of the members of the coop.

First of all, even a tiny food buying club is subject to zoning laws, sales tax laws and health department regulations. If you have a paid manager, you must comply with state and federal employment laws. Even if your workers are all volunteers, if the

volunteers are earning extra discounts for their labor, you may have a problem with employment laws (see the chapter "Volunteers and the Law").

The biggest problem for a coop operating with no legal status is the potential liability of the individual members if someone is injured at the coop, if someone decides to sue the coop or if the government decides you should have filed tax returns and hits you with back taxes and penalties. The members themselves will be sued, individually and separately. The IRS will bill the members, as individuals, for the coop's taxes. The courts will probably rule that you are operating as a partnership and hold all partners (all members) individually and personally liable for all debts and lawsuits against the coop. If the coop has a board of directors, the directors may find themselves personally liable for the coop's taxes and debts and the medical bills for the volunteer who injured his back lifting a 100 pound sack of soy beans.

Even an "unofficial" coop can and should obtain liability and workers compensation insurance to protect itself from injury claims. But you can't find anti-Internal Revenue Service insurance, and you can't be sure that a lawsuit won't be greater than the amount of your insurance coverage.

We highly recommend that you pick an appropriate legal structure for your cooperative and formally adopt that structure — put it down in writing. If you have been in business for awhile, operating without any legal structure, now is the time to set one up. Your good luck may continue, but why take such a big chance?

Corporations

A corporation is a legal entity in itself. It is seperate from its owners (the people who own shares of stock or memberships) and from the people who run it. In effect, it is a ''legal person'' and can make contracts, accumulate assets, borrow money and, of course, pay taxes. Corporations are licensed by the state; the rules under which they operate vary from state to state.

The most attractive feature of a corporation is its limited liability. As a member or stockholder, you need not worry about losing your personal possessions to pay a debt or court judgement owed by the corporation. As a partner in a partnership, remember, your personal assets are vulnerable. In a corporation you usually can only lose your investment, nothing more. There are, however, exceptions to the limited liability. Someone who grossly mismanages the corporation or who participates in transactions which are unfair to the corporation (usually for the person's own benefit at the expense of the corporation) can be held personally liable for his or her actions. A corporation will not shield you from personal liability that you normally should be responsible for, such as not having car insurance or acting with gross negligence. Professionals such as doctors cannot hide behind corporations to protect themselves from malpractice suits. As to financial commitments, many banks, before lending money to a small corporation, will require the stockholders or officers to co-sign as personal guarantors of the loan. Stockholders can be held personally liable for back taxes owed by the corporation; there is no limited liability when the IRS is trying to collect.

There are many other advantages and disadvantages to corporations; they are all covered in the following chapters. The remainder of this section will review the three basic kinds of corporations — for-profit, non-profit and cooperative — and some variations within these three categories.

For-Profit Corporations

This is your usual corporation. When people think of corporations, this is what they think of. The business is there to make a profit.

Corporations come in all sizes. They can be as large as General Motors or as small as your neighborhood pasta shop which has decided to incorporate. Small corporations may sometimes benefit from special legislation not available to larger businesses. We discuss this later in the ''Closely Held Corporation'' and ''Sub Chapter S Corporation'' chapters.

The owners of a corporation are the people who invest in it by purchasing shares of stock issued by the company. The company issues the stock to raise capital. The more shares you purchase, the greater your investment, and, usually, the larger your voice in major decisions since each share usually gets one vote. The procedure of one vote for each share of stock is unlike the cooperative principle of one vote per member regardless of how many shares of stock a member holds.

Most small corporations issue only one class of stock, called ''common'' stock, and voting power goes along with the number of shares you own. Some corporations issue a second class of stock, called ''preferred'' stock, which usually pays higher dividends and usually does not come with voting rights. Preferred stock is a common way to raise investment money and is covered in the chapter ''Financing Your Cooperative''.

The overall management of the corporation — that is, the people who set policy — is the board of directors. The board is elected by the shareholders. The day to day operations are handled by the officers who are appointed by the board. In a small corporation the directors are often also the officers and the shareholders.

Except in some small corporations, shares of stock are usually freely transferrable. The shareholder can sell the stock at any time for whatever price someone else is willing to pay for it. Cooperatives usually try to put some restrictions on the free transferrability of shares of stock, since owning a share of stock is more than being an investor — it's being a member of the cooperative.

Unlike partnerships, corporations do not automatically dissolve when a shareholder departs or dies. A corporation continues to exist until the shareholders vote to liquidate it (or until a court liquidates it in bankruptcy). This ongoing corporate life is known as "perpetual existence".

A corporation may hire its owners, the shareholders, as employees; partnerships and sole proprietorships cannot. This difference is important because owner-employee benefits such as health insurance can be written off as deductible expenses on the corporation's tax return. Partnerships can also take a tax deduction for employee benefits paid; but because partners are not considered employees of their partnership, benefits purchased for the partners are not tax deductible.

Corporations pay income taxes on their profits. Corporate profits are actually taxed twice (called "double taxation"): once as corporate income and again when distributed to shareholders as dividends; the shareholders have to declare the dividends as taxable income on their personal tax returns. Small corporations, including cooperatives, can usually avoid double taxation by paying out all their income as salaries and bonuses so that the corporation's profit is zero. As long as the owner-employees' wages and bonuses are reasonable for the kind of work they do (comparable to wages paid for similar work in other businesses) the IRS will probably not challenge the procedure. In this way, the corporation pays no income tax. The employee-owners pay taxes on their wages, which is basically the same amount of tax they would have paid on their dividends. The corporate profit is, therefore, only taxed once.

The corporation also has the option to retain some of its profits and not distribute them as wages or dividends, though the IRS does have a limit on the amount of retained earnings allowed. The retained earnings are taxed once, to the corporation. If they are ever distributed in the future, the shareholders will have to pay taxes on the dividends the year they are distributed.

We would like to point out that this discussion of dividends and retained earnings has nothing to do with patronage refunds. Although patronage refunds are sometimes called dividends and are sometimes retained by coops, the refunds are totally different than the dividends and retained earnings of conventional for-profit corporations.

Some people will say that banks lend more readily to corporations. The stable, lasting image of a corporation is more secure than a partnership which may dissolve when a partner leaves. However, don't rely too much on this. It is likely that when you first incorporate, a bank will still require stockholders to sign as personal co-signers of the loan and maybe even pledge their personal assets (a house perhaps) as security before the corporation will get the loan.

Many coops organize as for-profit corporations. It is easier to qualify as a for-profit corporation than as a non-profit corporation (which is very restricted) or as a cooperative corporation (becuse many states do not recognize this form, and many of those that do recognize cooperative corporations often have specific definitions and limitations).

Being a for-profit corporation does not mean you have to earn a profit. You can pay reasonable wages and bonuses, lower prices, make donations and otherwise cut down on the profit you would make, thereby giving the money to local people instead of to the government. An accountant can help you with this.

Through all this maneuvering to eliminate profits, however, you should realize that profit, in and of itself, is not evil. Even for a coop dedicated to "food for people, not for profit," sometimes a profit is essential for the survival of your business. The entire concept of profit, unfortunately, is too often muddy and confusing. A section in the Bookkeeping chapter, "The Politics of Profit," attempts to clear up the confusion.

Closely Held (Small) Corporations

It's not only the big guys who incorporate. Many small, sometimes family-owned businesses incorporate to take advantage of the limited liability provision. But these small corporations usually do not want to permit free trading of shares of stock. They don't want just anyone to be able to purchase a share and become an owner. They want to limit share ownership to the few people directly involved. If a stockholder leaves, dies or becomes disabled, the business wants the first right to purchase the shares. The shareholders also intend to appoint themselves directors and officers and hire themselves as employees. Many worker coops and some producer coops are in this situation.

"Closely held" is the common name for corporations which place restrictions on stock ownership and transferability. In some cases, closely held corporations may receive special recognition by state and federal agencies exempting the corporation from some securities laws and from obtaining some stock permits.

Some states allow businesses to incorporate as

"close corporations", a legal term for certain closely held corporations which meet certain state requirements. While all "close corporations" are closely held, not all closely held corporations are "close".

Closely held corporations must be structured according to strict federal and state regulations. Close corporations in particular may be subject to certain requirements on how profits must be distributed which may cause coops problems with the IRS. If you are interested in closely held corporations, talk to an attorney or an accountant.

Sub Chapter S Corporations

A federal tax provision benefitting small corporations is found in Sub Chapter S of the Internal Revenue Code. It allows small corporations (and joint stock companies and associations as well) to be taxed in the same way partnerships are. The corporation itself pays no federal income tax. The stockholders as individuals, like the partners in a partnership, pay the taxes on their personal tax returns. This avoids the double taxation of the corporation's profits. However, in Sub Chapter S corporations, each stockholder must pay federal taxes on all the dividends to which he or she is entitled whether or not all the profits have been distributed. (The corporation will probably want to keep some of the profits to finance capital improvements and expansion and for reserves.) In the usual corporation, the stockholder only pays taxes on the dividends actually paid.

Another advantage of Sub Chapter S is due to some complex tax laws which allow current business losses to be carried back to prior years to offset prior years' taxes, bringing immediate tax refunds. Any business, corporation or otherwise, can avail itself of operating loss carryback laws. But if a corporation is brand new and sustains a loss, there are no prior years to carry the loss back to. In the case of a Sub Chapter S corporation, the loss passes through to the stockholders. They in turn can carry the loss back to their personal prior years' returns even though the business did not exist then. Losses of a regular corporation (or any other business) that cannot be carried back can be carried forward to offset the future years' earnings, but the business must wait a full year or more to get the refund.

Sub Chapter S status has many restrictions. There can be no more than 25 shareholders. None of the shareholders may be non-resident aliens. All the shareholders must be individuals or estates; another cooperative cannot own a share. No more than 20% of the corporation's income can come from royalties, rents, dividends, interest, annuities or other "passive investment income". The corporation must apply for a Sub Chapter S status either in the first 75 days of its tax year or any time during the preceding tax year. And that's not the entire list of restrictions. What's more, Sub Chapter S is a federal tax law. Many states do not recognize Sub Chapter S for state income taxes. If you are interested in Sub Chapter S we suggest you talk to a lawyer or an accountant.

Sub Chapter S status isn't really necessary for cooperatives. As a cooperative, your group can take advantage of a federal tax structure similar to the one for Sub Chapter S corporations, without worrying about proper filing and other Sub Chapter S restrictions. It is called Sub Chapter T, and any for-profit corporation or cooperative can qualify. Sub Chapter T is discussed later in this section.

Non-Profit Corporation

People who form a cooperative often think that since they do not intend to make a profit, they can incorporate as a non-profit corporation and not have to pay federal and state taxes. People have heard that non-profit corporations can receive grants from federal agencies, foundations, corporations and wealthy individuals. Some people find that their state's laws require coops to be structured as non-profit corporations. Some people like the term "non-profit" and what it stands for and want their coop to be able to say it is a non-profit corporation.

Much of what people think and have heard about non-profits is misleading. Much of it is incorrect. Much of it correct, but...

Non-profit status is not available to some coops and is, in fact, not even desirable in many situations. Non-profit *tax exempt* status, a separate category from simply being non-profit, is very difficult to obtain. And even after obtaining tax exempt status, only certain non-profit tax exempt corporations come under the IRS rules which enable them to receive grants.

We should start at the beginning. What is a non-profit corporation? Most states define a non-profit corporation as one which will not distribute "gains, profits or dividends" to its members during the life of the corporation. Generally speaking, non-profit corporations may not distribute patronage refunds because such refunds are considered "gains, profits or distributions". There are exceptions to this rule and we discuss them below.

A coop which plans to engage in a profit making activity can still obtain non-profit status. What is done with the profits, not whether profits are or are not made, determines if a coop can be non-profit.

A non-profit corporation may retain the profits for its own use. The corporation may donate the profits to other non-profit corporations. The corporation may also pay out its profits in the form of wages to member-employees. As long as the wages are reasonable — comparable to wages paid for similar work in similar fields — the IRS will not interfere. If the wages are much higher, the IRS will call the excess "dividends" which non-profits may not legally distribute. Members wages are taxable to the members regardless of the tax status of the corporation.

Non-profit corporations may not issue corporate stock or certificates of ownership. Most states allow non-profits to issue memberships if the corporations want to; issuing memberships is usually optional. Most non-profit coops are exempt from registering their memberships as securities and obtaining stock permits. Some states have specific definitions, responsibilities and privileges for members of non-profit corporations.

Non-profit corporations have the same benefits common to all corporations: perpetual existence, company paid fringe benefits for member-employees and limited liability. As with other corporations, the limited liability provision in a non-profit coop has its own limits. Officers in a non-profit corporation are personally liable for federal corporate taxes and penalties if the coop does not pay.

Like all other corporations, non-profits are chartered by the states and not by the federal government. Obtaining state non-profit status is not difficult if you meet the definition and adhere to the above requirements. So if your state requires coops to be structured as non-profit corporations, or if you are determined to have "non-profit" in your name because you like the flavor of it, non-profit status is available to you.

State non-profit status will exempt you from paying state income taxes, state employment taxes and the state franchise tax which is a minimum state income tax imposed on corporations.

Federal non-profit tax exempt status is only available to non-profit corporations which meet certain IRS requirements. Section 501(c) of the Internal Revenue Code spells out which non-profits are eligible for tax exempt status. Many of the categories within Section 501(c) do not apply to coops. But if your coop is a social club, a cemetary company, a group legal service, a credit union or a farmer coop, you may be eligible for a tax exemption. These specific categories, however, are not eligible to receive grants.

The major reason most people seek tax exempt status is to be eligible to receive grants. But only certain tax exempt corporations qualify. Corporations which do qualify for this special status can receive grants from government agencies and private foundations and can receive tax deductible donations from corporations and individuals. These particular non-profits are also eligible for low mailing rates, they are exempt from social security and unemployment taxes, and they may sometimes be exempt from property taxes.

This special category is Section 501(c)(3) of the Internal Revenue Code. It applies only to non-profit corporations which are organized and operated for charitable, religious, scientific, literary or educational purposes.

A charitable purpose, in addition to its conventional meaning, can be defined as providing services "beneficial to the public interest". Charitable purposes include providing services and facilities to senior citizens or to blind people or to an ethnic group; defense of human and civil rights; a public interest law firm; promotion and development of the arts. For example, the Delaware Theater Company of Wilmington was granted tax exempt charitable status. The company's charter states that the theater will be accessible to and will provide special programs for young people and senior citizens. The IRS ruled that the theater was established "for the public good", and that was good enough for the IRS.

Groups falling in the "religious purpose" category are churches of all types, traditional and unconventional.

A scientific purpose is one carried on in the public interest. A scientific purpose would not be one which is incidental to a commercial operation such as the design or construction of equipment. Scientific research will usually qualify if the results are

made available to the public. The IRS defines scientific in conventional, Western terms. ESP, parapsychology and other non-traditional sciences are not likely to qualify.

A literary purpose does not mean any kind of publishing or distribution. A commercial publishing enterprise cannot usually qualify. The material published or distributed should be "directed towards the betterment of the community". Publishing materials for the handicapped or publishing educational materials, for example, could qualify. It is okay to sell the publications; you don't have to give them away. One non-profit publisher we know, THYB Publishing Company of Glen Ellen, California, was formed for the sole purpose of publishing and distributing *The International Bill of Human Rights*, a United Nations document. The company qualified for and was granted 501(c)(3) status. The IRS also granted this status to Ms. magazine. Among the arguments which won Ms. its tax exemption is that the magazine is used extensively in classrooms to teach children about sexual stereotypes.

Educational purposes qualifying for tax exempt status are very broad. Almost anything which provides "useful information beneficial to the community" can be considered an educational purpose. Child care coops, tutoring programs and public discussion groups would probably qualify. You do not have to organize as a conventional institution with a regular faculty and student body.

Even if you are able to qualify under Section 501(c)(3), you have yet another IRS hurdle to jump though it's not a difficult one. Within this code section are two classes of tax exempt corporations: public charities and private foundations. Public charities are churches, schools, hospitals, medical research organizations, public safety organizations and "publicly supported" organizations. An organization is publicly supported (and, therefore, a public charity) if it receives at least a third of its income from gifts, grants, contributions, membership fees, admissions, sales of merchandise, performance of services or furnishing of facilities. The income-earning activities must be related to the exempt purpose of the corporation.

Private foundations are 501(c)(3) corporations which do not qualify as public charities. Private foundations are subject to restrictions and certain excise taxes not imposed on public charities. The tax deductibility of donations to private foundations is more limited than donations to public charities.

The tax exempt categories are well defined. They strictly limit tax exempt status to particular types of organizations. Even though we present various possibilities for qualifying under the federal tax exempt law, the fact is most coops do not qualify. Tax-exempt status is routinely denied if the organization carries on a business with the general public similar to the business engaged in by for-profit corporations. For example, a federal appeals court ruled that a non-profit pharmacy operated by a senior citizens group, selling drugs at cost to the elderly and handicaped, is not tax exempt because it "operates for a substantial commercial purpose". The pharmacy, the court said, relies financially on customers rather than on charitable contributions and competes with profit-making drugstores. The pharmacy also does not provide drugs below cost to needy customers, something the court also noted. As another example, a cooperative which was formed to provide members with free exchange of personal services including home maintenance, minor repairs and transportation, was ruled not eligible to be a tax exempt corporation because it operated chiefly for the economic benefit of its members.

There are two confusing areas of law non-profit corporations must deal with — confusing because state and federal laws are sometimes different. You may find yourself taxed one way by the state and another way by the IRS. The bookkeeping, as you can imagine, can easily become a nightmare.

The first area is patronage refunds. As we explained earlier, patronage refunds are considered "gains, profits or dividends" which non-profit corporations are forbidden to distribute. If your state recognizes you as a non-profit corporation, the state will not allow you to distribute patronage refunds. If you don't obtain federal tax exempt status, however, the IRS does not consider you to be a non-profit corporation for tax purposes, regardless of your state designation. Therefore, the IRS does allow distribution of patronage refunds. You are, in effect, two different types of corporation in the eyes of two different taxing authorities.

Now, we'll muddy the water a little more. In some states, non-profit corporations may also be cooperative corporations. Some states require all cooperative corporations to be non-profit as well. If you are able to obtain non-profit status and cooperative corporation status, your state will allow you to distribute patronage refunds. If you do not obtain tax exempt status from the IRS, then both the state and the IRS will allow patronage refunds.

If you do obtain federal tax exempt status, however, remember that you may not distribute patronage refunds even though the state may now allow them. The situation is just reversed but once again, you are two different types of corporations.

Keep in mind, throughout this confusion, that no state or federal law **requires** a coop to make patronage refunds. There are always other ways to distribute a coop's earnings, and they are discussed throughout this book. If eliminating patronage refunds will solve a lot of your legal problems, you should consider this option.

The second confusing area of law involves ownership of a non-profit corporation and ownership of the corporation's assets. Although states do not allow members to receive distributions of gains, profits or dividends during the life of the corporation, many states do allow members to receive and keep the corporate assets on dissolution of the corporation. If the corporation held onto its profits over the years, when it closed its doors for good the members are entitled to receive the profits. The profits, if distributed to the members, will be taxable to the members.

This state law only applies, however, if a non-profit corporation did not receive federal tax exempt status. A 501(c)(3) tax exempt non-profit corporation is not allowed by law to distribute any of its assets to its members on dissolution. When a 501(c)(3) corporation goes out of business, all remaining assets of the corporation must be turned over to another 501(c)(3) organization. A non-profit corporation which has 501(c) tax exempt status — different, you'll remember, than 501(c)(3) — may on dissolution be able to distribute its assets to its members in certain situations.

As you can see, non-profit status is not a simple category to define or to obtain. It is not something you should attempt without the help of a competent accountant or attorney.

"Not For Profit"

We've noticed that many small coops who are not legally set up as non-profit corporations, but who are operating without a profit motive, use the expression "not for profit" to describe themselves.

"Not for profit" is not a legal term. No state, to our knowledge, either authorizes or prohibits its use.

We would like to offer a word of caution to those of you using "not for profit" in your name or in your advertising. Some people might consider the term "not for profit" misleading. They might think you are trying to pass yourselves off as a non-profit corporation. Some people might consider this fraud. The chance of this happening is remote. We have never heard of any "not for profit" coop having such trouble. But you might want to contact your state's attorney general office (try the charitable trust division) and get an opinion.

The Open Education Exchange is a "free" university operating throughout the San Francisco area. It is the largest and one of the oldest free U's in the country. Bart Brodsky and Janet Geis were two of the original founders of the Exchange. Today, they are its co-ordinators:

The corporation was just a group of academics with non-profit status, an independent educational group. We got in under their umbrella. They gave us carte blanche and they put me on the board. It's important to have non-profit status. We have a publication; mailing is cheaper, substantially cheaper. There's contributions, which in the last year we've just started asking for. Free public service announcements on radio and TV. As a 501(c)(3) we can elect to pay social security or elect not to. That's a lot of money out of your salary.

We're tending to talk about non-profit as opposed to profit in kind of a corrupt fashion: okay, what can you get out of this status? People simply think of it as a tax category. We also like to feel we're setting an example, setting up a model that has applicability in other areas, not just adult education. There's a legitimacy we're striving for. It's all too easy to say we're just taking care of our own little group over here in the corner.

We've actually been told that banks don't trust us. Because most non-profit corporations are usually set up on the basis of funding grants that run out. And so as a non-profit corporation we're less viable than profit-making corporations. So we're at a disadvantage. It was harder to get insurance as a non-profit corporation. We had a hell of a time getting liability coverage for our front office and coverage for our cars. The agent said it was because we were non-profit, because we had an organization that was untried and untested. Because we were non-profit, we might not be as secure or as stable. Because non-profit corporations usually self-destruct, especially new ones, when the grants run out.

Cooperative Corporation

A cooperative corporation is a consumer, producer or worker coop which has incorporated under its state's cooperative statutes. The cooperative principles we've discussed throughout the book — no profit motive; one member, one vote; distribution of patronage refunds — are part of cooperative corporation law in most states.

Cooperative corporations are entitled to benefits common to all corporations: limited liability, perpetual existence, tax deductible fringe benefits for member-employees. Cooperative corporations may also get additional advantages such as the following:

1. Being able to use the word "cooperative" in your name. Many states require you to incorporate as a cooperative corporation in order to use the word "cooperative" or "coop".

2. Issuing memberships instead of shares of stock. These memberships are limited to actual members. Members are usually restricted by state law from transferring their memberships to someone other than a new member or the cooperative itself. The purpose of this restriction is to make sure that only people involved in the coop will own memberships. In most states, the coop will be permitted to repurchase memberships from inactive members. Restriction on the transfer of shares of stock of a cooperative organized as a for-profit corporation is also usually possible though it is not written into law the way memberships in a cooperative are. It also requires a statement in the corporation's bylaws. Also, the term "membership" may be more attractive to a coop than "stock", the latter having a more conventional business ring to it. For-profit corporations cannot issue memberships.

3. Possible exemptions from, or simpler procedures for registering your memberships with the federal Securities and Exchange Commission and with the similar state agency.

4. Paying out patronage refunds based on participation. Sub Chapter T, which allows any coop to distribute patronage refunds, is a federal law and is not recognized by many states. States specifically allow cooperative corporations (and, in some states, only cooperative corporations) to distribute patronage refunds.

5. Possible exemption from stock permit fees required of most for-profit corporations.

Though organizing as a cooperative corporation may seem the most appropriate form for cooperatives, in fact relatively few coops are so organized. This is largely due to the fact that many states make it difficult for coops to incorporate as cooperative corporations. Each state has its own coop statute and no two are exactly alike. In order to be a cooperative corporation you must meet your state's qualifications. Some states have no general coop statute at all; only large agricultural coops qualify. Of the states with coop statutes, some require coops to be non-profit corporations, some allow consumer coops only and others restrict the type of business coops may undertake. A handful of states do have excellent coop statutes which allow any type of cooperative to incorporate under the cooperative corporation rules. If your state's coop laws are too limiting or non-existent, you may be able to incorporate in another state; it's called "foreign incorporation". The chapter "State By State Coop Laws" at the back of the book lists the coop statutes for all 50 states, the District of Columbia, Puerto Rico and the Virgin Islands and also provides information about out-of-state incorporation.

Sahag Avedisian, the Cheeseboard Collective, Berkeley, California:

Being in a collective is a good way to take your political and philosophical beliefs and make them a mainline part of your life. You no longer have to talk about being liberal or doing something that's politically correct because your own workplace frees you personally to pursue your personal interests. If the world were somehow a collective place economically, I think art would blossom. All the energy that goes into our survival would be freed.

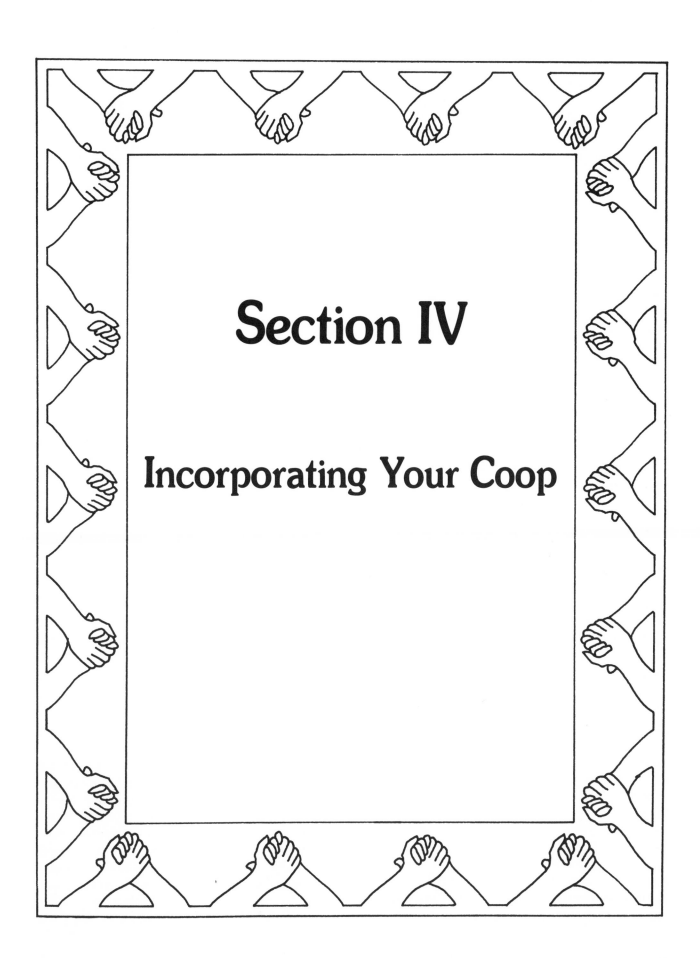

Section IV

Incorporating Your Coop

The pine tree is the ancient symbol of endurance and fecundity. More than one pine is used to signify cooperation. The trunks of the trees are continued into roots which form the circle, the ancient symbol of eternal life, typifying that which has no end. The circle represents the all embracing cosmos which depends upon cooperation for its existence.

— James Peter Warbasse, first president of the Cooperative League of the U.S.A.

Incorporating Your Cooperative

If your cooperative intends to become a corporation, you will probably need the help of an accountant or an attorney. Corporation law is complex. Even so, you should be knowledgeable in the workings of corporations. This chapter will briefly explain what the articles of incorporation and bylaws are, describe the people who make up the corporation, outline the ways coops which incorporate differ from usual corporations, and note a few legal and tax considerations for coops. The general discussion will apply to all corporations whether for-profit, non-profit or cooperative. However, each state has its own particular wrinkle to the law. Your coop will need to do some research to learn the precise legal and tax requirements for your particular type of corporation. We will conclude this chapter with examples of articles of incorporation and bylaws filed by several different cooperatives.

Articles of Incorporation

Articles of incorporation are like the constitution or charter of the cooperative. They set out the basic framework and policy. The articles should be written in general terms. Once written, they are usually more difficult to amend then bylaws; so save your specifics for the bylaws. The articles typically include:

1. The cooperative's official name and address.
2. The purpose of the cooperative. This should be stated in very general terms. For example, if your coop is organized as a for-profit corporation, the ar-

ticles might say the purpose is "to engage in any lawful activity". As a cooperative corporation, your purpose might read, "to engage in any lawful activity primarily for the benefit of the members who shall be the primary consumers (or producers) of the goods and services of the cooperative". You want to be certain to cover all possibilities because the direction of the coop may change in the future. If the coop is set up as a tax exempt non-profit corporation, your purpose must include the wording which defines it as a non-profit: "Organized under Section 501(c)(3) of the Internal Revenue Code for charitable, religious, educational, scientific or literary purposes",etc.

3. The number and names of the original directors on your board.

4. Whether stock or memberships will be issued (one or the other) and the total number of authorized shares or memberships. "Authorized" means available for sale. You select however many shares you wish to make available; they don't all have to be sold. Once you pick a number, you will not be able to issue more than the authorized number without obtaining a new stock permit from the state. Although you can authorize a million shares if you want, we suggest that you authorize no more shares than you anticipate actually issuing. If you incorporate as a cooperative corporation, some states will not allow the coop to commence operation until a certain percentage (20%, 25%, sometimes 50%) of the authorized shares are sold. If your state has such a restriction, you want to be sure to keep the number of authorized shares low enough to meet the state requirements. Check your state's rules in the chapter "State by State Coop

Laws'' at the back of the book. The number of authorized shares is an important decision from a legal standpoint and will require professional help.

5. Many states specify that certain operations or procedures are governed by the articles of incorporation. It is necessary for you to research your state's laws to find out what must be mentioned in the articles in addition to the above basics.

Bylaws

Bylaws flesh out your articles of incorporation. They are a set of rules for your coop to follow. Bylaws can be very general or quite specific. The more specific you get, the more you limit yourself but the easier it is for members and others to understand exactly what you are trying to accomplish; there is less likelihood of confusion or disagreement. States often specify that the bylaws govern certain operations or procedures. Where your state law specifies that bylaws govern a given situation, be sure your bylaws cover that situation. Below is a list of items commonly found in bylaws. Many of these items, such as restrictions on transferring shares and methods for amending the bylaws, are often dictated by state law. You will have to study your state's law and make sure your bylaws do not conflict with the law. Bylaws typically include:

1. The name and location of the coop.
2. How it will carry out its purpose.
3. The principal office of the coop.
4. Who can be a member or shareholder including any restrictions on owning and transferring memberships.
5. Privileges and responsibilities of members. For example, what is the minimum amount of purchases a member must make in order to remain active in a consumer coop? In a worker coop, how many hours must a member work? Can a member be expelled? How?
6. When and where membership meetings will be held. Most coops always have an annual meeting. Special meetings can be called at the request of a certain percentage of the members. Notice of the meetings must be given.
7. The number of directors, the length of their term in office, how they are elected, when they should meet, how they can be removed, how many constitute a quorum to conduct business (a quorum is the minimum number of directors who must be

present at a meeting in order to vote and make decisions; typically it is 50%).

8. The voting rights of members, which is usually one vote per member regardless of the number of shares owned.
9. The names of the officers.
10. The method for amending the bylaws.
11. The distribution of patronage refunds.
12. How the coop will distribute its assets if it dissolves (presumably it would be in proportion to the participation of each member).
13. Any other items you want to specify or your state requires.

Directors

In traditional corporations, the directors have the responsibility to set the basic policy for the corporation. They approve the annual budgets and major contracts. They are responsible for the records of member meetings and elections and for the annual financial statements. The board also selects the professional help — the accountant and attorney.

In some very small cooperatives, the board of directors is often just considered one of several committees with no more power than anyone else. It exists mainly for legal purposes. The major decisions are made by the members meeting as a whole. Other coops may give the board varying degrees of responsibility and control over the operations of the coop. The larger the coop, the more power the board usually has, just because it's difficult for a lot of people to collectively oversee a large corporation.

But large or small, the directors have important legal responsibilities to the coop and to the coop's customers, creditors and suppliers. Even if a board of directors is only a figurehead committee, directors still have the same legal responsibilities as any corporation's directors. Some states specify that a corporation "shall be managed by the board of directors". If your state makes such a distinction, then you know the buck stops there, no matter what your bylaws say. When a coop is sued, the directors' names will be on the complaint. The concept of limited liability may not always extend to directors on the board if a court determines that the board acted negligently or did not fulfill its duties.

Directors are under a duty to do the best they can for the corporation. Directors may be held liable for dealings which are irresponsible or where they seek personal gain at the expense of the corporation. This is not usually going to be a problem in small coops nor is it likely to even be one in large coops. But though this law on the "fiduciary duty" of the directors is basically concerned with large corporations where directors can take advantage of their position to make lots of money, boards of directors of coops should be aware of it.

Most states specify a minimum and maximum number of directors, often between 5 and 25. It is probably best to have an odd number of directors, to prevent a tie vote. Experience has seemed to show that in larger coops, the minimum should be 7 and the maximum 13.

The terms should be staggered. If it is a nine member board, for example, three might be elected each year, each serving a three year term. A seven member board might have four elected one year and three the next, each serving two years. This way, you always have continuity.

Although the board of directors may have ultimate authority in running the coop, the directors themselves have no authority as individuals. The authority is a group authority and may not be delegated to one or a few directors.

Boards of directors usually meet once a month. Notice of directors meetings must be given in advance. The law requires that a quorum be present in order for the directors decisions to be binding. The minimum quorum is usually 50% of the directors unless your state allows (and your bylaws specify) otherwise.

––––––––––––––

Open Education Exchange:

We've talked to a number of people who've worked with boards of directors involved with day to day operations, boards of perhaps 20 to 30 people. To get a quorum together was a big thing. Then to try to make a decision with 20 people is almost impossible. It's the same kind of thing that happens with a collective. When you have a board of directors that is so large and everybody has a vote, it's hard to have a consensus. We know of one non-profit corporation that folded mostly due to disagreements as to how people wanted to do it. People who

worked there were on the board. It got into staff disagreements and that kind of problem which couldn't be resolved. Certain people just left, and those were the main people who were holding the group together.

One of our board members had been on the board of a corporation and it couldn't work out policy. It was hard to get the board together, hard to find out what people wanted. It became little political power blocks, two or three people. He got very disgusted. He's encouraged us to keep the board small, make sure you know who's on it, keep the thing personal.

––––––––––––––

Officers

The officers — the president, vice president, secretary and treasurer — are responsible for the day to day business of the corporation. They are usually elected by the board of directors, though in small coops the members could elect them. Either the board of directors or the bylaws set out the specific duties of the officers. In small coops, the officers are often designated for legal purposes only and have no real power; managers and small groups or the entire membership makes the day to day decisions. State law, however, often gives officers "legal authority" to enter into obligations and contracts on behalf of the corporation. It does not matter whether your coop grants your officers authority or even specifically forbids it. If the party with whom the officer contracts believes the officer had the authority, the contract is binding. This is known as "apparent authority". Pick responsible officers.

A person may be both a director and an officer. In fact, a few states require the president to sit on the board.

Shareholders/Members

In the traditional corporation, the shareholders or members of the corporation elect the board of directors but otherwise have little say in the operation of the business. In most states shareholders also must vote on any amendments to the articles of incorporation. In small cooperatives, the members or shareholders often exert a lot more power and input, acting in place of the board and the officers in making decision.

There are laws governing the rights of shareholders and members. The following chapters will discuss these rights.

Voting

In the traditional for-profit corporation, each share of stock is worth one vote. The people who own the most stock have the most votes and thereby control the corporation. Owning a few shares of General Motors stock gives you little say in the management of the company.

Cooperatives work differently. An essential element of being a true coop is that each member has only one vote no matter how many shares of stock the member might hold.

One member, one vote is required by state law in most cooperative corporations and non-profit corporations. If your coop is organized as a for-profit corporation or if the law does not specify one member, one vote, you need to make this voting arrangement clear in your bylaws.

Many state laws specify that, in for-profit corporations, voting goes with the shares: one vote per share. If your state has such a requirement, you want to be sure to set up your coop so every member gets one share of stock and that no one may hold more than one voting share.

Sharing in the "Profits"

Corporations make profits. Cooperatives have "surpluses" or "net savings" or "net margins". This is more than a twist of words. Cooperatives are not in the business of making profits. They're in the business of providing goods and services and work to their members. Any surplus belongs to the members.

In the usual corporation, profits are distributed in proportion to the number of shares you own. In a cooperative, the surplus is distributed in proportion to the business a member does with the cooperative. In a worker cooperative, the business done with the coop would be the number of hours worked by the member.

Cooperative corporations would, under most state laws, distribute patronage refunds rather than dividends. A non-profit corporation is not al-

lowed by law to distribute any part of its income to members except, of course, as wages. A coop set up as a for-profit corporation may find legal restrictions in some states on distributing surplus on the basis of patronage rather than on stock ownership. Even though everyone in the coop may own equal shares, some members will have done more business with the cooperative than others. Check with your lawyer or do some legal research. If this is a legal problem for you, you can just as effectively return the surplus to the members by lowering prices in a consumer coop or raising wages and benefits in a producer or worker coop. You may also keep the surplus for reserves or for new equipment.

Transferring Shares or Memberships

People buy stock in large corporations in the hope that the value will rise and that the company will make a profit and pay dividends. Usually anyone can buy the shares of stock. People own stock in small conventional corporations primarily to control ownership of the company but also with the hope that the value will rise and that they may someday sell out and retire.

A different set of rules is necessary for coops. If a cooperative's share of stock (or membership) was freely traded or allowed to be sold for what it would fetch on the open market, outsiders not interested in the principles of the coop, outsiders only interested in the coop making money, could gain control by buying up a majority of the shares. This would defeat the coop's purpose. There are ways to protect a coop from this (the one member, one vote rule discussed above is a good place to start).

If the coop is a non-profit corporation, by law no stock is issued nor are there dividends paid to people who hold memberships, so there is no possibility for speculation.

A cooperative corporation may be able to issue stock or memberships, though some states limit them to memberships. If only memberships are issued, there is no problem since there is no speculative value to them. Only a member can own a membership. If stock is issued, restrictions on its transfer to non-members is often provided for in the law, but it should also be stated in the articles or bylaws and on the stock certificates.

Cooperatives organized as for-profit corporations issue stock and need to protect themselves. They must include a provision in the articles of incorporation or bylaws (states may differ on this) indicating that the cooperative has the first right to buy back the stock when a member leaves or dies. The price should be what the member paid for it (housing coops sometimes allow a limited increase for cost of living). State laws usually require that these restrictions on transferring shares be written in a noticable size of type (the actual size is specified by law) on each stock certificate. Since any errors in this procedure can be costly if not ruinous to a successful   cooperative, it may be wise to have a lawyer run this through.

Stock Permits

States require corporations to obtain permits to issue stock. Sometimes the permits are open-ended and allow the corporations to issue as many shares as they want to whomever they want. Sometimes the permits are for a limited number of shares and must list name, address and possibly other data about each member. Sometimes the permits are for a limited time period such as one or two years.

Some states define memberships as stock and require the same permits. Other states exempt memberships. Some states automatically grant cooperative corporations an exemption from obtaining stock permits.

The federal government usually requires the stock and the memberships to be registered (called "qualifying" the stock) under federal securities law. There are several exemptions, however, which apply to most small coops.

The federal Securities and Exchange Commission (SEC) gave an opinion in what they call a "no action letter" that securities issued by a worker cooperative were not securities as defined by the federal law and thus did not have to be registered (Yellow Cab Cooperative Association, no action letter dated January 15, 1978). The SEC had earlier made a similar ruling involving an agricultural supply coop (United Stated Supplies Inc., no action letter dated March 14, 1977). This seems to indicate that the SEC recognizes the difference between shares issued by cooperatives where no personal gain is intended and shares issued by traditional profit-oriented businesses. The United States Supreme Court also noted this distinction in a case involving a housing cooperative. The court ruled that the coop's shares had none of the characteristics that are usually associated with share ownership in the commercial world, especially noting the fact that the shares were not purchased in the hope of making a profit but rather for acquiring living space (United Housing Foundation Inc. Vs. Forman, 421 US 837, 1975).

The federal securities law allows exemptions for "small offerings". This is defined as having fewer than 100 shareholders, which is not a problem for most small producer and worker coops. However, consumer coops usually reach higher memberships and would have difficulty qualifying. The law also requires that the total sales price of all securities sold in any 12 month period be under $100,000 — not a likely impediment to small coops.

Another possible federal exemption which might be more helpful to consumer coops is the "intrastate exemption". You do not have to register your stock with the SEC if all shareholders are residents of the state and if the coop is incorporated and doing business exclusively in the state. The residence requirement is strict. If, for example, your coop's membership includes college students who are actually residents of another state, your coop will not qualify under this exemption.

Special Federal Tax Considerations — Sub Chapter T

Cooperatives organized as for-profit or cooperative corporations may receive special federal tax benefits under Sub Chapter T of the Internal Revenue Code. These benefits are not available to the usual profit-oriented corporation. A coop which has qualified as a tax exempt non-profit corporation may not make use of the Sub Chapter T provisions; but if your coop is a non-profit corporation subject to income taxes, Sub Chapter T may also be helpful to you. To qualify under Sub Chapter T, your coop must be run cooperatively as defined by the Internal Revenue Service. This basically means that:

1. Control is by the members — one member, one vote.

2. The coop is primarily interested in providing goods and services and/or labor to its members rather than in making profits.

3. Any money distributed out of income must be in the form of patronage refunds rather than traditional dividends.

Some interpretations of Sub Chapter T cite two

other requirements for eligibility, though the IRS apparently does not pay close attention to either of these:

1. Should the coop ever dissolve, the remaining assets must be distributed to members and former members on the basis of patronage over the life of the coop. You may want to include something to that effect in your bylaws. Be sure to keep detailed records of each member's involvement so if the IRS ever challenges your coop, you'll be covered.

2. At least 50% of your business must be with members if you are a consumer coop; or at least 50% of the people in a producer or worker coop must be members. Only in very large consumer coops, where many sales are made to non-members, this is likely to be a problem. This rule was originally intended to apply to farmer coops — a kind of producer coop — and most people feel that it shouldn't necessarily apply to consumer coops. The IRS may very well agree.

Here's how Sub Chapter T works: A cooperative is allowed to return all or part of its surplus (net margin, net savings) to its member-patrons and not pay corporate taxes on the amount returned. This return is called a patronage refund and must be based on the amount or percentage of business (or labor if a worker coop) a member has done with the coop. For example, if one member of a consumer coop made purchases equal to 2% of all purchases made by members, that member is entitled to 2% of the patronage refunds. Similarly, in a producer coop, a member whose products yielded 2% of the coop's earnings would receive 2% of the refund. In a worker coop, though the same reasoning applies, the actual method of payment is usually different. A worker who works 2% more hours would usually receive additional wages reflecting this. Thus at the end of the year you may not even have a surplus. If you did, you would probably pay it out by raising wages. Nevertheless, a worker coop could also pay out patronage refunds based on the percentage of labor each member provided the coop.

As the law is written, in order for the coop to avoid all income taxes, the distribution of the surplus must be to all patrons, both members and non-members. However, few coops will distribute to non-members since that would defeat the goal of full membership participation in the coop. Why should someone become a member if they can get benefits without it? So unless the cooperative earns all its income from business with its members, it will have to distinguish between a surplus resulting from business with members and a surplus from business with non-members. The surplus from business with non-members, unless distributed to the non-members, will be taxed as corporate income — whether it is distributed to members or not.

Sub Chapter T law requires that there be a "pre-existing obligation" by the coop to pay patronage refunds in order for the coop to qualify. Be sure to include a provision in the articles or bylaws indicating that you intend to distribute your surplus from member business in the form of patronage refunds. This provision fulfills the requirement.

Patronage refunds are taxable to the members of the coop on their personal tax returns, except in the case of consumer coops. Where the patronage refund is in return for purchases of goods and services for personal, living or family use — like buying food from a food coop or housing from a housing coop — the member does not have to pay federal taxes on it. These refunds are considered discounts rather than income.

The IRS must be notified, on a form 1099, of each member who receives over $10 in taxable patronage refunds.

Most coops do not like the idea of distributing all of the surplus even if it is to avoid taxes. They need cash to pay for new equipment, improvements and expansion, and to hold in reserve for emergencies. Sub Chapter T acknowledges this need by allowing coops to distribute part of the surplus, retain the rest and still not pay taxes on any of the surplus (assuming the surplus is based on member business only).

With the consent of the members, the coop may pay as little as 20% of the patronage refund in cash and retain the rest. The amount retained is considered either a loan from the member to the coop, which must eventually be repaid to the member, or increased equity, in which case the coop issues additional shares or memberships to the member. The additional equity may be more desirable to the coop because the coop does not have to worry about repaying the loan. But if the coop has a policy to limit individual members' investments or if state law limits individual members' investments, a loan may be the only option.

Members must consent to the lower patronage refunds either in writing or by having it stated in the bylaws. Consent is necessary because the members must pay personal income taxes on the full refund — on the cash and non-cash portions. That is why at least 20% must be paid in cash: to guarantee that the member will have enough money to pay the taxes. Even if a patronage refund is non-taxable, as is the case in most consumer coops, member consent is required to withhold part of the patronage refunds and the 20% rule still applies.

For many years the federal government would not recognize worker coops as qualifying under Sub Chapter T. However, several cases and IRS rulings have changed that (Puget Sound Plywood Inc. v. Commissioner, 44 T.C. 305 acq., 1965; Linnton Plywood Assoc. v. United States, 236 F. Supp. 227, 1964; Rev. Rul. 71-439, 1971-72, Bull. 321). Worker cooperatives may now distribute surpluses to its member-employees as patronage refunds. The refunds are based on the number of hours worked by each member. If some employees are not members, the coop must pay corporate taxes on the non-members' contribution to the surplus unless the coop also distributes refunds to them. The refunds are taxable income to the employees.

The cost of keeping records on members' business with the coop can be very high. You should seriously consider whether your coop is best served by paying patronage refunds at all. A small but growing coop might be better off returning the surplus in other ways such as by lowering prices, raising wages, paying year-end bonuses or some combination of these. Bonuses, by the way, must be "reasonable". If the IRS decides that the bonuses are unreasonable (too high), they will declare the unreasonable part of the bonus a taxable dividend which the corporation is illegally trying to pass through as a bonus. The bonus would have to be a very substantial amount for the IRS to consider it unreasonable.

If your coop never intends to have more than 25 members, it can organize as a Sub Chapter S corporation and pass all the profits through to the members. The corporation itself pays no income taxes. Sub Chapter S was discussed in the section on corporations. An accountant can be very helpful in these matters.

The discussion of Sub Chapter T applies to federal tax law only. Many states do not recognize these special tax provisions and do not allow any exemptions from double taxation. Many states will impose corporate income tax on Sub Chapter T corporations even though the IRS doesn't. In most states, your coop must be organized as a cooperative corporation to pay tax-free patronage refunds for purposes of state taxes. Fortunately, state taxes are much lower than federal taxes.

Sample Articles and Bylaws

Following are copies of the actual articles of incorporation from three coops: the Swallow, a retail worker coop; Mendocino Distribution, a trucking coop; and Homestead Exchange, a medium-sized consumer coop. All three, you should note, are brief and to the point.

Following the articles are copies of the actual bylaws of the above three coops and those of Bookpeople, another worker coop. Each set of bylaws offers different ideas and different ways of expressing those ideas. The Swallow and Bookpeople are employee owned and operated businesses; their bylaws emphasize the concerns of the employee-members. Bookpeople's bylaws, by the way, make no mention of membership requirements and how a person becomes a member. Bookpeople spells this out in separate written employment procedures. Most coops, however, include membership requirements in the bylaws. Mendocino Distribution is primarily a trucker for rural food coops and most of its members are other coops. Homestead Exchange is a retail food cooperative and its members are the consumers.

These articles and bylaws are reprinted here to serve only as samples. Your own articles and bylaws must address your specific needs and your state's requirements.

ARTICLES OF INCORPORATION

OF

THE SWALLOW COOPERATIVE, INC.

ONE: The name of this corporation shall be The Swallow Cooperative, Inc.

TWO: The purpose of this corporation shall be to conduct any lawful business primarily for the benefit of the members who shall be the ultimate producers of the goods and services of the Corporation. The earnings, savings, or benefits derived from the activities of the Corporation are to be used for the general welfare of the members or to be distributed equitably among the members on the basis of their participation in production.

THREE: The principal office of the Corporation is in Alameda County, State of California.

FOUR: The number of directors of the Corporation shall be five.

FIVE: The current directors, who shall serve until the next annual meeting are (5 people named).

The post office address of each director is (street address), Berkeley, California.

SIX: The corporation shall have no capital stock. It shall issue memberships to all workers of the corporation as provided in the Bylaws. No member will have more than one membership. There will be no cost for membership.

Dated: _____

ARTICLES OF INCORPORATION

OF

THE HOMESTEAD EXCHANGE COOPERATIVE, INCORPORATED

ONE: The name of the corporation is The Homestead Exchange Cooperative, Incorporated.

TWO: The purposes for which this corporation is formed are:

(a) To promote individual self-reliance and community self-sufficiency through the establishment of a cooperative marketplace uniting producers and consumers as shareholders.

(b) To conduct lawful business in accordance with the principles of the International Cooperative Alliance, primarily for mutual benefit of the shareholders through production, purchase, sales, storage, distribution, and provision of merchandise and services.

(c) To conduct such other activities as will serve the economic, educational, political, recreational and cultural welfare of the shareholders.

THREE: This corporation shall have, exercise, and possess all the rights, powers, and privileges generally granted to a cooperative corporation by the laws of the State of California.

FOUR: The principal office for the transaction of business of this corporation shall be in Mendocino County in the State of California.

FIVE: This corporation is authorized to issue two classes of shares, to be designated as follows:

Class A - membership shares
Class B - sustaining shares

The total number of shares which this corporation is authorized to issue is one hundred thousand (100,000) shares.

The number of membership shares shall be ten thousand (10,000) shares.

The number of sustaining shares shall be ninety thousand (90,000) shares.

The par value of all shares shall be ten dollars ($10.00).

The aggregate par values of all shares shall be one million dollars ($1,000,000).

Each shareholder shall have one vote regardless of the number of shares owned.

No shareholder shall own more than four (4) percent of the total number of membership shares issued and outstanding at any time.

The amount of capital with which this corporation will begin business is ninety (90) dollars.

SIX: There shall be nine (9) directors. The names and addresses of the persons acting as initial directors are listed below.

(9 people named)

IN WITNESS WHEREOF, the undersigned, including (or being) the persons hereinabove named as the first Directors, have executed these Articles of Incorporation on (date of signing), 19__.

(typed names and signatures)

ARTICLES OF INCORPORATION

OF

MENDOCINO DISTRIBUTION COOPERATIVE, INC.

ONE: The name of this corporation is Mendocino Distribution Cooperative, Inc.

TWO: This corporation is formed for the following purposes:

(A) The primary purpose is to acquire and distribute food, tools, materials, and services to members who are ultimate consumers of such food, tools, materials and services pursuant to Article 12202 of the California Corporations Code.

(B) Without in any way limiting the foregoing, the objectives, purposes, and powers of this corporation are:

(1) To engage in the sale of consumer goods, primarily for the benefit of its members, and to distribute the earnings, savings, and other benefits arising from such activities in such manner as the membership will decide.

(2) (a) To provide research, marketing and other services for those consumer members who may be ultimate agricultural producers, processors of such locally produced agricultural products, and/or manufacturers utilizing primarily local materials and resources.

(b) To distribute the earnings, savings, and any other benefits as might accrue from such activities, for the general benefit of the consumer members and the community at large, as the membership shall determine.

(c) To thereby provide a mechanism for the exchange of locally produced commodities, goods, and services, and an enhancement of the local economy.

(3) To advance the cooperative concept of an economic system having service as its motive, and to join or otherwise associate with cooperative societies and other organizations for the purposes of mutual aid and the creation of a viable and stable economy.

(4) To have, possess, and exercise all the rights, powers, and privileges generally granted a cooperative corporation by the laws of the State of California.

THREE: This corporation is organized pursuant to Part Two, Division Three, Title One, of the Corporations Code of the State of California, relating to cooperative corporations.

      FOUR: The principal office for the transaction of business is to be located in the County of Mendocino.

      This corporation will be composed of no more than 250 members.

      FIVE: Board of Directors

      (A) The number of Directors of this corporation shall be five.

      (B) The names of the Directors and the addresses of the persons who are to act as the first Directors of this corporation, until the election of their successors, are (5 people named).

Dated: _____

BYLAWS OF

THE SWALLOW COOPERATIVE, INC.

A California Corporation

ARTICLE 1.   PURPOSES AND POWERS

The purposes for which this cooperative is formed and the powers which it may exercise are set forth in the Articles of Incorporation.

ARTICLE 2.   MEMBERSHIP

SECTION 1.   REQUIREMENTS FOR MEMBERSHIP

Any person may become a member by working for the cooperative in return for such wages as may be determined by the Directors. No charge may be levied for membership. However, the Directors may set such requirements for the acceptance of new members as may be fair and equitable to the cooperative and to the individual members, old and new.

SECTION 2.   PRIVILEGES OF MEMBERSHIP

Each member is entitled to one vote. Each member is entititled to work for the cooperative in return for a just wage.

SECTION 3.   MEMBERSHIPS NONASSESSABLE

The members of the cooperative shall not be assessed for the debts of the cooperative.

SECTION 4.   TERMINATION OF MEMBERSHIPS

The Directors may terminate the membership of any member who has not worked for the cooperative for a period of one year and who has not participated in organizational activities for one year. Such termination may occur only after written notice is sent to the member at his or her last known address. Such termination will not affect any rights of the member as may have already accrued under ARTICLE 4 of these bylaws.

SECTION 5.   TRANSFER OF MEMBERSHIPS

Memberships shall be nontransferable.

SECTION 6.   MEMBERSHIP CERTIFICATES

The officers will prepare and distribute membership certificates to each member of the cooperative.

ARTICLE 3. MEMBERSHIP MEETINGS

SECTION 1. TIME AND PLACE OF MEETINGS

Membership meetings will occur annually on the first Tuesday in March of each year at 8:00 p.m. at the offices of the cooperative at (street address). No notice need be given of such meetings regularly held.

SECTION 2. SPECIAL MEETINGS

Special meetings may be called by the Board of Directors or by a written petition of ten percent (10%) of the membership. The Directors must give written notice by mail of such special meetings at least ten (10) days before the meeting is to be held. This notice will describe the reason for the special meeting.

SECTION 3. QUORUM

At any membership meeting, the presence in person of ten (10) members or such lesser number as shall equal five percent (5%) of the total membership constitutes a quorum for the transaction of business. If a quorum is not present, any meeting may be adjourned from time to time by those present until a quorum is present. Notice need not be given of the time of reconvening. If balloting is conducted by mail on any issue or election, the number of members voting by mail shall be included in determining whether quorum requirements are satisfied with respect to matters on the mail ballot.

SECTION 4. VOTING BY MAIL

The Board of Directors in the first instance, or when directed to do so at a membership meeting, may conduct a vote of the membership by mail on a specific issue or issues or election. The procedure for conducting such balloting shall be established by the Directors.

ARTICLE 4. DISSOLUTION

The cooperative may be dissolved by a two-thirds vote of the membership. On dissolution, any reserves of the cooperative in excess of the outstanding financial obligations of the cooperative shall be distributed to the members. Such distribution shall be to each member in the proportion that the labor performed by such member stands to the total amount of labor performed by all members of the cooperative.

If, after due diligence, any member cannot be found, that member's distributive share of the proceeds upon dissolution shall be turned over to such recognized cooperative organization as a majority of the members may determine.

ARTICLE 5. DIRECTORS AND OFFICERS

SECTION 1. NUMBER AND TERM

The number of Directors shall be no less than five (5) nor more than eight (8). The Board of Directors may fix the exact number of Directors. This provision relating to the number of Directors may be amended only by a majority vote of the membership. A Director shall serve for one year.

SECTION 2. MEETINGS

Regular meetings of the Board of Directors shall be held on the first Tuesday of March in each year, immediately following the regular membership meeting. No notice need be given of such meetings regularly held. The Board of Directors may hold special meetings from time to time upon notice or upon waiver of notice signed by all the Directors.

SECTION 3. OFFICERS

The Board of Directors will appoint a president, vice-president, treasurer and secretary. The office of secretary and treasurer may be held by one (1) person.

ARTICLE 6. RESERVE FUND

The Board of Directors may set up a reserve fund equal to ten percent (10%) of net earnings for any fiscal year.

ARTICLE 7. AMENDMENTS TO BYLAWS

These bylaws may be amended by the Board of Directors or by a majority of a duly constituted quorum of the members at a membership meeting. Provided, however, that if the amendment is made at a membership meeting, then the proposed amendment must have been submitted to the entire membership by mail at least ten (10) days prior to the membership meeting.

The bylaws may also be amended by the written consent of a majority of the members of the cooperative.

The bylaw provision relating to dissolution of the cooperative may be amended only by a vote of two-thirds (2/3) of the membership at a meeting or in writing.

ARTICLE 8. BUSINESS PRACTICES AND PRINCIPLES

All the business of the cooperative shall be conducted cooperatively, i.e., for the benefit of the cooperative and all its members.

BYLAWS OF

THE HOMESTEAD EXCHANGE COOPERATIVE, INCORPORATED

ARTICLE 1. NAME AND PRINCIPAL OFFICE

The name of this organization shall be The Homestead Exchange Cooperative, Incorporated, hereinafter referred to as "The Cooperative," and its principal office shall be in the City of Ukiah, Mendocino County, California.

ARTICLE 2. IDENTITY AND PRINCIPLES

(A) The Cooperative is a member-owned-and-operated business dedicated to serving the entire community and conducted primarily for mutual benefit of the shareholders. The primary purpose is to engage in the business of providing food and other products to members, who shall be the ultimate consumers of such products.

(B) The principles adopted by the Cooperative in order to fulfill the purposes of the organization as stated in the Articles of Incorporation shall be:

(1) Democratic control in all areas of the organization;

(2) One member/one vote;

(3) Open membership;

(4) Limited dividends on capital, in accordance with state law;

(5) Patronage refunds based on purchases;

(6) Neutrality in religion and partisan politics;

(7) Advancement of the cooperative movement; to be accomplished through education and association with other cooperatives.

ARTICLE 3. ORGANIZATIONAL DOCUMENTS

In addition to these Bylaws, there shall be Articles of Incorporation chartering the organization, an Administrative Code detailing the operations of the Cooperative, and a Membership Agreement between the Cooperative and its members.

ARTICLE 4. STRUCTURE

(A) Control and ownership of the Cooperative is held by the members.

(B) Administration of the Cooperative is delegated to the Board of Directors.

ARTICLE 5. MEMBERSHIP

(A) Definition of Membership

(1) A member of The Homestead Exchange is anyone who owns one (1) "A" or "Membership" share.

(2) An active member of The Homestead Exchange is a member who has purchased fifty dollars ($50.00) of goods or services during the year.

(B) Share Purchases

(1) "A" or "Membership" Shares. Ownership of an "A" share shall constitute a lifetime membership. Each member may own only one (1) "A" share. Each "A" share costs ten dollars ($10), and allows the shareholder one (1) vote.

(2) "B" or "Sustaining" shares.

(a) "Fair Share." All Homestead Exchange members shall agree to the "Fair Share" policy as a means of implementing cooperative ownership of the business. Members shall accumulate capital in their "B" share account up to a total of ninety dollars ($90). This shall be accomplished by direct purchase of "B" shares at ten dollars ($10) each and/or by allocating eighty percent (80%) of a member's patronage refund to the member's "B" share account.

(b) "Limited Dividends on Capital." In accordance with the state laws governing cooperative corporations, dividends on membership shares, if earned and declared, shall not exceed five percent (5%) per annum.

(c) Termination of Membership.

i) Shareholders may sell their shares back to The Homestead Exchange, to be paid within one year, in a form to be determined by the Board of Directors.

ii) Sale of a member's "A" share constitutes termination of membership.

ARTICLE 6.   MEMBERSHIP MEETINGS

(A)   An annual meeting of the general membership of the Cooperative shall be held on the second Saturday in February at the Cooperative's chief place of business or at a place designated by the Board of Directors.

(B)   Special meetings of the membership may be called by a majority of the Directors or by written petition signed by at least ten percent (10%) of the members and filed with the Board.

(C)   Notice of annual and special membership meetings shall be given at least ten (10) days in advance, in writing, by mail to all members and by posting a notice of the meeting in a conspicuous place in the Cooperative's chief place of business at least two (2) weeks in advance.

(D)   A quorum at annual or special membership meetings shall be five percent (5%) of the current membership or fifty (50) members, whichever is less.

ARTICLE 7.   BOARD OF DIRECTORS

(A)   The Board of Directors shall consist of nine (9) duly elected members. The Directors of the Board shall serve without compensation for a term of two (2) years and may serve more than one (1) term and such terms may be consecutive. The terms of the Directors shall be staggered so that approximately half the Board is elected each year. In even-numbered years, four (4) Directors shall be chosen, in odd-numbered years five (5) Directors shall be chosen. Election of the Directors of the Board shall take place as follows:

(1)   The opening of nominations shall be on December 15 of each year. Any active member may be nominated to serve on the Board.

(2)   The closing of nominations shall be on the second Monday of the following January. Nominees are then contacted and asked to write a statement of purpose in seeking the position of Director.

(3)   These statements of purpose, together with ballots, shall be mailed to all members by the fourth Monday in January. Each member shall have four (4) or five (5) votes; (in even-numbered years four (4) Directors will be chosen; in odd-numbered years five (5) Directors will be chosen)--no two (2) of which shall be cast for the same nominee.

(4)   Ballots may be mailed or brought to the Cooperative's chief place of business. Balloting is closed at the

start of the annual membership meeting, and the votes shall be tallied during that meeting. The four (4) or five (4) candidates receiving the most votes shall be the new Directors. In the event of a tie vote, a runoff election shall be held. The new Board of Directors takes office at the first regularly scheduled Board meeting following that annual meeting.

(B) No more than two (2) employees of the Cooperative may serve on the Board of Directors at one time.

(C) Regular meetings of the Board of Directors shall be held once a month at a time and place to be determined by the Board. A quorum for meetings shall be five (5) directors.

(D) An emergency meeting of the Board of Directors may be called by the Board as quickly as all available directors can be notified and a quorum of five (5) directors duly assembled.

(E) A Chairperson, Vice-Chairperson and Secretary of the Board shall be elected by the Directors at the first regular meeting following the annual meeting. They shall serve for one (1) year in that capacity.

(F) A vacancy on the Board created by whatever reason shall be filled by a person chosen by a majority of the remaining directors. Such person shall serve for the balance of the vacated term.

(G) Duties of the Director are to attend all regular meetings of the Board and to fulfill other such duties as shall be determined by the Board. Failure by a Director to attend three (3) regular meetings during one (1) year shall require resignation from the Board.

(H) The Board of Directors shall be empowered to conduct the business of the Cooperative pursuant to ARTICLE FOUR of the Articles of Incorporation of The Homestead Exchange Cooperative, Incorporated.

(1) All meetings of the Board shall be open to all members and to the general public except those meetings (or portions of meetings) dealing with personnel.

(I) Decisions of the Board shall be based on a simple majority, including the votes of members in attendance at Board meetings. In the case that a vote is against that of a majority of Directors of the Board, the matter will be referred to the full membership of the Cooperative for decision. A two-thirds (2/3) majority of the votes cast by a quorum of the members shall decide the question when this circumstance arises.

ARTICLE 8. OFFICERS OF THE COOPERATIVE
(THE CORPORATION)

(A) President. The Chairperson of the Board of Directors shall also serve as President of the Cooperative (the Corporation).

(B) Vice-President. The Vice-President of the Cooperative (the Corporation) shall be elected by the Board from among store management personnel.

(C) Secretary. The Secretary of the Board of Directors shall also serve as the Secretary of the Cooperative (the Corporation) and shall keep or cause to be kept all minutes of the Board and membership meetings. Such minutes shall be kept in a minute book at the principal office of the Cooperative. A copy of the Articles of Incorporation and the Bylaws of the Cooperative and a list of all members shall be kept in such minute book. Inspection of such minute book shall be available to all members at any time.

(D) Treasurer. The Treasurer of the Cooperative (the Corporation) shall keep or cause to be kept all financial records of the Cooperative and shall prepare or cause to be prepared regular statements of financial standing for the Board and the members.

ARTICLE 9. PATRONAGE REFUNDS AND DIVIDENDS

(A) Patronage refunds and dividends shall be declared on an annual basis.

(B) The Board of Directors will determine the amount available for patronage refunds. This figure will be divided among the active members, prorated in proportion to purchases. The refund for each shareholder shall be allocated as follows:

(1) Eighty percent (80%) of the amount will be reinvested in the Cooperative in the form of "B" shares, until the amount of "B" shares owned by the shareholder is equal to ninety dollars ($90).

(2) Twenty percent (20%) of the refund will be returned directly to the shareholder, in a form to be determined by the Board.

(3) When a shareholder owns a "fair share," or ninety dollars ($90) of "B" shares, one hundred percent (100%) of the refund will be returned directly to the shareholder, in a form to be determined by the Board.

(C)   The Board of Directors will determine the amount available for dividends on "B" or sustaining shares not to exceed five percent (5%) return on the value of the shares. This figure will be divided among the shareholders in proportion to the number of shares owned. The form of payment shall be determined by the Board.

(D)   No dividend or investment shall be paid on "A" or membership shares.

(E)   In order to comply with the provisions of the Internal Revenue Code designating patronage refunds as non-taxable when attributable to personal, living, or family items or taken into account as an adjustment to basis of property, membership in this Cooperative (Corporation) constitutes consent by each member to include in the member's gross income for federal income tax purposes the amount of any patronage refund which is paid by this cooperative in money or allocated and distributed as a patronage refund, except the part of such amount that is properly taken into account as an adjustment to basis of property or is attributable to personal, living, or family items. All of the terms in this Section shall have the same meaning as under the Internal Revenue Code.

ARTICLE 10.   ADOPTION AND AMENDMENT OF BYLAWS

(A)   Adoption and amendment of the Bylaws shall be by two-thirds (2/3) majority of the Board of Directors and by two-thirds (2/3) majority vote of the votes cast by the membership. Proposal amendments to the Bylaws shall be made known to the membership by mail and by posting in a conspicuous place at the Cooperative's chief place of business.

(B)   Know all men and women present that the undersigned Secretary of the Cooperative (Corporation) known as The Homestead Exchange Cooperative, Incorporated does hereby certify that the above and foregoing Bylaws of this corporation were adopted by a two-thirds (2/3) majority vote of the membership at a duly held meeting on the _____ day of ____19__, and that the same do now constitute a timely and exact transcription of the Bylaws adopted and are the Bylaws of said Cooperative (Corporation).

_____
Secretary of the Corporation

BYLAWS OF

MENDOCINO DISTRIBUTION COOPERATIVE, INC.

ARTICLE 1. NAME

The name of this corporation shall be MENDOCINO DISTRIBUTION COOPERATIVE, INC.

ARTICLE 2. PURPOSE

The purpose of the cooperative is as set forth in the Articles of Incorporation. To meet this purpose, the cooperative is intended to be a central organization for cooperative associations. It shall encourage and promote food supply organizations within Mendocino County. Through its activities it shall provide prime quality food at the lowest cost possible. Its efforts shall ensure the long-term economic stability, general welfare, and cultural development of our local residents and communities.

ARTICLE 3. OFFICES

The principle office of the cooperative shall be located in Mendocino County, California.

ARTICLE 4. MEMBERSHIP

SECTION 1. (a) Any organization which is in sympathy with the aims and purposes of this cooperative, irrespective of the race, nationality, political opinion or religious belief of its members, shall be eligible and may apply for membership in the cooperative.

(b) In any vote of the general membership, each member organization shall have one and only one vote.

(c) Acceptance of membership application is subject to specific approval of the Board of Directors.

SECTION 2. Membership dues shall be set at an annual rate by the Board of Directors, and are non-transferable and non-refundable.

SECTION 3. The cooperative may be dissolved by a three-fourths majority vote of the Board of Directors, or by a vote of the general membership at the discretion of the Board. Upon dissolution, any reserves of the cooperative in excess of the outstanding financial obligations, may be either:

        i) turned over to such organization as the membership may decide; or

        ii) returned to the membership. The method of dispersal of reserves shall be determined by a majority vote of the membership.

SECTION 4. Any membership may be terminated for good cause by a two-thirds majority of the full board.

ARTICLE 5. GOVERNMENT AND MANAGEMENT

SECTION 1. The cooperative shall be responsible to its members.

SECTION 2. The administration of the cooperative is vested in the Board of Directors, who shall be responsible to the membership.

SECTION 3. The management and operation of the business may be performed by paid employees responsible to the Board of Directors.

ARTICLE 6. DIRECTORS

SECTION 1. Each member organization may select, in a democratic manner, a representative to the Board. The Board of Directors shall consist of the number of representatives so selected, at all times remaining within the limits set by the State of California, being a minimum of five and a maximum of twenty-five. In addition, and within those limits, the Board may appoint directors-at-large, which number shall not exceed two-fifths of the total board. Directors-at-large shall have full voting rights and be entitled to hold office in the corporation.

SECTION 2. No director shall receive remuneration for his Board activities, except reimbursement for approved expenses shall be permitted.

SECTION 3. The term for each and every director shall be for one year.

SECTION 4. The directors shall meet on the second Monday of January, April, July, and October. Fifty percent of the current directors shall constitute a quorum and the consent of fifty percent of the current directors shall be required for official action.

SECTION 5. All meetings shall be open.

SECTION 6. Each Board member shall have one vote. Decision-making shall be by consensus as far as is practicable.

SECTION 7. A director may send an alternate or proxy to any meeting, and this alternate may vote for the director in his or her absence.

SECTION 8. Absence from two of three consecutive meetings shall constitute grounds for removal from the Board. At least one week prior to removal, notice shall be sent to both the director and the member organization represented by that director indicating the intent of the Board.

SECTION 9. Neither directors nor members shall be personally liable for the debts, liabilities, or other obligations of the cooperative or its member organizations.

ARTICLE 7. OFFICERS

Officers shall consist of president, vice-president, and secretary-treasurer. The officers shall serve at the pleasure of the Board.

ARTICLE 8. BOOKS OF ACCOUNTS

SECTION 1. The fiscal year shall be the calendar year.

SECTION 2. The cooperative shall keep and maintain adequate and correct accounts of its properties and business transactions, and these shall be open to all members upon request of the secretary-treasurer.

ARTICLE 9. AMENDMENTS

These bylaws may be amended, altered, or repealed, in whole or in part, by a two-thirds majority vote of the directors.

BYLAWS OF

BOOK PEOPLE EMPLOYEES ASSOCIATION, INC.

STATEMENT OF PURPOSE

OF

BOOK PEOPLE EMPLOYEES ASSOCIATION, INC.

doing business as

BOOK PEOPLE

Our primary policy goal is to promote the financial sol-
vency of the corporation in order to provide for the needs and
general welfare of our shareholders/employees. We will further
pursue policies designed to promote and encourage independent
trade book distribution, retailing and publishing. We will
maintain a democratic structure of total ownership by employees
and try to promote this idea within the industry and in the economy generally.

ARTICLE 1. OFFICES

SECTION 1.

The principal office of the Corporation shall be at (street
address). The Corporation may have offices at such other places
within and without the State of California as the Board of Directors may from time to time designate.

ARTICLE 2. MEETINGS

SECTION 1. PLACE OF MEETINGS

All annual meetings of the shareholders shall be held at
the principal office of the Corporation, and all other meetings
of shareholders and all meetings of the Board of Directors shall
be held either at the principal office or at any other place
within or without the State of California which may be designated
either by the Board of Directors or by the written consent of
all persons entitled to vote at such meetings given either before
or after the meeting and filed with the Secretary of the Corporation.

SECTION 2. MEETINGS OF SHAREHOLDERS

The annual meeting of shareholders for the election of

directors and the transaction of such other business as may be brought before the meeting shall be held between October 1 and October 31 of each year. The exact date is to be determined by the Board of Directors.

A special meeting for any purpose or purposes may be called by the President at any time and must be called by him upon receipt of a written request, specifying the purpose of the meeting, from shareholders of record owning thirty percent (30%) of the shares outstanding. The business transacted at any special meeting shall be confined to the purposes stated in the notice thereof.

Each shareholder shall, at every meeting, be entitled to one vote in person or by proxy for each share of stock registered in his name; provided, however, that any meeting of the shareholders at which directors are elected, each shareholder shall be entitled in voting at such election to cumulate his votes and give one candidate a number of votes equal to the number of directors to be elected, multiplied by the number of votes to which his shares are entitled, or distribute his votes on the same principle among as many candidates as he thinks fit.

The Board of Directors may fix a time, not exceeding forty (40) days preceding the date fixed for any meeting of the shareholders or for the payment of any dividend or the making of any distribution, or for the delivery of evidence of rights or evidence of interests arising out of any change, conversion or exchange of capital stock, as a record time for the determination of the shareholders entitled to vote at such meeting or to receive any such dividend, distribution, rights or interest, and in such case only shareholders of record at the time so fixed shall be entitled to notice of, and to vote at such meeting or to receive such dividend, distribution, rights or interests. The Board of Directors at its option, in lieu of so fixing a record time, may prescribe a period not exceeding forty (40) days prior to the date of such payments, distribution or delivery during which no transfer of stock on the books of the Corporation may be made.

SECTION 3.   ACTION BY SHAREHOLDERS WITHOUT MEETING

Any action which, under any provisions of the California General Corporation Law, may be taken at a meeting of the shareholders, except approval of an agreement for merger or consolidation of the Corporation with other corporations, may be taken without a meeting if authorized by a writing signed by all of the persons who would be entitlted to vote upon such action at a meeting and filed with the Secretary of the Corporation.

SECTION 4.   MEETINGS OF DIRECTORS

The annual meeting for the election of officers and the

transaction of such other business as may come before the meeting
shall be held immediately after the annual meeting of the shareholders, and no notices thereof need be given. Other regular
meetings shall be held, without notice, at such times as may,
from time to time, be determined by the Board. Special meetings
may be called from time to time by the President. Directors
will meet at least twice a year without officers, to prepare for
the officer's reviews.

SECTION 5. NOTICES

Notices of the annual meetings and of special meetings of
shareholders shall be given not less than five (5) days prior to
the date thereof, and notices of special meetings of directors
shall be given at least two (2) days prior to the date thereof.
Notices of adjourned meetings need not be given if the time and
place to which the meeting is adjourned are announced at the
meeting at which the adjournment is taken. Any meeting of the
Board of Directors, although held without notice, at which every
director shall be present, without protesting prior thereto or
at its commencement the lack of notice to him, shall be valid
for all purposes.

Whenever any notice is required to be given to any shareholder or director by law or by these Bylaws, it may be given
personally or by mail, telegram or other form of written communication, charges prepaid, addressed to him at the principal
office of the Corporation or by an announcement posted at the
principal office of the Corporation on a bulletin board designated by the Board of Directors for that purpose.

SECTION 6. WAIVER OF NOTICE

Any notice required to be given by law or by these Bylaws
may be waived in writing, either before or after the time
referred to in such notice, by the person entitled to such notice.

SECTION 7. QUORUM

The presence in person or by proxy of the holders of record
of a majority of the shares of the Corporation then outstanding
at any meeting of the shareholders, and the presence of a majority of all the directors at any meeting of the Board, shall constitute a quorum for the transaction of business at such meeting;
and unless otherwise provided by law or in these Bylaws, the act
of a majority of a quorum shall be the act of the shareholders
or the Board of Directors, as the case may be. In the absence
of a quorum, any meeting may be adjourned from time to time by
the vote of a majority of the shareholders or directors present
without further notice. At any such adjourned meeting at which
a quorum shall be present any business may be transacted which
might have been transacted at the meeting as originally convened.

SECTION 8. ACTION BY BOARD OF DIRECTORS WITHOUT MEETING

Any action required or permitted to be taken by the Board of Directors may be taken without a meeting if all members of the Board shall individually or collectively consent in writing to such action. The written consent or consents shall be filed in the minute book of the Corporation. The action by written consent shall have the same effect as a unanimous vote of directors.

ARTICLE 3. BOARD OF DIRECTORS

SECTION 1. GENERAL PROVISIONS

All corporate powers shall be exercised by or under the authority of, and the business and affairs of the Corporation shall be controlled by, a Board of five (5) directors. Each director must be a shareholder. No person shall hold both a seat on the Board and the Office of Executive Vice-President at the same time.

Directors shall be elected at the annual meeting of the shareholders, and in such election the shareholders shall have the right of cumulative voting. In such election the candidates receiving the highest number of votes up to the number of directors to be elected shall be elected. Each director shall hold office until the next annual meeting or until his successor shall have been duly elected and qualified. Any director may resign at any time by giving written notice to the Corporation, and unless otherwise specified therein the acceptance of such resignation shall not be necessary to make it effective. Any vacancy in the Board of Directors, however arising, may be filled only by a vote of the shareholders.

Immediately after the annual meeting of the stockholders, the members of the Board shall meet with the executive vice-president and then proceed to elect a chairman, adopt rules of order, and elect officers, before proceeding to other business.

ARTICLE 4. OFFICERS

SECTION 1. ELECTED OFFICERS

The Officers of the Corporation shall be a President, an Executive Vice-President, a Secretary and a Treasurer, each of whom shall be elected by the Board of Directors at its annual meeting and shall hold office at the pleasure of the Directors. Any Officer may be removed by the vote of a majority of the entire Board of Directors at any meeting of the Board. Any Officer may resign at any time by giving written notice to the

Corporation, and unless otherwise specified therein the acceptance of such resignation shall not be necessary to make it effective.

In addition to the powers and duties prescribed in these Bylaws, such Officer shall in general exercise the powers and perform the duties incident to his office as well as such other powers and duties as may from time to time be assigned to him by the Board of Directors. Officers will serve as non-voting members of the Board.

SECTION 2. SUBORDINATE OFFICERS, EMPLOYEES AND AGENTS

The Board of Directors may appoint and may remove such other Officers, employees and agents as it shall deem necessary, each of whom shall hold office for such period, have such authority, and perform such duties as the Board may from time to time prescribe. The Board may delegate to any Officer or committee the power to appoint and remove any such subordinate Officers, employees or agents.

SECTION 3. OFFICERS

Under the direction and control of the Board of Directors, the Officers shall have the following specific responsibilities:

(a) President. The President shall preside at all meetings of the Shareholders and shall be the corporation's principal representative at all trade functions and before all legislative and/or governmental hearings, provided such representation has been approved by the Board. The President shall be consulted as to which other Officers and employees additionally shall represent the Corporation at any public function. The President may delegate these responsibilities and, in his/her absence, the Board shall assign these duties to other Officers or employees.

(b) Executive Vice-President. The Executive Vice-President shall be the chief executive officer of the Corporation; he/she shall have the general management of the affairs of the Corporation and its officers, employees, and agents.

(c) Treasurer. The Treasurer shall have the care and custody of all the funds and securities of the Corporation. He/she shall be required to submit monthly progress reports to the Board and an annual report to the Shareholders setting forth in full the financial condition of the Corporation. He/she shall at all reasonable times exhibit his/her books and accounts to any director or shareholder upon request. The Treasurer, with the Secretary, shall be responsible for issuing, transferring, and re-purchasing stock certificates at the direction of the Board and in accordance with the Corporation Bylaws. It shall be the duty of the Treasurer to pay all bills incurred by the

Corporation. All bills must be approved by the Executive
Vice-President and the Treasurer. Checks may be signed by
the Treasurer or other Officers or employees as designated by
the Board. During the absence or disability of the Treasurer,
the Board will delegate these duties to other Officers or
employees.

(d) Secretary. The Secretary shall keep the minutes of
the Board of Directors and the minutes of the Shareholders. He/
she shall affix and attest the same to documents when duly
authorized by the Board. The Secretary shall attend to the
giving and serving of all notices to him/her and to all duties
incidental to his office. The Secretary shall keep a roll of
Stockholders, showing their places of residence and the date
they became Stockholders. He shall further keep a roll of all
employees with dates and nature of employment, incorporating
significant changes in status where appropriate. He shall be
co-responsible with the Treasurer for issuing, transferring, and
re-purchasing stock certificates. During the absence or disability of the Secretary, the Board shall delegate these duties to
other officers or employees.

SECTION 4. SALARIES

The salaries of all officers provided for in ARTICLE 4,
SECTION 1 of these Bylaws shall be fixed by the Board of Directors. The salaries of other officers and employees shall be
fixed by the General Manager in accordance with guidelines established by the Board, but salaries so set by the General Manager
shall be subject to review by the Board.

ARTICLE 5. CAPITAL STOCK

SECTION 1. CERTIFICATES

Certificates of stock certifying the number of shares owned,
shall be issued to each shareholder in such form, not inconsistent with the Articles of Incorporation, as shall be approved by
the Board of Directors. Such certificates shall be numbered and
registered in the order which they are issued and shall be signed
by the President or a Vice-President and by the Secretary or an
Assistant Secretary, and the seal of the Corporation shall be
affixed thereto. All certificates exchanged or returned to the
Corporation shall be cancelled.

SECTION 2. TRANSFER OF SHARES

Transfers of shares shall be made only upon the books of
the Corporation by the holders, in person or by attorney, and on
the surrender of the certificate or certificates for a like number of shares, properly assigned. Transfers of shares shall be

made in accordance with the provisions of ARTICLE 5, SECTION 4 of these Bylaws.

SECTION 3. ISSUANCE OF COMMON STOCK

All shareholders shall own an equal number of shares of the Corporation's Common Stock. The Board of Directors shall authorize the issuance of shares of Common Stock and administer the provisions of ARTICLE 5, SECTION 4 of these Bylaws in such a manner that each holder of Common Stock shall own the same number of shares as every holder of Common Stock.

SECTION 4. RESTRICTIONS ON TRANSFER OF COMMON STOCK

The following restrictions on transfer and obligations for sale and purchase are imposed on all shares of the Corporation's Common Stock which may hereafter be issued for the purpose of restricting ownership of Common Stock to employees of the Corporation or its subsidiaries:

(a) _Restriction on Transfer._ Except as provided in this Section, no shares of Common Stock nor any interest therein shall be validly sold or otherwise transferred, with or without consideration, either voluntarily, involuntarily, or by operation of law, and no purported transferree shall be recognized as a shareholder of the Corporation for any purpose whatsoever.

(b) _Obligation of Corporation to Purchase Common Stock._ Whenever any holder of Common Stock ceases to be an employee of the Corporation or a subsidiary of the Corporation, by reason of his resignation, involuntary termination, death, disability or incapacity, or for any other reason whatsoever (referred to as "termination of employment"), the Corporation shall have the obligation to purchase, and the holder of the Common Stock shall have the obligation to sell to the Corporation, all shares of Common Stock owned by the holder of such Common Stock. Within thirty (30) days after the end of the month in which termination of employment of a holder of Common Stock occurs, the Corporation shall give written notice to such holder of the total purchase price to be paid for his shares of Common Stock, the place of payment, and the Payment Date. In the case of the death or incapacity of a holder of Common Stock, the notice shall be given to the holder's legal representative if the Corporation shall have received evidence of his appointment. The term "holder of Common Stock," as used herein, shall include a shareholder's legal representative who shall be bound by all of the provisions of this Section. For purposes of this Section, a "full-time employee" shall mean any employee who devotes at least three (3) full days a week to the business of the Corporation. The Board of Directors may grant an employee a leave of absence which will not constitute a termination of employment under this Section.

(c) <u>Purchase Price</u>. The consideration to be paid by the Corporation or its nominee for shares of Common Stock to be purchased under this Section shall be an amount equal to the purchase price paid by the shareholder for such shares of Common Stock. The purchase price shall be paid by the Corporation in cash against delivery of the certificate or certificates representing the holder's shares of Common Stock properly endorsed for transfer. Nothing in this paragraph (c) shall prevent the Corporation from paying the consideration for the purchase of any Common Stock in any lawful manner if mutually agreed to by the Corporation and the holder of such stock.

(d) <u>Payment Date</u>. The purchase price for shares of Common Stock shall be paid by the Corporation to the holder of Common Stock at the time specified in the notice provided for in paragraph (b) which shall not exceed one hundred twenty (120) days following the end of the month in which the termination of employment occurs (the "Payment Date") provided that as of the Payment Date and after giving effect to the purchase, the Corporation has funds legally available to purchase all shares of Common Stock owned by the shareholder. If the Corporation does not have such funds legally available, the Corporation shall give written notice to that effect to the holder and the obligation of the Corporation to purchase such shares and the Payment Date shall be postponed until such time as the Corporation shall have funds legally available for such purchase; and at such time the Corporation shall give written notice to that effect to the holder, whereupon the holder shall have the obligation to tender for sale to the Corporation, and the Corporation shall be required to purchase, such shares. The determination as to whether there are funds legally available for purchase of Common Stock shall be made solely by the Corporation through its Board of Directors and the determination shall be conclusive and binding on the holder.

(e) <u>Subordination of Corporation's Obligation to Pay for Stock</u>. The obligation of the Corporation to pay the purchase price for any stock to be purchased pursuant to this Section shall be subordinate to the claims of general creditors of the Corporation, whether such claims arose before the Corporation's obligation to repurchase or thereafter. Any amount which the Corporation is obligated to pay need not, prior to the Payment Date, be set aside or held in trust by the Corporation for the benefit of the person entitled thereto.

(f) <u>Order of Purchase</u>. If the Common Stock of two or more shareholders is to be acquired by the Corporation under the provisions of this Section, the Corporation shall pay the full price to each of them in order in which their termination occurs.

(g) <u>Designation by Corporation of Other Purchasers</u>. Whenever the Corporation is obligated to purchase Common Stock upon a termination of employment under this Section, the Board of Directors may designate another person who is not then a shareholder and who is, or on the Payment Date will be, an employee of the Corporation or a subsidiary of the Corporation to purchase all such shares of Common Stock. Such designation may be made by the Corporation by giving written notice to the holder of the Common Stock to be purchased at any time prior to the Payment Date. In the event any person designated by the Corporation for any reason fails to make the purchase, subject to the provisions of paragraph (d), the Corporation shall be obligated to complete the purchase.

(h) Notice. Any notice provided in this Section to be given by the Corporation shall be deemed to have been duly given if delivered to the holder or his legal representative in person or if mailed by first class registered or certified mail, postage prepaid, addressed to the holder at the last known address of the holder as such address appears on the records of the Corporation or addressed to the holder's legal representative if the Corporation has been notified of such representative's address.

(i) Legend on Certificate. All certificates for shares of Common Stock issued by the Corporation shall bear on their face a legend referring to the restrictions upon transfer of such shares imposed by the provisions of this Section.

ARTICLE 6. GRIEVANCES

SECTION 1. GRIEVANCE COMMITTEE

The members of the Board of Directors shall appoint a Grievance Committee to hear and determine grievances of employees regarding wages, hours, work assignments and other terms and conditions of employment and disputes between two or more employees concerning such matters. The Grievance Committee shall act according to the written procedures which shall be established by the Board of Directors and recorded in the Internal Policy.

ARTICLE 7. BANK ACCOUNTS AND MISCELLANEOUS

SECTION 1. CHECKS, DRAFTS, ETC.

All checks, drafts and other orders for the payment of money, notes, acceptances, and other evidences of indebtedness issued in the name of the Corporation shall be signed by such officers, employees, or agents of the Corporation and in such manner as shall be determined from time to time by resolution of the Board of Directors. Endorsements for deposit to the credit of the Corporation in any of its duly authorized depositaries may be made, without countersignature, by the President, the Treasurer, or any other officer, employee, or agent of the Corporation to whom the Board of Directors, by resolution, shall have delegated such power or by hand-stamped impression in the name of the Corporation.

SECTION 2. BANK ACCOUNTS AND DEPOSITS

The Board of Directors may from time to time authorize the opening of, and the deposit of funds of the Corporation in, general and special bank accounts with such banks, trust companies, or other depositaries as the Board may select and may make such rules and regulations with respect thereto, not inconsistent with the provisions of law or of these Bylaws, as the Board may deem expedient.

SECTION 3. CORPORATE SEAL

The seal of the Corporation shall contain the name of the Corporation and the words "Corporate Seal 1971 California."

Bookpeople is an employee owned and operated book wholesaler, in business over ten years. Steve Hargraves and Terry Nemeth describe its organization:

Everybody who works here owns an equal number of shares in the company. There is a six-month probationary period when someone comes to work here. At the end of that probationary period, if you decide that you want to get involved in an employee-owned company, you have to buy into the company. There's nobody who owns a piece of Bookpeople who doesn' work here. That's part of the bylaws. There can't be outside owners.

Everybody has the same amount invested. Those who didn't have the money borrowed what they could when they bought in. Some were able to borrow $1,500, some were only able to borrow $500, some weren't able to borrow anything. Those people put up a note, to be paid off within a year out of their pay checks.

If you leave, the company buys back your share. You get back exactly what you put in. There are only as many outstanding shares as there are employees. It's one share per person. Somebody who's been here ten or twelve years can't acquire more shares than any other employee. Any company-owned shares are considered not issued and have no voting rights. We can issue more shares if we take on more people. Right now, we can issue twelve more shares without refiling with the state.

We've considered other ownership ideas in the past, looking for a possible way to reward people who've been here a long time. One of the things we considered was issuing some sort of preferred stock. But it's difficult to tamper with the stock situation without ending up with unequal ownership. We discussed it with lawyers a couple times, but nobody's come up with a really good way to do it. So we figured we'd just keep it the way it is.

We decided that in order to operate efficiently within this employee ownership, we needed to set up a fairly standard business hierarchy. And in order to prevent our being constantly in meetings, the employee-owners elect representatives once a year. If all our policies had to come up to the vote of 35 people, we would be grossly inefficient.

The representatives are the board of directors and they set company policy. Everyone has one vote for the board. The general manager is under the board of directors, is hired and fired by the board, the manager's salary is set by the board. The general manager sets everybody else's salary with the help of individual department heads. The department heads more or less govern the different disciplines in the business: buying, office management, promotion. sales and warehousing-fulfillment.

Any overall policy that we have or significant changes in the way we do business would have to be approved by or the idea would have to come from the board. Individual business policies like a particular discount policy can be originated by a department head with the general manager's approval. So in the day to day business, policies can change some, just through the general manager, if they're small and if they relate to one particular aspect of the business. If they relate to a more general sense of the business direction, it needs board approval. There's an attempt as consensus but if a majority is the best you can get, you live with that. There is an attempt and a tendency to get unanimous agreement on the board, but it doesn't always happen. But it happens more often than not.

Directors serve a one year term. A lot of times, for the first three or four months, directors are just becoming acquainted with the company policies; they haven't previously worked on that level. So it slows down the board's functions for the first four months of every term. After that they become better educated board members. Usually the way the board works, you always have two or three or four people who were on the last board, so you have some carry over year to year, which I think is very important. If we had to have five new board members every year it would be a whole lot more chaotic than it is. Enough people have run for election each year who were on the last board, and enough of those people were respected enough to be re-elected. We've never set it up as a system where we have to have a carry over; but the company is just run that way. If you feel somebody is not doing a good job on the board, they're not there for that long. You don't feel helpless. Once a year

in October we vote for a new board. It's only a year down the road.

We have a general membership meeting once a month. We use the meeting to disseminate information, to give as much information to the general body as possible. And to get feedback from them directly. Departments are meeting themselves, department heads are meeting with the general manager. So we have the various avenues for getting information from the employee-owners to the people who operate the business day to day.

Although there's equal ownership, there are different job levels throughout the place which are paid differently. It's not like a collective in the sense that you come in, do whatever job is available, everybody gets the same amount of money, that kind of thing. There are particular jobs set up. We just feel that's the only way to get the work going day to day. Each department has job descriptions and there is a certain amount of money equated with each element of that job. So if you fufill that part of that job, you're entitled to that money. It takes it away from the realm of just merit raises — which we also have room to do — but it tries to be a little more fair in terms of what people actually do. It's always a difficult ratio to strictly administer because you have some people going to a new job and they think that just because they're doing the job, they should get the pay. These kind of things get worked out individually rather than as a general policy.

Everybody has an interest in who's coming to work here, but new employees are hired by the department heads. Everybody does not have a say in it. If you had 35 people doing the hiring...

New employees tend to have an exaggerated view of what being an owner-employee means: ''I should be able to determine my job, I should be able to determine where I work, I should be able to determine my pay.'' Those things aren't practically possible. Since I've been here we've gone through five different payroll plans in an attempt to some way fairly distribute the amount of money that's available for payroll. We've come up with the system where we attach a certain amount of money to certain jobs because it seems to be the least arbitrary of all. Yet it's very difficult to be completely non-arbitrary. At some point somebody has to make a judgment as to what kind of job you're doing. The very notion of a department head being able to tell an owner that not only aren't you doing a good job, you're doing such a bad job that we're going to have to put you on probation. It's a very difficult notion, it's tough.

There are no legal restrictions to firing an owner. The ownership is a result of being an employee. They can bring an grievance, though, to the board if they feel they've been unjustly fired. The board appoints a separate grievance committee of three people to hear the case. Since I've been here, we've had only one grievance, maybe two. We've had very few firings too. Most of the people, when it's time for them to go, leave.

No matter how well you try to explain to a new person who comes into this company what the dynamics of it are, how the tension is between standard business operating structure and the fact that it's employee owned, people tend to have certain expectations about the word employee ownership. They think it means, "I can advance through this company very quickly because I'm an owner and, uh, the next thing I know I'll be head buyer." Well, it's a small company and we just don't have that many slots. We can't create a new vice president in charge of marketing or something like that.

We deemphasize the business heirarchy. We don't have private offices. We don't have secretaries. Things tend to happen on more of a personal level. You don't go to the assistant manager who speaks only to the manager who speaks only to the vice president who speaks only to the president. People who are employees out in the warehouse could also be on the board. So the authority in some ways runs across business lines. Everybody here nas something to say and exercises their say. In any place where you have 35 employees you're liable to get 35 divergent views about any one particular issue. Working those out in some sort of balance between keeping the business profitable and also maintaining a democratically managed company becomes sort of a tension.

Because of a lack of hierarchy, too, you get some problems with the amount of experience people have in their particular jobs, the pressure they can put to bear on other aspects of

the company that they're not educated enough to handle. Just because you become an owner six months after you come to work here, you don't necessarily at that point know enough to really contribute a lot to setting the policy of the company. That's sometimes frustrating to people. A lot of people feel, "Well, I'm an owner, my say should be just as important as anyone else's." Sometimes you have to fall back on people who are experienced to give you some view of what is going to happen as a result of your new proposition. A certain amount of frustration is involved in old employees as well as new. Old employees have to deal with people who don't have as much experience but do have equal say. It's tough balancing those things off.

Part of what we do is provide everybody with the information they need in order to feel good about this job, in order to feel they have some input to it. When people have a chance to express what they feel about the place and have the information to make some decisions, they feel satisfied about what their place in the company is. Everybody here knows what our daily break-even is, everybody knows what yesterday's sales were. All they have to do is punch it in on the computer. They know how far above or below projection the sales were, they know what our budget is. They know, that in order to maintain the conditions here, in terms of medical benefits, in terms of the free lunches, in terms of payroll, we have to achieve our sales projections. More people are aware of how we get these books and what it means to us to get them out than any other place I've seen. You're not only concerned with your weekly paycheck but also with the profit-and-loss for the company that particular month, what does the balance sheet look like, where are we going, what's our policy on this particular matter. Everybody here is concerned with that. People have to be concerned with a wider aspect than just their particular job. Only in this particular kind of place would I be able to learn enough from working in the warehouse to make major decisions about the company as a whole. If I worked in a standard business in the warehouse, would they ever show me a profit-and-loss statement for any one month? Never. There was no way in hell anybody in that warehouse was going to see a profit-and-loss for that company so you could have made some kind of reasonable decisions.

People often volunteer to do some little part in somebody else's department. The people in that department are more than willing to let you do that, show you the part, tell you how it fits into their department and let you try to figure it out. You have the opportunity to learn a little bit about buying, a little bit about promotion, a little bit about publishing. If you approach it right, you can probably get more education out of an experience here than any other company I can imagine working for. If you want to learn the economics of the book trade, what publishing is all about, if you approach it right here you can find out anything you want to know. At most companies, you're cubbyholed and you learn one skill and that's it. Your skill doesn't apply to the whole company. After about 2 1/2 years at this company, the whole world opens up to you; I think it takes that long to learn all the ramifications of the book trade.

We probably get more volunteer labor out of the people who are here than any other company I have seen. People are willing to stay a couple extra hours at night just to finish up whatever it was they started. A very large percentage of the people have the attitude that they're not clocking in here and clocking out, but they're here to do certain jobs. If it takes an extra hour here, if they have to come in Saturday morning for a couple hours, they're willing to do it.

People work here for a variety of reasons. They're here for the company structure, some are here because we're distributing books, some are here because we're publishing books. To fit all those interests into one company with equal ownership, you get this ball that's bulging in different spots all the time. The thing is to keep the ball round and do away with the soft spots. That's the constant struggle. You always have to go back to giving the people as much information as possible. A lot of time you spend is unproductive, but productive in terms of a democratic corporation. Unproductive in terms of our outside fulfillment of orders, but productive in terms of educating the people in here to what the whole looks like.

My personal feeling is that running a company this way is a political statement to the rest of the country. If you want to go to the heart of the beast, the heart of the beast is economics. This is an economic entity that we're dealing with, this culture, this society. We're trying to develop a new way of looking at how to run a business. Employee ownership is dependent on the fact that this company must survive in this capitalistic, profit oriented system. If you can find a different way of approaching those economics, in some ways you're making a political move. That's the justification for me personally. I feel that it's worth it.

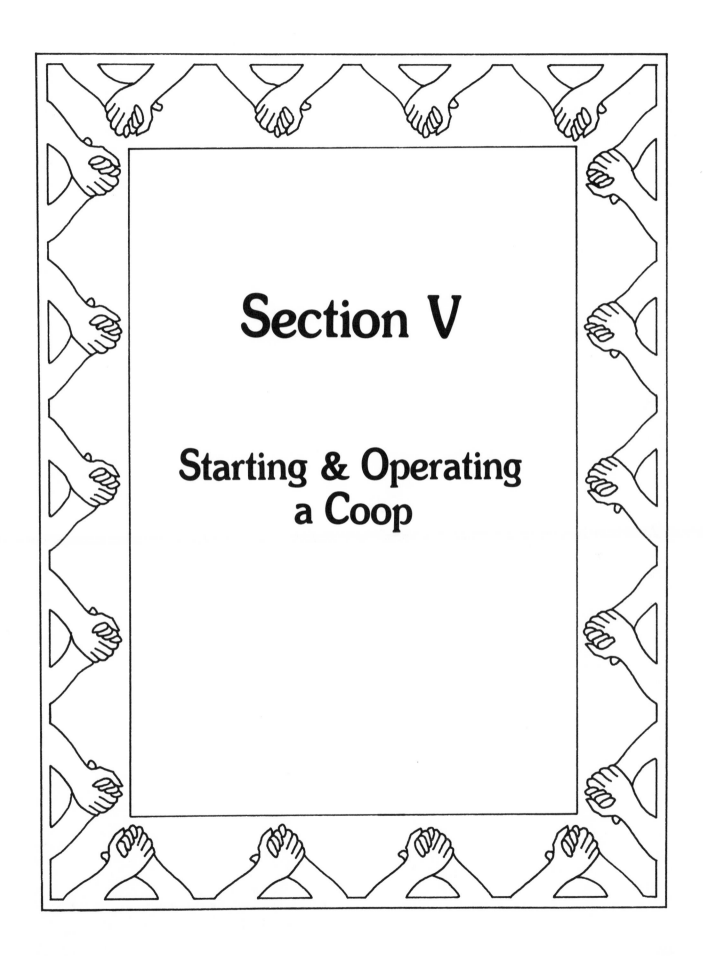

Section V

Starting & Operating a Coop

The world is run by those who stay to the end
of the meeting.

Most of this section of the book deals with legal, technical and formal aspects of starting and operating a coop. Most of the information applies to any coop regardless of its legal structure. Keep in mind, however, that your coop is started and operated by people, people with different ideas, backgrounds, educations and dreams, and with different levels of energy, dedication and competence. And people are forever fouling up, bypassing or otherwise subverting every legal, technical and formal rule ever put down on paper.

This section discusses the Internal Revenue Service. But no law in all of IRSdom is as difficult to deal with as your co-members in your coop. This section discusses personnel policy. But writing a personnel policy is one thing; getting the personnel to go along with the policy is something else again.

People are the challenge, but people are also the reason to try to make a cooperative work. People respond to people, to kindness and compassion, much more than they'll ever respond to rules and regulations. You need the rules so everyone knows how to proceed. But you need the human interaction and understanding to make the rules work.

Financing Your Cooperative

In many ways this is the most important chapter in the book. Without seed money a business is not likely to survive. Your coop is no exception.

Money is needed for pre-opening costs. initial operating losses, facilities, inventories, maintenance, professional services (accountant, lawyer), wages, utilities, insurance, taxes, emergencies and possibly expansion. At the beginning, the cooperative is not likely to be able to support the member-workers at anything near a decent wage. So the workers will need to find other sources of income for themselves as well.

Some types of businesses require less initial money than others. Service businesses — those providing a service such as repairs, maintenance, bookkeeping, consulting, etc. — usually have fewer initial expenses and require less capital than sales and manufacturing businesses (those providing goods). Many service businesses already own their own tools and can buy parts as needed. Service businesses, particularly those where you go to your customers rather than have them come to you, can sometimes be operated out of people's homes or away from high-rent shopping areas. By contrast, retail stores must come up with a lot of cash before the store even opens its doors, to stock the shelves. Retail sales businesses must have well stocked stores to attract customers. Retail stores usually must be in a good shopping location, which often means high rent. A manufacturing business or a wholesale operation ("wholesale" means sales to other businesses who will eventually resell your goods or use them in their own manufacturing processes) can often be located in low-rent areas, but these businesses must still have initial capital to purchase the raw materials and goods they plan to manufacture and resell.

Most businesses should not expect to break even for the first one to two years. Initial expenses are high and initial sales are slow. It takes a while for your customers to find you and for the word to spread about your new business. It will probably be two more years before the business becomes a growing successful concern, able to generate enough cash from operations to pay its own way. More than half of all small businesses fail in those critical first two years, over 80% in the first five years. Lack of money isn't the only reason; inadequate managerial and technical skills can pull a business down in no time. Still, having enough cash to launch your venture and keep it going in the hungry days is an important element in its success.

This chapter is designed to help your cooperative obtain capital for its initial operations and to keep it going during the difficult years.

Money From Members and Equity Capital

The first and most common source for seed money is the coop's members. Investments by members make up part of what is known as "equity capital". It belongs to the coop. The coop need not pay it back as it must with loans, though some coops have a proviso agreeing to pay back the investment if the member leaves and the coop can afford to make the outlay.

If the coop is a partnership, members invest by "buying into" the coop. The partners are actually only contributing money which, in many situations, can and will be returned to the partners at a later date.

If the coop has been formed as a corporation, members invest by purchasing shares of stock or purchasing memberships in the coop. A member's investment isn't always in money. Some coops, especially when beginning, will accept services such as rewiring or building shelves or will accept contributions of equipment. Be aware, however, that investments other than cash can sometimes result in complicated tax problems and can even sometimes result in additional income taxes for the investor. What's more, most states do not allow corporations to issue stock or memberships in exchange for future services. Many states also restrict issuance of stock or memberships in exchange for past services. You will need professional advice.

The coop's surplus (savings) earned from the operation of the business is also equity capital. These earnings are, you might say, "owned" by the coop in the same way that members' investments are "owned" by the coop, at least until the coop agrees to return them.

Below we discuss several different ways of obtaining equity capital from members and from customers. Many coops exist solely on equity capital, loans being so difficult to obtain and so much of a problem besides — because, sooner or later, you have to pay back a loan. If you ever do need or want a loan, the greater your equity capital, the more you will impress bankers and other lenders. A substantial amount of equity capital is an indication of a substantial (i.e. creditworthy) coop

Stock and Memberships

In most cooperatives, each member will only be permitted to purchase one share of voting stock or one voting membership, since an integral part of the cooperative philosophy is that each member get only one vote. In a consumer coop, the stock or membership is usually kept at a very low price to attract members, and so it isn't a great source of equity capital. In a producer coop, stock or membership sometimes costs substantially more — maybe a few hundred or maybe a few thousand dollars — in order to raise needed capital. But often you'll find that the members just don't have the cash and need to make payments over a period of time. State law sometimes restricts the maximum amount you can charge for a membership or stock certificate.

To obtain greater equity capital, a coop might also issue additional shares of non-voting stock. This non-voting stock is a different class of stock than the voting shares and is often referred to as "preferred stock". Some cooperatives ask their members to work up to a "fair share" amount of preferred stock over a period of time. "Fair share" is what the coop thinks each member should contribute to meet the coop's financial needs and to demonstrate a commitment by the members to the coop. For example, a consumer coop may charge individuals $5 to purchase a voting share and become a member. But then members are encouraged or required to continue contributing, possibly out of their patronage refunds, until they have reached their "fair share", be it $50 or $100 or $200 or whatever the coop decides (and the state allows).

Direct Charge

Direct Charge consumer cooperatives have become attractive because they provide a steady source of member investment and help build up the economic base.

The member is required to invest in the cooperative and pay a weekly charge or dues. Many direct charge coops require an investment of up to $100. There is nothing magical or legal about $100 as a basic investment; it just seems to be what most coops like to use as a nice rounded figure. Sometimes payment may be made in installments. The weekly charge is usually between $2 and $5. By requiring weekly dues, the cooperative is able to raise a continuing source of new money. Furthermore, the members are obviously encouraged to do most or all of their shopping at the coop and get the most out of the weekly dues.

Though direct charge coops are usually thought of as consumer coops, a variation of this approach could also be used by producer and worker coops. Any kind of coop which wanted to build up its equity could require its members to pay a weekly charge or dues. In producer and worker coops, the dues could be taken out of the member's paycheck.

Surcharge

One way to collect the required investment for each member, whether or not the coop is direct charge, is to add a surcharge of, say, 2% to each sale in a consumer coop, to each item in a producer coop, and as a deduction from each worker's wage in a worker coop. The amount would be applied to the member's fair share account. Once the member's fair share amount is reached, some coops continue the surcharge in the form of a member loan to the coop, usually repaid with interest in three to ten years.

Mark-ups

Every business needs to sell its products for more than it paid for them. Overhead and the cost of producing or obtaining the product must be recouped. Members need to be paid for their labor. The coop may also want a little extra cash on hand as a cushion for unforseen costs. For example, a clothes shop which buys sweaters for $30 each may, after taking all costs into account, have to sell the sweaters for $55. The difference between the base price (the cost to the coop) and the sales price is the mark-up.

A mark-up is not the same as a surcharge. A surcharge increases a member's investment in the coop; a mark-up does not. A surcharge could be added on top of the mark-up.

Retained Earnings

The profits — the coop's savings or surplus from operations — can either be distributed to the members or retained by the coop to help finance its operations. Many coops, particularly consumer coops, retain a percentage of their earnings as a regular operating procedure. Other coops, particularly worker coops, retain none of their earnings but distribute them all to the member-workers. The members are often working for minimal wages and need every dollar they can get. Unfortunately, this often leaves the coop with little or no operating funds. The result is that every unexpected expense brings on a crisis. It's called crisis management, and it's no way to run a business.

If at all possible, your members should agree to leave some of the earnings in the coop's bank account for emergencies and unanticipated cash needs. The policy regarding retained earnings should be stated in your bylaws or partnership agreement.

Depending on how your coop is legally structured, the retained earnings may or may not be taxable to the coop or to the members. The taxability of a coop's earnings is discussed in the chapters on organizing coops.

Loans and Grants

After equity capital, loans are the next most likely source of money for your coop. Some coops are also eligible for grant funds. This chapter discusses different sources of loans and grants.

Member Loans

Members should be encouraged to lend money to the coop, at a certain rate of interest, in addition to buying their fair share of the stock. In some cooperatives, members are encouraged or required to purchase "certificates of interest", a fancy term for a piece of paper which acknowledges that someone has lent the coop money, and the coop has obligated itself to repay the money with interest by a certain date. Certificates of interest are usually payable in three to ten years. The coop does not put up any collateral (any business assent as security for payment) for this kind of loan. Many states set the maximum interest rate a coop can pay.

Loans can also be obtained from members by tacking on an additional percentage to a member's purchases in a consumer coop or by withholding a percentage of a member's earnings in a producer or worker coop. The money thus obtained from members would become a loan much like a certificate of interest, repayable with interest at a later date.

Community Loans

This can be a promising source. Often you'll find people in the community whose hearts are in the right place and who would like to help your coop make it. One way to approach community people who are wary about whether your coop will make it and whether anyone else will lend to you, is first ask for a "pledge". A person who pledges a loan consents to make the loan sometime in the near future. When you have obtained pledges totalling the amount you want, then go back and collect the loan from each person. In this way, no one has the sometimes uncomfortable feeling of being "first" and wondering whether anyone else will ever give.

It probably is best if you borrow from a limited number of people. Most states have laws requiring you to obtain a securities permit if you borrow from more than a certain number of people. Check your state's law before you begin soliciting.

Loans From Other Coops

Some cooperatives have committed themselves to help others. The Wheatsville Food Coop in Austin, Texas obtained its first loan from a local federation of coops. One coop in Berkeley, California puts aside a certain amount to make available as loans to other coops around the state. You probably won't find a list anywhere of coops willing to help others with financial assistance. One usually hears about them by word of mouth.

Bank Loans

Banks will probably not lend you money to start unless the coop or a member puts up some security (collateral), often a house. Banks may lend you money later on when you've established yourself, but they may still require security. The banks will also often require a responsible individual member to co-sign the loan — to personally guarantee to repay the loan if the coop fails to do so. Banks do not generally like small coops. The coops seem too unstructured and perhaps too uncapitalistic for the bank's taste. You shouldn't feel too discriminated against, however; banks do not generally like to lend money to new small businesses, period. (There is one notable exception. The District of Columbia National Bank makes it a policy to help coops, giving loans to coops and to groups wanting to organize as coops in Washington D.C.)

Christopher Hale, Christopher Crooked Stitch Collective:

In the beginning, all of the business capital came from me. As we took on more and more workers and as the business expanded, I found all my money going back into the business in order to make it expand. We weren't working with any loans.

Then we introduced the idea of a dividend. If you invest a certain amount of money — we decided that $200 was one share — a percentage of the sale price of the garments went towards the dividends. There was this very complex system, but 10% of the selling price of a garment was the dividend. Depending on how much you invested, you got that percentage of the dividend.

Some people didn't have very much money to invest and some had a lot. When we did our calculations, we found out that we weren't charging enough for our garments and we were losing money. And the whole dividend got wiped out. In fact, in December we had a deficit, and to make it up each person had to return $65 in order to balance the books.

When we decided to make a real go of it as a collective, we decided that each member *had* to invest $400. Those who didn't have the money would achieve their investment by working without pay. Their dividend or their share of the profit would go towards the investment. If they want to leave the collective and withdraw their investment, they have a certain amount of time to let us know and then they can withdraw all their money. We have to pay it back to them.

We're at the point now where we're talking about trying to get a loan, trying to get out of the position where we're constantly financing ourselves, which is very limiting. The people who work in this collective, their major source of income is from this work and they need it as it comes in. And the money better be there. It limits our growth because as soon as the money comes in from a sale, it goes out. There isn't much profit; it's mostly just direct labor. If we do reach a point where we start being financed by the banks, all the labor and all the materials will be covered by the loan. When the money comes in from that, a percentage will go to pay the interest on the loan. It will be an increased cost but it also will probably be increased productivity and justify itself. We are still discussing it. People are very idealistic and would like to be totally self-financed but they don't have the money to do it.

———————————

Loan Guarantee Organizations

These groups will help your coop get a loan. They go to the lending agency (usually a bank, but it also could be a foundation or even a government agency) on your behalf and secure and guarantee the loan. In most instances, to qualify, your coop must have first tried to get a bank loan and been turned down. The interest you'll be charged will depend on which lending agency is giving you the loan; usually it is the going rate. You will end up paying more, however, because loan guarantee organizations make their money by charging your coop "points" — added interest or payment — usually between one and two percent. It may still be worth it, though. If you need the money as soon as possible, loan guarantee organizations should be able to get it to you quicker than if you yourself go through the application process to get a loan, particularly from a federal or state agency. Some loan guarantee organizations are partly state financed; others are privately run.

Find out if your community has a Small Business

Development Corporation. Ask at your bank or at a local Small Business Administration office. Beware that many loan guarantee organizations have been known to be rather sleazy operations. Check with other businesses which have received loans through them.

Federal Government Loans and Grants

There are many government agencies which give direct loans, guarantee bank loans and make outright grants to coops. Several books have been published which list these agencies and tell you how to make an application for a loan or grant. We list these books in the "Resource" section at the end of the book. These books, unfortunately, go out of date regularly. As administrations change, so do the policies of the agencies. So you will have to do research, make telephone calls, write letters.

To get you started, we list below just a few of the better known federal agencies which in the past have given loans, guaranteed loans or provided grants to coops.

Small Business Administration

The SBA makes loans to "small businesses". "Small", by their definition, is a business with as much as $22 million in yearly sales and as many as 1,500 employees. So there are a lot of big businesses in the SBA's small business loan program.

The SBA's definition of "business" is an organization whose purpose is to make money. So, coops structured as non-profit corporations are not eligible for SBA loans. Consumer coops are likewise not eligible. Producer coops are eligible only if their membership consists entirely of individual small businesses, such as would often be the case in a marketing coop. Employees purchasing a going business through an Employee Stock Ownership Plan (ESOP) are eligible for SBA loans. Worker coops which conduct a regular type of business activity are also eligible for SBA loans.

Being eligible for a loan and getting one, however,

are two entirely different stories. Some people say that the SBA does not really like coops and does not lend readily to them. One official in Washington indicated that California coops have a greater chance of obtaining SBA loans than coops in other states. This is probably because California has a very active coop movement. Coops owned by disabled people are also more likely to get an SBA loan.

The SBA does not make very many loans, period. They make about 20,000 loans a year, and only about 25% of the available loan funds go to new businesses. The bulk of the money is lent to existing and expanding businesses. The SBA makes no grants.

The loan program most applicable to new business ventures in one the SBA calls the 7(a) Program, also known as the Loan Guarantee Plan. Under this program, a commercial bank loans you money and the SBA guarantees up to 90% of the loan. The maximum 7(a) loan is usually $500,000 with a 7-10 year payback period. Maximum interest is currently a couple percentage points above the prime rate. The bank sets the exact terms of the loan.

The only direct SBA loans normally available to small businesses (money loaned to you directly by the SBA) are made through their Economic Opportunity Loan (EOL) Program. EOL loans are made to "economically and socially disadvantaged" businesses — primarily blacks, Native Americans and Spanish speaking people. The EOL loan ceiling is $100,000 and you have up to fifteen years to repay. The interest rate is lower than the loan guarantee rate.

The SBA will make loans for up to eighty percent of your starting capital (as opposed to a fifty percent bank minimum). You will be expected to have some of your own capital invested in your business.

Both 7(a) and EOL loans are only available to people who have been unsuccessful in obtaining financing through the private sector. In other words, first the bank has to turn you down; then the government may step in. To get an SBA loan, you will have to convince them that you have the ability to operate a business successfully and that the loan can be repaid from the earnings of your business.

SBA loans also come with strings attached. The agency has a set of operating guidelines you must follow which limits your freedom and flexibility somewhat. The SBA will periodically audit your books which can be both a help and a nuisance.

There are 86 SBA field offices in the country. Contacr the one closest to you or write Small Business Administration, Washington, D.C. 20416.

Farmers Home Administration

The Farmers Home Administration (FHA) has several different loan programs including:

1. Agricultural loans for the production of food for animals or humans. Money is also available to construct and improve farm homes and to develop and improve farm land.

2. Housing loans for groups of low income families in rural areas. Farmers Home Administration also makes money available for farm labor housing to non-profit farmworker coops.

3. Business guaranteed loans for profit and non-profit businesses in areas outside a city's limits. Farmers Home Administration guarantees the loan made by a private bank.

4. Alternative energy guaranteed loans for fuel alcohol production or other non-petrol fuel plants.

The interest rates vary with the type of program. A guaranteed loan will be around the prime rate, while FHA direct loans will probably be less. Collateral is required for some loans.

To be eligible, a coop must be recognized by the state as a coop. This usually means filing as a cooperative corporation with the state. You should check with your Farmers Home Administration county office (there are 2000 of them) or with one of the 300 multi-county district offices.

Obviously, farmworker cooperatives are likely candidates for Farmers Home Administration funds, both for money to buy property and to set up cooperative housing units. But consumer coops as well as worker and producer coops should also be able to qualify for Farmers Home Administration assistance. FHA also gives occasional grants.

Department of Housing and Urban Development

The Department of Housing and Urban Development (HUD) has three separate loan programs: a Direct Loan Program; a Mortgage Insurance Program (where HUD insures loans from approved lenders for long-term financing); and a Special Loan Program for low income people. There are several other programs within the low-income category, where a subagency of HUD will purchase mortgages or issue securities using the mortgages as guarantees.

The process of obtaining a HUD loan can get pretty involved. Rather than describe it in elaborate detail here, we suggest you contact a local HUD office. There is one in almost every major city; or write HUD, 451 7th Street S.W., Washington D.C. 20410.

Community Services Administration

CSA provides grants to coops. The guidelines for eligibility are broad, but the coop must be low income. CSA gives money to local community action agencies which distribute the funds based on need. CSA has an Office of Economic Development (OED) and Office of Community Action (OCA). OED has a Rural Development Loan Program which will lend to coops or to non-profit groups who will then reloan to coops (whether profit or non-profit). OCA gives grants for specific purposes, like housing, energy. etc. CSA has ten regional offices: Boston, New York, Philadelphia, Atlanta, Chicago, Dallas, Kansas City, Denver, San Francisco and Seattle. Or you can write the Community Services Administration, 1200 19th Street N.W., Washington D.C. 20410

Co·operators are
in the
HAPPINESS
BUSINESS

National Endowment for the Arts

Every time we turn around, the National Endowment is getting its budget trimmed once again. If it hasn't been totally wiped out by the time you read this, the Endowment has in the past been a good source of grant money for non-profit groups. The Endowment makes no loans. Decisions are made by a panel meeting in Washington D.C. Program information and application procedures can be obtained by writing the NEA, Washington D.C. 20506.

Minority Business Development Agency

MBDA helps minority businesses. At least 50% of the employees must be minorities. Most recipients are profit-making businesses and must have annual gross receipts of at least $150,000. The loans and grants are not made directly to the businesses or coops, but to "intermediaries" such as the National Economic Development Association. The NEDA has regional offices in Chicago, Dallas, Atlanta, New York, Washington D.C. and San Francisco, and district offices in many other cities. Or you can write the Minority Business Development Agency, 14th and Constitution N.W., Washington D.C. 20230.

Department of Energy

The DOE has provided assistance to energy coops. If you're involved in solar energy, gasohol, windmills, reclaiming old hydroelectric plants, etc., they may provide you with financing. Contact a local district office or write the Department of Energy, 1000 Independence Avenue S.W., Washington D.C. 20461

State, County and Muninipal Assistance

State and local agencies may also provide loans, grants and loan guarantees to cooperatives. The kinds of agencies you might try contacting are: state departments of commerce, energy, industrial development or economic development; state cooperative councils and departments of consumer affairs; cooperative extension offices; state arts councils or commissions; and local community action or development agencies.

Grants from Private Sources—
Foundations and Corporations

There are several foundations which have been particularly helpful to coops. Others would be too if they were approached and educated on how coops work. Though it isn't as well known, large corporations also give over $2 billion to groups each year. However, corporations, in order to get tax write offs, will only give money to groups which have qualified under federal law as non-profit tax exempt organizations.

Though non-profit coops have the best chance of obtaining grants, coops not so organized can still find many donors who will help them out. Foundations often give money to groups who are not recognized as non-profit if the activity being funded would qualify as non-profit tax-exempt activity under federal law. Take a look at the "Non-profit Corporation" chapter in this book.

There is also a way your coop can get around not being non-profit and receive grants from corporations. Find a public foundation which would be willing to act as your sponsor. Public foundations are community oriented non-profit organizations supported by government and public agencies, organized under Section 501(c)(3) of the Internal Revenue Code. A public foundation which chooses to sponsor your coop will become the recipient of the money by acknowledging your activities as its own, but will then channel the money to you. There are, in fact, public foundations which specialize in this. The "Resource" section at the back of the book lists publications which have names and addresses of foundations, corporations and other organizations which give grants and loans to coops. But they are only the tip of the iceberg. Use your imagination. Contact local foundations and corporations and community groups. Non-profit coops in your community should also be a helpful source of information.

Volunteers

People donating their labor to make the cooperative work is not only important financially in reducing the number of paid employees but enriches the spirit of working for a common cause. Often when a coop begins, the members agree to work without pay to set it up. Even later, many coops will rely on volunteers to keep costs and prices down.

Donations in Kind

Someone may offer an old truck no longer being used, another member has wood you can use for shelves. You might also ask local community groups for donations. The IRS, however, may get into the act by claiming that the donations are income to the coop. You probably should check with your accountant.

Federal government surplus property may be donated to non-profit educational and public health organizations. Non-profit coops may qualify. All types of personal property (not real estate) is available: tools, office equipment and supplies, furniture, hardware, vehicles, boats, airplanes, construction equipment and many other items. The program is administered by, and the property is distributed by the states. Contact your state controller's office or write Federal Surplus Personal Property Donation Program, General Services Administration, Federal Supply Service, Washington D.C. 20406.

Shows and Sales

Don't forget the concerts, dances, shows, cake sales, garage sales, open houses.   They not only bring in some money (which, by the way, is taxable income) but unite the members in a spirited cause.

Sympathetic Landlords

Check around. You should be able to find a landlord who is more concerned with your being good tenants than with making a huge amount of money off the rent. The Food Coop at the University of California in San Diego was offered their space at a very low rent. The university as landlord was more interested in providing a congenial food service to the students than making money off the rent. The school also contributed $3,000 to the coop for equipment.

College Interns

The Sacramento, California Food Coop convinced several business students at the local college to get first hand experience by doing a time-management study for the coop free of charge. The results helped the coop use its personnel more efficiently, at less cost per worker-hour. The students got credit from the school.

Credit From Suppliers

When you are just getting started, most suppliers and wholesalers will want cash on delivery. After a few orders, however, suppliers will start extending you credit. Thirty days is common. Some supliers will offer a small discount, usually 1% or 2%, if you pay sooner. As you get established and known in the community, most of your suppliers will extend you credit.

The National Consumer Cooperative Bank
NCCB — The Coop Bank

"The Congress finds that user-owned cooperatives are a proven method for broadening ownership and control of market participants, narrowing price spreads, raising the quality of goods and services available to their membership and building bridges between producers and consumers and their members and patrons. The Congress also finds that consumer and other types of self-help cooperatives have been hampered in their formation and growth by lack of access to adequate cooperative credit facilities and lack of technical assistance. Therefore, the Congress finds a need for the establishiment of a NATIONAL CONSUMER COOPERATIVE BANK which will make available necessary financial and technical assistance to cooperative self-help endeavors as a means of strengthening the nation's economy." — Excerpt from Public Law 95-351, *National Consumer Cooperative Bank Act.* Statement of Findings and Purpose.

History of the Bank

With the signing of Public Law 95-351 by President Carter on August 20, 1978, the National Consumer Cooperative Bank (NCCB) was born. The dream of many cooperators, consumer advocates and legislators had finally become a reality. Leaders in the effort included Ralph Nader and Sam Brown, consumer advocates; Art Danforth, cooperative author; Ester Peterson, Director of the White House Office of Consumer Affairs; Senator Thomas McIntyre (D-NH); Congressman Fernand St. Germain, (D-RI); The Cooperative League of the U.S.A. (CLUSA); and many other individuals and organizations active in the cooperative movement.

The long, hard struggle to establish the NCCB spanned a good part of the twentieth century. It is not uncommon for new businesses to have problems laying their foundations and getting going. The NCCB was no exception. There were start up difficulties which originated both from within the organization and outside of it.

The downturn of the economy and a change in presidential administrations threatened the NCCB with extinction almost before it had even opened for business. But a well-coordinated nationwide group of cooperators and cooperative groups who call themselves "Friends of the Bank", along with the help of key senators and representatives, enabled the NCCB to survive, much leaner in funding but victorious. Not only did the NCCB survive, it has been transformed into a truly cooperative corporation owned by its members, no longer another arm of the government as it was originally set up.

Organizational Structure

The Coop Bank has its headquarters in Washington D.C., and there are eight regional offices located in different geographical areas of the United States. Final decisions on all loans are made by the loan committee which operates out of the national headquarters. However, coops seeking NCCB assistance are required to apply through the regional office which serves their area. (See the list of regional offices and areas served at the end of this chapter).

A fifteen member Board of Directors sets bank policies and governs its operations. Of the fifteen, twelve directors are elected by Coop Bank stockholders and three are appointed by the President of the United States. The three presidential appointees represent small business, low-income cooperatives and the government.

Stock in the NCCB is divided into three different categories. Class A stock is owned by the U.S. Treasury in return for the funds advanced to start the Bank. It is being converted to Class A debt which must be repaid within 40 years.

Class B stock is required to be purchased by the Bank's cooperative borrowers. These coops must purchase between one and ten percent of the value of their loan in Class B stock. The percentage is determined by the Bank and is based on the amount of the loan. The cost of Class B stock is usually added to the amount of the loan requested.

Class C stock is available for purchase by any coop eligible to borrow from the Bank.

Currently no other classes of stock are offered by the Bank. However, it does have the power to make other offerings and sell stock to other public and private investors.

It is interesting to note that the NCCB does not adhere to the traditional cooperative policy of one member, one vote regardless of the number of shares owned. This situation has met some resistance from Bank staff and other cooperators, so it may change.

Here's how stockholder voting rights are set up. Class A stock, which is being converted to Class A debt, does not carry any voting privileges. Class B stockholders have five votes plus one additional vote for every 5000 members. Housing cooperatives holding Class B stock get one additional vote for every $500,000 in loan amount. Other coops get one additional vote for every $100,000 in loan amount. Class C stockholders are entitled to one vote. By law, no single coop can control more than 5% of the total vote. Contact your NCCB regional office for additional information on stock purchase procedures and current stock offerings.

Loans

A nationwide survey conducted prior to drafting the Coop Bank legislation indicated that most cooperatives had difficulty obtaining credit, not because they were not creditworthy, but rather because most bankers do not understand the cooperative, not-for-profit way of business. Hence, the extreme need for the Coop Bank.

The Bank's Statement of Policies reads, in part:

"Coops are not subsidized by the Bank; it makes market rate loans to cooperatives that meet conventional credit tests. It is required by Congress to be a prudent lender; to survive, it must make loans to creditworthy, efficient cooperatives. ...The Bank will strive to be an understanding and creative lender. It will conduct its affairs in a financially sound manner. ...The Bank will strive to be sensitive and responsive to the needs of cooperatives that are new, that serve low-income persons, that use non-traditional management techniques, or that have been deprived of credit in the past. The Bank will attempt to respond to the diverse needs of its clientele by customizing loan programs, terms and conditions to the specific needs of each individual borrower. If an applicant does not initially appear creditworthy, the Bank will help find a way to correct the deficiencies."

The Coop Bank offers three types of loans: Title I loans, available to creditworthy coops; Title II loans, also known as "Self Help Capital Advances", available to coops which do not meet the creditworthiness requirements; and Technical Assistance Contracts, which are loans to be used to hire consultants and advisors. No grants are given.

The Bank offers the Title I loans to creditworthy cooperatives. The loans are usually made on a long-term basis and always at market rate interest. The statutory allocation of loan funds requires that no more than 30% be made to housing cooperatives, no more than 10% be made to producer coops and the balance be made to consumer coops. Also, the Coop Bank must make its best effort to make 35% of its loans to low-income cooperatives or cooperatives primarily serving low-income people.

Title II loans are available to coops which are not eligible for regular Coop Bank loans. These are coops too new to have a financial history and coops in temporary financial trouble.

Title II loans are administered by the Self Help Development Fund, a separate organization affiliated with the Coop Bank. The Bank oversees the operations of the Fund. The Bank's directors may serve on the Fund's board, Bank personnel may work for the Fund, and the Bank can make contributions to the Fund.

Technical Assistance Contracts, available through the Bank or the Fund, are loans to finance board member and staff training in coop management, financial planning, legal concerns, marketing, membership services, coop principles and housing coop conversions. The Bank contracts with "technical assistance providers" — organizations such as Cooperative League of the U.S.A. (CLUSA) and North American Students of Cooperation (NASCO) — to work with and assist your coop. The Bank then bills your coop for the cost of these services; they are, by the way, not cheap. The contracts are limited to a maximum of $3,000. Terms are negotiable and payment can be deferred up to one year when necessary.

How to Get a Loan From the Coop Bank

The Bank's loan application process is not a simple one. In fact, it is more difficult than applying for a conventional business loan from your local bank or financing a piece of equipment bought from a dealer or manufacturer.

The Coop Bank is required to be a prudent lender. Like any other bank it needs to make good loans, loans that will be repaid. If it didn't, it would fail and the Coop Bank experience would become a negative factor in the cooperative movement as a whole.

To be eligible for assistance from the Coop Bank, your cooperative must:

1. Be a legally incorporated entity. For-profit, non-profit and cooperative corporations are eligible. Coops set up as partnerships, associations or other non-incorporated structures are not eligible for Coop Bank loans.

2. Be "chartered or operated on a cooperative, not-for-profit basis to produce or supply goods, services or facilities for the benefit of its members as ultimate consumers or primary producers of such goods, services or facilities." The words "chartered or operated" means that your coop does not have to be incorporated under the cooperative corporation laws of your state as long as your articles or bylaws include this stipulation.

3. "Make membership available on a voluntary basis to all persons who can make use of the coop's services and are willing to accept the responsibilities of membership" and without discriminating on "social or political grounds or on the basis of race, religion, age, sex, marital status, sexual preference or handicap." A close reading of this requirement suggests that most worker cooperatives would be excluded from obtaining Coop Bank loans because worker coops usually restrict membership. This, however, is not the case. Worker coops are eligible for Coop Bank loans. The intended purpose of this requirement is to prohibit discrimination.

4. Observe the cooperative principles of giving voting control to members or stockholders on a one member, one vote basis, and take positive steps to insure economic democracy and maximum participation by members of the cooperative, including holding annual meetings of the membership.

5. Allocate or distribute net savings to members or patrons in proportion to their patronage or labor in the coop.

6. Limit dividends paid on voting stock according to the Coop Bank's guidelines.

7. If a producer or worker coop, at least 70% of the workers must be members.

What else will the Bank look for in assessing your eligibility for a loan? As with any bank, the guidelines are never hard and fast. They include obvious factors such as the coop's ability to repay the loan but they include more intangible factors too. How loyal is the coop's membership? Is the coop providing useful goods and services? How closely does the coop work with other community-based groups?

The Bank's loan office will conduct a credit analysis. Where feasable, a loan officer will make a fact-finding visit to the coop. The Bank will evaluate the coop's financial status, management performance and skills. The loan office will also study the coop's potential impact on small business in the neighborhood.

The application process for Title I and Title II loans, or any loan for that matter, is basically the same. The first step should be getting your financial books and records together so that you can accurately assess your needs. Once you have established the amount you need to borrow and what you will use it for, you must also be able to show that you will be able to repay it. It is a good idea during this step to seek the professional help of an accountant or financial counselor if you don't have such a person on your staff. This will enable you to be as realistic as possible with your needs, assessments and projections for repayment. Your loan proposal will be reviewed by similar type professionals on the Bank's Loan Committee and they will see whether you have done your homework or not.

The Coop Bank is here to help coops. Don't be afraid to ask for assistance. Actually you should contact your regional office during the early stages of the loan process. Get information on the Coop Bank's current lending policies, eligibility requirements, application procedures, etc. Obtain a current loan application and instructions for its completion. Experience shows that the loan application and review will take from three to six months and that the Coop Bank is not particularly eager to make loans of less than $10,000. This lower limit is generally due to the time and paperwork involved on both sides. However, we know one worker coop which got a $7,500 loan from the Bank.

Seek the assistance of another cooperative which has successfully gone through the loan process with the Coop Bank. Request a copy of their completed loan application and see how it could aid you in completing yours. Talk with the people who prepared the application and who dealt with the Coop Bank staff. You will find that other cooperatives are eager to cooperate. Sometimes they don't know their help is needed; most times we are afraid to ask. If you don't know of other cooperatives in your area who have dealt with the Coop Bank, ask at the Bank's regional office.

The information requested by the Coop Bank to complete the loan application will be very useful to your cooperative whether or not you get a loan. It will include a description and history of your coop, your membership, the market it serves and your management systems. You will be asked to describe, in narrative form, your financial needs, your financial structure and your past and projected financial performance. In addition, you will be required to provide past, current, and projected financial statements, schedules of depreciable assets, cash flow projections and your organizational documents such as articles of incorporation, bylaws, job descriptions, personnel policies, etc.

It sounds like a lot of work to get all of these items together in a concise, organized manner, but it is definitely worth the effort. You will find that by going through the process you learn many important things about your coop, its past successes and failures, its current needs, and its prospect for the future.

When applying for a loan or assistance from the Coop Bank, be clear in your understanding of what the Coop Bank expects from your cooperative. You should work with your regional office while preparing your application. To help the flow of communications we suggest that your coop designate one person to act as your representative to the Bank.

Be thorough, submit a complete, accurate, honest and realistic application. Remember, your application is usually the Bank's first formal introduction to your cooperative. It is important to make a good first impression; it lasts the longest and it is usually accurate.

Once you have submitted your application, follow through on it. Contact your regional office to make sure they received your application. It is a good idea to send it "Return Receipt Requested" just for good measure. Find out who your loan officer is and make personal contact with that person. Encourage dialogue and express your desire to answer any questions or to provide any additional information the loan officer might need in making a credit analysis. Keep the Coop Bank informed on any new developments in your cooperative which might affect their decision. Be patient with the Bank as it goes through its review process but don't be silent, don't just sit back and wait.

If your loan request is approved, you will find that the Coop Bank will work with your cooperative in setting the terms and conditions of your loan. There will be active participation on both sides.

If, on the other hand, the Bank determines that your cooperative is not creditworthy, the Bank will not flatly deny your loan request, tell you to go away and slam the door. The Bank will make sug-gestions which will hopefully steer your cooperative into a healthier condition. Heed the suggestions, welcome the assistance, request active participation by Bank staff in getting your cooperative on the right track to success.

Offices Of The National Consumer Cooperative Bank

National Headquarters

National Consumer Cooperative Bank
2001 S Street, N.W.
Washington, D.C. 20009
(202) 673-4334

Region I (New England) — Massachusetts, Maine, New Hampshire, Vermont, Rhode Island, Connecticut

Battery March Building, Room 1116
89 Broad Street
Boston, MA 02110
(617) 223-5234

Region II (Mid-Atlantic) — New York, New Jersey, Puerto Rico, Virgin Islands, Maryland, Pennsylvania, Delaware, District of Columbia

90 Church Street, Room 801B
New York, NY 10007
(212) 864-3333

Region III (Southeast) — South Carolina, Georgia, Alabama, Virginia, North Carolina, West Virginia, Kentucky, Tennessee, Mississippi, Louisiana, Arkansas, Florida

315 King Street, Room 210
P.O. Box 2730
Charleston, SC 29403
(803) 724-4113

Region IV (Great Lakes) — Michigan, Indiana, Ohio, Illinois

144 W. Lafayette Boulevard, Suite 608-612
Detroit, MI 48226
(313) 226-2400

Region V (Midwest) — Minnesota, South Dakota, North Dakota, Wisconsin, Upper Michigan, Iowa, Missouri, Kansas, Nebraska

> LaSalle Building, Room 450
> 15 South 9th Street
> Minneapolis, MN 55402
> (612) 725-2305

Region VI (Southwest) — Texas, Oklahoma, New Mexico, Arizona, Colorado

> 221 West Lancaster, Suite 301
> Fort Worth, TX 76102
> (817) 870-5587

Region VII (West) — California, Nevada, Hawaii, Pacific Territories

> 1330 Broadway, Suite 1017
> Oakland, CA 94616
> (415) 273-7576 or (415) 523-3425

Region VIII (Northwest) — Washington, Oregon, Alaska, Montana, Idaho, Utah, Wyoming

> Market Place North
> 2001 Western Avenue, Room 150
> Seattle, WA 98121
> (206) 442-0706 or 0699

Coop Bank Toll-Free Number: 800-424-2481

You can call the Bank between 9 a.m. and 5 p.m. (Eastern Standard Time) to obtain general information quickly on most matters related to the Bank's operations, including application procedures, eligibility requirements, and publications. Should the staff member responding to your inquiry be unable to help you, he/she will refer you to someone else who can.

Bank's Approved Policies

The NCCB Approved Policies have been released in final, published form. The 28-page booklet contains credit and lending policies for the Bank and the Office of Self-Help Development and Technical Assistance, guidelines for technical assistance delivery, and the Bank's low-income definition, voting rights policy, loan appeals procedure and public observation rules. For a free copy, write or call:

> Publications NCCB
> 2001 S Street, N.W.
> Washington, D.C. 20009
> Toll-Free (800) 424-2481

Taking The Next Step Toward A Cooperative Bank: What Coops Can Do

Buy stock. Coops that borrow from the NCCB are required to buy Class B voting stock. Non-borrowing coops must apply to buy voting stock (Class C). Non-borrowing coops must submit a copy of their bylaws, articles, a short history of the coop, and a letter requesting Class C stock. They should also list a contact person the Bank can call with any questions. This information is sent to the Office of the Treasurer, NCCB, 2001 S Street, N.W., Washington, D.C. 20009. The Bank will then rule on the coop's eligibility to buy stock and send out a prospectus. Coops can hasten this process by including payment with their request; the Bank will return the money if the coop is ruled ineligible. Shares cost $100. Coops need to buy only one share in order to vote. Call the Treasurer's Office at (202) 673-4378 with further questions.

Neither Rome, the Coop Bank, your cooperative nor the cooperative movement was built in a day. We have all arrived together at the crossroads of opportunity for positive growth. If we continue with patience, commitment, and support for each other, we will succeed.

Bookpeople:

We don't have the money sometimes to go out and do exactly what we want to do. We're limited to how the business does in any particular year and the shareholders. It provides for an undercapitalized company. When you figure that you've got 30 to 40 employees and they're the ones providing the capital, it's not going to be that much to begin with. The only way we could conceivably build up our basic capital besides putting profits back into the company is to expand and get a lot more employees, which is not really practical.

We once made an application for a bank loan and were turned down. We actually heard a rumor that we didn't get it because we were an employee-owned business. They would never come out and say that to us, but they suggested that to us. Its sort of put our backs up a little bit.

Lots of times, banks want major stockholders to co-sign a loan, and there are no major stockholders. They want a person to take responsibility for that loan. I even ran into that with a car loan. We bought a car for the sales rep. I went down to the bank, and the guy kept insisting that we put it in my name. He wanted my personal references, where I bank, stuff like that. He wasn't interested in the company taking out a loan. When I got the loan payment book, my name was on it. I had to call them up and say, "Listen, we went over this over and over again. The company was taking out a loan. I'm not taking out a personal loan." We finally got it straightened out but it was pretty ridiculous. They don't think in those terms. They wanted a major shareholder. I was going to sign it as manager of the business, which was only an officer position, and they wouldn't hear of it. They wanted it to be in my name.

Sometimes it's been a benefit that we don't have the money to make grandious moves in the trade, to do exactly what we want to do. Sometimes its been a benefit that everything we've done new has taken a long time — to find information, to explain it to everybody and to have everybody's input. It's hindered us and it's helped us. In the long run I think it works out better.

Insurance

Insurance — what insurance you must have , what insurance you'd like to have, how much you can afford, how much risk you're willing to take — should be completely worked out before you begin operation.

How easy or difficult it is to obtain insurance and how much the insurance will cost depends primarily on the kind of business you are engaged in, the location of the business and similar factors. Insurance companies, however, are sometimes hesitant to issue policies to unusually structured businesses, particularly small coops and non-profits. Like banks, insurance companies view these ventures as being more unstable than conventional businesses. Another problem is that ownership interests and areas of legal responsibility often appear somewhat hazy. Owners and members come and go a lot, particularly in the early days, and this lack of continuity of ownership makes insurance companies uncomfortable. Insurance is available but you may have to work harder to find it.

To be sure of complete protection, all members of the coop as well as the coop itself should be specifically named on the insurance policy. This is important on property insurance policies: if one of the members is not listed on the policy, the insurance company can, in some cases, reduce the payment on a claim. This is even more important on liability policies because an uninsured owner or member could be the defendant in a large lawsuit.

If your coop is a club (such as a food buying club) again all members should be named as additional insureds on your insurance policies. Not all insurance companies write policies for clubs so be prepared to shop around.

The different kinds of insurance available to you include:

Vehicle Insurance. Liability coverage is mandatory in many states. The same coverage available to you on your personal auto is available on a business vehicle; the premiums, however, are usually higher for business vehicles.

Workers Compensation Insurance provides wage, disability and death benefits to employees injured or killed on the job. Most states require employers to carry workers compensation for all employees. In nearly all states, a state board determines the premiums to be charged, but insurance companies can pay dividends (i.e. refunds) after the policy has expired if you have a low loss record. Premiums increase with the number of employees you have and vary dramatically with the occupation. Workers compensation insurance for a roofer is roughly ten times higher than for a grocery clerk.

Partners in a partnership, officers in a corporation and members of a coop are often not considered employees and may be exempt from workers compensation insurance. Volunteers may also be exempt but we encourage you to have workers comp or other coverage on all volunteers. There are im-

110

portant and often tricky legal distinctions between owners, members, volunteers and employees which may require professional help. Don't take a chance by leaving workers unprotected. It is not fair to your workers, and if someone got hurt on the job, it might involve you in a lawsuit.

Every state's workers compensation laws are a little different in how they cover volunteers. Volunteers do not always receive the same workers comp benefits as regular employees and often have to go through more elaborate procedures if they have claims.

An alternative to workers comp for volunteers, a special accident and health policy, is available. This policy will pay when volunteers are injured on the job. The volunteer must prove he or she was injured while on the job. For information, write C.I.M.A. Insurance, 4200 Wisconsin Avenue, Washington D.C. 20016 (In California, write Consortium For Human Services, P.O. Box 1183, San Jose, CA 95108).

Fire and Extended Coverage. Basic fire insurance covers fire and lightning losses to your equipment and inventory and to your premises. Extended coverage protects against storms, most explosions, smoke damage, riot and damage caused by aircraft or vehicles. Your lease may require this coverage. If you own the building or have a substantial investment in goods or machinery, you shouldn't be without fire and extended coverage insurance.

Be sure your policy includes a "right of subrogation" clause which covers neighboring businesses if a fire breaks out in your store and does damage to the neighbor's premises. A fire in your small office may do minimal damage to your furniture, but what about the smoke and water that destroyed $20,000 worth of Persian rugs in the business next door? You could be liable for the damage. If you lease, sometimes the owner of the building will have right of subrogation coverage for the tenants and neighbors.

The cost of fire and extended coverage insurance varies widely and is based upon the location of your property and the degree of fire protection in your community, the construction of the building (insurance for frame buildings is much more expensive than insurance for concrete buildings), the nature of your business and the nature of neighboring businesses. If you move into a building next to a woodworking, upholstery or dry cleaning operation, your fire premiums will be high even if your business is a low fire risk. A sprinkler system in your building will sharply reduce your premium.

Theft, Vandalism, Malicious Mischief. For many people, this kind of insurance is an unaffordable luxury. The cost of theft insurance depends largely on the type of merchandise you stock and on the type of theft protection on your premises — alarms, bars on the windows, door locks, etc. An investment in some security protection is certainly as important as an investment in theft insurance.

Liability Insurance pays lawsuits brought against your business because of bodily injury or damage to others' property. A customer in your store slips and falls, breaks a leg and slaps you with a $100,000 lawsuit; it's not uncommon. Over and above any mandatory insurance, liability coverage is unquestionably the most important to a business.

Premiums are usually based upon the square footage in the store; the bigger the store, the higher the premium. If you are a manufacturer or a contractor, premiums increase as your annual sales and payroll increase.

Liability insurance does not cover owners of a business, employees, volunteers and other workers. Coops have an unusual problem involving members. Working members are not covered by liability insurance. Working members are considered owners or employees and must be covered by workers compensation insurance or some other accident policy. Non-working members, however, should be able to get coverage under the liability policy. This is not a usual insurance situation and should be thoroughly discussed with your broker.

Products Liability refers to insurance coverage for any product manufactured by the insured. This coverage applies to the product once it leaves the manufacturer's hands and covers the manufacturer in case the ultimate user of the product sues for bodily injury or property damage. The courts generally hold manufacturers strictly liable for any injury caused by their product, sometimes even when the product has not been used correctly. As the number of lawsuits increases, so does the cost of the insurance: products liability insurance is the fastest rising insuranace cost next to doctors' and hospitals' malpractice insurance.

Bonds. Surety bonds guarantee the performance of a job. If you are unable for any reason to complete a job, your surety company must do so. Many contractors have such bonds to protect their customers and require them of sub-contractors. Surety bonds are most often used in the construction industry and are always required on public construction contracts. Surety bonds are difficult to obtain for new businesses and are often impossible to obtain unless you have $20,000 or more of liquid assets, such as cash, receivables and inventory. Fidelity bonds are placed on employees, insuring the employer against theft or embezzlement by bonded employees.

With all insurance, weigh the risks against the cost of the policy — and expect the rates to climb every year even if you have no claims. Shop around, too: different insurance companies offer different rates and different payment plans. Insurance agents can put together a package policy for you, combining all your coverage under one contract.

We are partial to independent agents because they are not tied to one company and can piece together the best insurance package to fit your needs and your pocketbook. We suggest you pick an agent who will devote time to your individual problems, who will at no extra cost survey your entire situation and recommend alternative methods of insurance, pointing out the advantages and disadvantages of each.

We also suggest that, if possible, you locate an agent who has experience with coops, someone who likes what you're doing and — most important — has the contacts to find the unusual insurance you may need and the unusual insurance company who will insure you. Ask other coops for recommendations.

Before you sign your insurance policy, read it — the whole damn thing. Get explanations for anything you don't understand and be sure all your members are fully and individually covered.

Permits and Licenses

Most business licenses and permits are required and administered by local governments — the city if you live within city limits, the county if your business is not in an incorporated city. Some businesses must also have state and federal licenses. Even though you may be exempt from income taxes, sponsored by the community or otherwise out of the business mainstream, you are still usually required to obtain these local permits.

This chapter will describe the different types of licenses and permits typically required by states and municipalities and those currently required by the federal government. Regulations, however, vary from city to city and state to state and they are changing and multiplying all the time. You should make it your responsibility to contact state and local government agencies to learn the most recent requirements and restrictions.

Fictitious Name Statement

When a business goes by any name other than the owner's legal name, the business is being operated under a fictitious name. In a partnership, unless all of the partners' names are included as part of the business name, the business has a fictitious name. A corporation's legal name is not considered a fictitious name; but if a corporation does business under a name other than the official name of the corporation, it is using a fictitious name.

People doing business under a fictitious name are required to file a fictitious name statement with the county in which they do business. The county will charge a filing fee, usually $10 to $25. Filing a fictitious name statement prevents any other business in the county from using the same business name.

In addition to filing for the name, you will be required to publish the fictitious name statement in a newspaper "of general circulation" in the county, the theory being that the public has a right to know with whom they are doing business. The county clerk can provide you with a list of acceptable "general circulation" newspapers. Publication costs can be relatively low — $15 to $30 — if your county has one of those newspapers that specialize in running legal notices (and little else). If not, small-time newspapers almost always charge less than large circulation dailies. You will be required to renew your fictitious name periodically, usually every five years.

For the specific fictitious name requirements for your locality, contact the county clerk's office, usually located in the county administration building at the county seat.

Local Business Licenses

Just about every business in the country must get a local business license which is merely a permit to do business locally. "Local" may refer to either the municipal or the county level and sometimes to both. Local business licenses can cost anywhere from $10 to as much as $500 and must be renewed annually or bi-annually. The fee is sometimes based on annual sales volume or the number of employees. Businesses operating under a fictitious name will usually not be able to get the local license until they have filed the fictitious name statement. Contact city hall or the county clerk for specifics.

Other Local Permits

Your business may be required to conform to local zoning laws, building codes, health requirements, fire and police regulations. Restaurants, night clubs, taverns, groceries, child care homes and retail establishments in general are most likely to be subject to these additional regulations. You should contact your local government before you open your doors, even before you sign the lease. You may find the regulations so demanding that you cannot afford to meet them. If you do not get the proper permits or meet the building requirements, the city can and will shut you down.

State Occupational Licenses

If your coop provides a service to the public (as opposed to selling or manufacturing goods) the business itself and possibly all the workers may be required to have state occupational licenses. States have traditionally licensed doctors, lawyers, CPA's, contractors and a few other proessionals. Recently, however, demand for consumer protection has brought about state licensing of dozens of additional occupations. Auto mechanics, stereo and TV repairpeople, marriage counselors, plumbers, even dry cleaners, to name a few, are often licensed. Occupational licenses are usually issued for one or two year periods and, as always, for a fee. Some of the occupational licenses require the licensee to pass a test; some have education and experience requirements. Contact the state agency administering consumer affairs to inquire about possible licensing of your business. State offices are always located at the state capital and usually in the larger cities around the state.

Sales Tax and Seller's Permits

Unless you live in a state with no sales tax, you will be required to collect sales tax from your customers and remit the tax to the state. Every state's sales tax laws are a bit different: many states exempt food, labor and shipping charges from sales tax; some states want only a report of your taxable sales; others want a breakdown of sales, taxable or not. Depending on the dollar volume of your business, you will have to prepare either monthly, quarterly or annual sales tax returns on which you report your sales and pay the taxes collected.

Every state which collects a sales tax issues "seller's permits" (also called "resale permits") and every business which sells goods must have one. Some states will also reqire a security deposit from you before issuing you a seller's permit, which is the state's way of guaranteeing that you will collect and remit sales tax when you sell your goods to your customers. The amount of the deposit is often based on your own estimate of expected future income; so you can minimize the deposit by being conservative and estimating low initial income. If you file sales tax returns on time and pay the taxes owed, in about two years the state will return your deposit. States will sometimes allow you to put your security deposit into a special interest-bearing bank account. When you apply for your seller's permit, the state will give you a full set of sales tax rules and procedures. Service businesses which do not sell parts or inventory are usually not required to obtain a seller's permit.

Besides registering you as a seller, a seller's permit gives you the right to buy goods for resale — both finished products and raw materials — without paying sales tax to your supplier. Only goods which will be resold in the normal course of business can be purchased in this manner. You may not use your seller's permit to make tax-free purchases of office supplies, tools and equipment or goods to be used for personal, non-business purposes.

Businesses selling wholesale goods and raw materials must also obtain a seller's permit, allowing them to sell their resale goods to another business without charging sales tax. The wholesale business will often be required to keep a detailed record, by customer, of the tax-exempt sales. States usually provide wholesalers with a special form for this purpose.

Other State Regulations

Truckers and taxi cab operators usually must register with the state's Public Utilities Commission. Businesses operating factories or other poten-

113

tial air and water polluting equipment must often meet state Air and Water Resources Commission requirements. Employers may be subject to state wage and hour laws and ocupational safety and health laws administered by the state Department of Labor or Department of Industrial Relations. Employers must have state employer identification numbers. States often have laws regulating finance charges imposed on customers.

Federal Identification Numbers

Sole proprietorships are identified by the proprietor's social security number. All other coops must obtain a Federal Employer Identification Number, even if you are not an employer. Fill out form #SS-4, free from any IRS office. Partnerships with no employees (partners, remember, are not employees) should note on the form, "For Identification Only". Otherwise the IRS will automatically start sending you payroll tax returns to fill out. Also see "Employers" below.

Federal Licenses

The federal government licenses all businesses engaged in interstate commerce, common-carrier transportation, radio and television station construction, manufacture of drugs, preparation of meat products and investment counseling. You should contact the Federal Trade Commission, Washington, D.C. 20580 for specific licensing requirements.

Exporting and Importing

Any business which will be exporting goods to foreign countries must have a Validated Export License from the Department of Commerce for each shipment. Write the Office of Export Administration, Department of Commerce, Washington, D.C. 20233.

You do not need any special permit to import goods into the United States but you should be aware of customs procedures which are lengthy if the value of your shipment is over $250 (including shipping costs), and customs duties, which can run from nominal amounts to as much as 110% of the value of the imported goods. Contact a local U.S. Customs office.

Securities and Exchange Commission

Incorporated coops may be required to "qualify" their stock or membership certificates — register them and have them approved by the federal (and possibly the state) government. The chapter "Stock Permits" discusses this further.

Any incorporated coop with more than 500 members and $1,000,000 or more in assets must file a financial statement with the SEC. When you start to get that big, you should consult a lawyer.

Employers

All employers must have a Federal Employer Identification Number, the same identification number mentioned above under "Federal Identification Numbers". Fill out form #SS-4, free from any IRS office. The number serves two purposes: identifying the coop, and setting it up in the IRS computer as an employer. When you get your ID number, you will also receive all the forms and instructions for keeping payroll records and preparing payroll tax returns.

Your state will also probably require you to obtain a similar state identification number.

Some employers are subject to the minimum wage and equal-opportunity employment laws which come under the Fair Labor Standards Act and the Civil Rights Act Title VII. All employers must comply with Occupational Safety and Health Administration (OSHA) regulations. Complete information about these laws is available from the U.S. Department of Labor, Washington, D.C. 20210.

Federal Trade Commission Regulations

Businesses which impose finance charges on credit customers must explain those charges in carefully worded statements according to Truth in Lending Act requirements. Businesses which guarantee merchandise, sell by mail or sell or manufacture clothing, fabrics, packaged goods or labeled goods are subject to Federal Trade Commission regulations. You can obtain copies of all FTC laws from the Federal Trade Commission, Washington, D.C. 20580.

Bookkeeping

Bookkeeping is a system to record, summarize and analyze your financial activity — your sales, purchases, credit accounts, cash, payrolls, inventory, equipment. Your "books" — your ledgers and worksheets — are the bound papers on which the bookkeeping activity is recorded or "posted."

Your books are your only source of complete information about your operation. Without a complete set of books you find yourself trying to evaluate your business by looking at isolated areas, such as cash and inventory — these being the most observable (and also the most misleading). If, for example, you price your product based solely on its cost to you plus some arbitrary markup — a common mistake with beginners — you could be selling at a loss and not even know it. Accurate books can tell you, almost at a glance, the pulse, temperature and general well being of your venture. They can tell you if you're making money or losing money and why.

All members should learn to read and understand ledgers. It isn't hard; it's not like learning French or learning to read music. Bookkeeping involves basic English, adding, subtracting and common sense.

Though everyone in the coop should have at least rudimentary bookkeeping knowledge, your business is much more likely to succeed if at least one member is a bookkeeper, someone who not only understands bookkeeping but enjoys it as well. If your books are kept by someone who is simply following someone else's instructions or by someone who is only doing the job because no one else will do it, if the bookkeeper finds the work tedious and boring, the books will suffer and so will your coop. Inaccurate, incomplete or non-current ledgers will provide inaccurate, incomplete and untimely information about your business.

Income and Expense

All your members, employees, volunteers and even your customers would better understand your business (and economics in general) if they understand what income is and what comprises expenses.

Income is sales of goods or services or both. Income is also donations received. Income may arrive in the form of cash (a cash sale or a donation), the promise of cash in the future (a credit sale) or goods and services (traded or donated).

Incoming cash is not necessarily income. Loans to the venture are not income, and they are not expenses when repaid. Capital contributed by members is not considered income. Sale of stock is not income. Members' capital and stock sales are investments; a business does not make money (i.e. generate income) when an owner or member invests in a business.

When a customer pays an old bill or pays up on a credit account, the incoming cash is not income. The income was recognized and recorded when the credit sale was made. You do not record income a second time when the bill is paid.

Most people with no bookkeeping knowledge think that the $5,000 deposited to the bank account this month means $5,000 of income came in. It is very important that the sources of incoming cash be identified and explained: this much sales (real income), this much paid-up old bills (income recorded last month or the month before), this much a bank loan or a member's contribution (not income at all).

Outlays of money can be equally confusing. Some are expenses and some are not. A repayment of a loan, as mentioned above, is not an expense; the interest paid is an expense. Repayment of capital to members is not an expense. Rent, telephone, utilities, supplies, insurance, advertising, permits and licenses, and postage are all expenses.

Your biggest expense, your inventory, is not legally an expense until you sell it. The expense is called "cost of goods sold". If you spend $10,000 stocking your store, until you make a sale, your expense (your cost of goods sold) is zero. If during the year you sell $8,000 of the $10,000 stock — your cost, not the sale price — you have an $8,000 expense.

Income taxes on the business are certainly expenses, but federal income taxes are not deductible on the federal return. State income taxes are deductible on the federal return but not on the state return.

Payroll is an expense but a complex one. Wages paid to employees who are not members and the payroll taxes on those wages are basic business expenses. Wages paid to members are also expenses; but depending on how your business is legally structured, these wages may or may not be tax deductible. Owners can usually set their own wages, and this causes much confusion and misunderstanding when you get into the often touchy issue of profit.

The Politics of Profit

"Food for people, not for profit" is probably the best known expression in the anti-profit culture. The people who want to operate or associate with enterprises which have "non-profit" in their names (because of the philosophy, not because of the cheaper postage rates) need to understand what the word "profit" means. Because, when you get right down to it, no organization can function without profit.

"Profit" has, particularly for some people with cooperative ideals, become synonymous with excessive profit, with greed and callousness. Oil companies and agribusiness and munitions manufacturers seek as much profit as they can get their grubby hands on, to the detriment of the earth and all its inhabitants. But small, community oriented businesses must have a profit as well, not to exploit, but to survive.

Even the accountants have varying definitions of profit. Basically, when your total income exceeds all of your expenses, you've made a profit. But what's an expense? What about fair wages for the people who've worked to make the venture successful? Are those "expenses" or is that "profit"?

Here are some examples from income tax law. A sole proprietorship — a one owner business — is required to pay income taxes on the profit the business earns. Expenses allowed by the Internal Revenue Service in determining profit include all the regular business deductions — cost of goods sold, overhead, employee wages, etc, — but do not include any wages paid to the owner. The owner of a sole proprietorship is not an employee of the business for tax purposes; the owner's salary is not an allowable business deduction on the tax return. The profit is the owner's wage (whether the owner draws it or not) and the profit is taxable to the owner at the same rate a wage would be taxed. No profit, no wage. So if a grocer, a sole proprietor, sells food to the community for $10,000 more than the grocer paid for the food, is that "food for people" or "food for profit"?

Tax laws are structured differently for corporations and partnerships than they are for sole proprietorships. Partners can pay themselves wages — called "guaranteed payments to partners" — and show the wages as expenses in computing the partnership's profit. Corporation owners can set their own salaries and pay themselves as full-blown employees with withholding and all the trappings. The owner's wages are deductible expenses in computing the corporation's taxable profit. The partners pay taxes on their guaranteed payments and the corporation owners pay taxes on their wages, the same amount of taxes they'd pay if their businesses were sole proprietorships. Using the example of the $10,000 grocery business, the partners in the grocery could pay themselves a $10,000 wage and the partnership shows no profit selling food to the community. The corporation owners could pay themselves a $10,000 wage and the corporation makes no profit selling food to the community.

Owners of corporations can even go so far as giving themselves enough of a bonus at year end so the corporation shows a zero profit even if it makes a lot of money. It's a tax gimmick many corporate owners use. Within reason, it's legal. So the tax return of the Corner Grocery Inc. shows that it made no profit selling food to the community, yet the owners paid themselves $100,000 in wages. So, what's a profit?

In addition to providing a fair wage, profit is necessary to have as a reserve in case things are not going quite so well next year — to offset an unexpected loss. Profit is necessary to buy new equipment when old equipment breaks down or when you decide to expand. Without a small cushion provided by profit, every financial problem becomes a crisis.

The entire concept of profit and fair wages should be explained to the people you work with and the people you serve. Any financial statement you prepare should show your wages as expenses of operation. Explain to the community that it's impossible to know in advance what actual expenses you'll incur and what volume of sales you'll generate. If your goal is to pay yourselves a fair wage and charge no more than necessary, some years you'll succeed and break even, some years you'll make a little more, some years you'll make a little less.

People who see the word "profit" and read "greed" can cause themselves and their community enterprises needless grief. They could even unwittingly bring about the demise of a business that deserves to flourish.

Open Education Exchange:

We had a number of values when we started. One was, hopefully, the development of a community. Another was to do a school, to create an economic alternative for the teachers who participated. And hopefully there was a little bit of save-the-world. All along, we were trying to create an institution that worked. We were willing to use whatever organizational structures worked to maintain and insure the survival of the organization. It was the service that we felt was important. We started in a sense with a charismatic structure and, over the years, we evolved to a bureaucratic structure.

We started with a lot of volunteers from a collective communal restaurant that was on its way to disintegration. A few of the people in th commune liked the idea of a school. They were listed as staffers. The people, I think, volunteered a part time commitment the way you might volunteer to work at the Free Clinic. They liked the sense of a new project starting. They could tell that a few of us were very much dedicated. Many of the people were subsidized; they were receiving government aid of some kind such as SSI or welfare.

The amount of energy you put in determined the amount of say you had over things, because you were there when something was to be decided. I thought of it in a sense that the expertise determined the authority, and that is the way it was going to be. I could have said, okay I'm the director of the school, or something, but I did everything possible to avoid taking a label or a title. For a couple of years we worked without titles. But we had a problem with people who asked, who's in charge, who can I talk to about a special problem? And even the staff people were asking — maybe we should say something about who's got responsibility for certain things.

We tried to operate on a consensus basis. We'd get togehter. The task would be relatively simple, like who's going to put the papers out or who's going to answer the phones. We had schedules for people. These kinds of decisions were hacked out in a consensus. But at the time we had very clear values that we all held, so it wasn't difficult to arrive at consensus. I think a main factor was that no one was making money except for the people who were teaching classes. So none of us had any conflicts over that.

As the school changed, the staff people changed. They'd take responsibility for a little while. We had one woman who was a volunteer. She was an older woman, her husband owned a business, and she was just looking for something to do. She was a wonderful person, but after awhile it just wasn't exciting or interesting anymore. After a couple months, she left. She said she thought the job would be more exciting. She said this is just filing papers. It stopped being so much fun to work in the office and do what was needed. There were a lot of cards to be filled out, a lot of forms. People who were volunteers, they were doing it because they wanted it to be fun and interesting; and this was work.

The staff was unpaid for a year and a half. I was operating for the first two years on the naive assumption that once we could afford to pay minimum wage to our staff, all our problems would be over. If you could get volunteers to work, think how dedicated people would be if they could get minimum wage. This would be the greatest thing in the world.

When we first started employing people it worked out all right. We still had the feeling that we were all working together. We didn't want to be employers, and I stressed that. We still wanted to operate on a consensus basis. We weren't telling these people what to do.

For awhile, we kept on hiring maybe what you'd call alternative types, people who had political consciousness or moral consciousness. We were trying to pick people whose primary goal, motivation for working, was not money. We were trying to find people who would be more involved in it than just a job. A lot of people we hired on that basis weren't that good at paperwork. Minimum wage turned out not to be enough to obtain the skills that were necessary to feed an increasingly large, voracious paper machine.

We had differences of opinion over finances. They thought if we had any surplus money in one month, we should just spend it all, raise everybody's salaries. If we needed the money next month, we could just ask our students to donate. I said, well, we're not doing crisis management here. We're trying to have more of an even flow from one month to the next. I felt that asking the people who were taking classes to donate more money was like pulling our your last card.

A lot of the people — by no means all — were approaching the job trying to work out a personal agenda. They were dumping, we felt, a lot of things into the organization that were totally apart from the service we were trying to perform. They had a personal problem, they somehow felt the problem was going to be worked out by the job. They were looking to it to solve everything because it was this alternative, funky job and people who worked there should spend time with them, care about them, really get into it heavier than maybe people had time for.

Many of the people didn't want to commit more than three or four hours a day. Most of the people didn't want a five day a week job. But here we were, willing to work seven days on it. And when the teacher payroll had to go out, we were there til twelve or one. There were deadlines. We'd be there all night if we had to be.

Some things I missed out on, in terms of ordering priorities. Some things started sifting out as more important and some things sifted out that we had to do a certain way. Maybe had we been different people with different personalities, almost inevitably it would have sifted out in a different way. We were making a commitment. We found that we could work more effectively and efficiently in a hierarchical structure. Finally, reluctant-ly, we eventually accepted the fact that we were bosses. We had to hire people who could do certain tasks. Their politics was secondary to their willingness to do the job that had to be done. We decided to hire people to do clerical jobs who had clerical experience. We'd look for personalities we thought we could get along with, but we would be looking for expertise and experience. It would be easier to have someone who looked at it as a job. There wouldn't be so many hassles to work out. Our ads for staff used to say, "Fun atmosphere, community organization." Now when we advertise, we say "Educational corporation, responsibility, so many years experience, clerical"; and then at the end we'll add, "Mellow atmosphere".

One of the things we try to do now is to deal with people individually in regards to their salaries. We don't make it a group thing where everybody's comparing what they're making. All sorts of jealosies come out and all sorts of problems. We also found out that when we were paying everyone the same, when someone new came to us they would start at the same salary everybody else was making. The established staff got upset about it because they had been working there, they had experience and they were committed. They thought that the person starting shouldn't get the same amount. So we don't discuss wages. We found that some things, if we don't make a big deal out of it, we don't have to somehow find the one correct rule to live by, because it's so damn difficult.

Personnel

In the early stages of a coop, the process for becoming a member-employee is usually very informal. New people are added because they are available, because they have a friend who is already a part of the group, or because they have useful experience, ideas or skills needed by the group. This informal manner of bringing in new people works better with smaller groups (2 to 10 people or so) than it does with larger groups. In a small group, the members are familiar with each other's goals and ideologies, and this familiarity facilitates acceptance and trust of a new member brought into the group at the recommendation of an existing member.

Eventually, as a coop expands and becomes more established, the informal structures of membership and staffing must change. More formal procedures should be developed for bringing in and dealing with new member-employees. Actually, this makes it easier for everyone involved. The group develops a personnel policy and a set of hiring procedures. The prospective new member-employee is introduced to an organized and understandable sequence of events which will result in either getting or not getting the job. Prior to hiring anybody, your coop must be clear on your organization's goals and needs. If not, how can you expect to prepare an adequate job description or accurately represent what your coop is to a prospective employee?

You must also be certain that you will be able to afford another employee. Sometimes the answer is not strictly a matter of financial consideration. It is often a matter of asking (and answering) questions like: What if we don't hire another person? Are current employees going to burn out? We all need to get paid more, but without more help, how will we keep up with our increasing business? The lines at the cash register are moving too slow; what are we going to do? In some situations you can't afford not to hire a new person; the right person, with proper training, will more than "pay" for himself, both psychologically and financially. Bear in mind, however, that the monetary cost of hiring a new employee will be 10% to 15% higher than the additional gross payroll. This is due to federal and state payroll taxes imposed on the coop as employer and to the cost of workers compensation insurance.

Prospective employees should be given an accurate picture of your coop's goals and needs and a detailed job description for the position. The prospective employee will then have a fair basis to determine whether your coop meets his or her needs. Both the needs of the employer and the employee must be met in order to successfully work together. If either's needs are not met, the relationship between you as employer and the individual as employee will never survive.

Job Descriptions

People work best if they know what they are expected to do and what they can expect of their employer. Therefore, it is helpful to have a job description for all job positions in your coop. Wherever possible, it should be thorough, specific and include the following:

1. Position title.

2. General Description — overview of scope of the job.

3. Specific Duties — the more specific, the better (where possible, indicate % of time devoted to each duty.)

4. Minimum Requirements — experience, skills, education.

5. Supervision — employee is accountable to whom?

6. Time Requirements — hours/days worked.

7. Evaluation — how and when they are done and who does them.

8. Range of Pay — regular time/overtime; frequency and amount of raises.

9. Benefits — health plan, vacation leave, sick leave, retirement.

10. Commitment to cooperative principles.

If the position is being filled because another employee is changing jobs or leaving your organization, the current job description (if one exists) should be reviewed and revised where necessary to include all aspects of the work to be done. Ask the employee who is moving on to help in the review process or in the preparation of a job description if one doesn't exist.

Sahag Avedisian is a member of The Cheeseboard Collective, Berkeley, California:

Membership meetings should be run however the people feel the most comfortable. It's hard to analyze the effectiveness versus the efficiency of the structured versus the chaotic meeting. If it's chaotic, which I personally like, then people who don't generally talk will check what they've been hearing with other people, under the din of a chaotic meeting. I think that phrasing engenders a lot of creativity. Some of the problems the structured meeting tries to avoid are not avoided. It's supposed to allow people to talk, to prevent people from dominating the meeting. But that's not true. People who have a lot to say will say it, whether it's anarchy or structured. People who don't want to say anything, tend to say nothing anyway. At least in a chaotic meeting, there's a way for people who don't talk to act.

The Personnel Policy

No matter what the size of your coop, it's a good idea to have a personnel policy. Your personnel policy should not be an undefined one that "everybody understands." It should be clear, concise, written and available to all members. This does not mean that it has to be permanently cast in cement. Special circumstances do come up, needs change. Flexibility is a virtue.

There is no perfect formula for the ideal coop personnel policy. Policies will vary from coop to coop depending on the coop's size and structure. For example, a coop with a hierarchical management structure will have a personnel policy quite different from that of a coop where total equality in the workplace is the goal.

Seek the help of other coops in your area. Ask them about their personnel policies, how they do it, what works, what doesn't work. If they have any written policies ask to read them and see how the policies fit or could be adapted to fit your organization. Remember, we are not alone. We don't have to do everything by ourselves from scratch every time.

The basic elements that should be covered in any personnel policy are:

Organizational Structure (Chain of command). An organization chart is helpful here. Define who has the authority to hire and fire.

Policy of Equal Employment Opportunity and Affirmative Action.

Hiring Procedures. Job opening advertising, interview process, training, trial period, etc.

Evaluation Process. Frequency, by whom, method.

Grievance Procedures. Identify who handles grievances and how.

Firing/Termination Procedure. Basis for firing, authority to fire and employee's appeal process.

Length of Commitment Expected.

Policy of Agreeing to Work Together to promote a harmonious, effective workplace.

Business Hours. Days and hours open.

Holidays. Open/closed, religious, paid or unpaid.

Full-time/Part-time Employee. Definition of each.

Compensation. Pay dates, pay scales, periodic raises, cost of living increases, bonuses, policy on advances.

Overtime. Is it mandatory? How is it compensated?

Vacations. Paid or unpaid, length, how accrued, when taken, accumulation.

Sick Leave. Paid or unpaid, how accrued, accumulation.

Other Types of Leave. Maternity or paternity, family emergencies, mental health days (good in avoiding "burnout"), leaves of absence, jury duty. Paid or unpaid.

Fringe Benefits. Health plans, retirement and profit sharing.

Volunteer Worker Policy. Jobs available, benefits.

A thorough personnel policy that incorporates the elements listed above will clarify the position of member-employees as well as that of the coop as employer. It will provide a useful, efficient tool in dealing with problem situations which do arise in employee/employer relationships whether your coop is a six-person bakery collective or a consumer food cooperative with a staff of fifty.

Below, we expand upon some of the basic elements we've listed and share some experiences other coops have had in this area.

Who Does The Hiring?

Who has the authority to hire new member-employees? Does the entire membership make a collective decision? Do you want to set up a formal personnel committee?

Many coops act as an integral unit and all members together administer the personnel policy. The prospective member might be interviewed by a committee or by the coop as a whole. Many coops require that consensus be reached before any new member is asked to join.

Other coops have a hierarchical management structure. They often have personnel committees, typically composed of one or two members of the board of directors, the general manager and perhaps one or two other members of the coop. The personnel committee may be a standing (ongoing) committee or it might be formed whenever the need for personnel arises.

Equal Employment Opportunity

Federal laws prohibit discrimination based on race, color, religion, sex or national origin. It is a good idea to make a statement about equal employment in your personnel policy. For more information about the laws, write the Department of Labor, Washington D.C. 20210. Some states also have equal employment opportunity laws similar to those of the federal government. Other states have conflicting laws, and some states have no such laws. Where there appears to be a conflict between state and federal governments, federal courts have ruled that federal law takes precedence. You should get some professional advice.

Hiring Procedures

Finding applicants for most jobs is not hard. On the contrary, there are usually more applicants than you really have time to deal with. If care is taken in advertising the position available, a lot of time and effort will be saved.

You should provide a summary of the job available (title, duties, payscale, full or part-time), and the basic qualifications an applicant must have.

You should have a system set up to screen responses to your advertisement. For the initial screening it is good to have a formal and impersonal method for gathering information about people. It is not necessary that all people interested in a job get a written application or have a personal interview. Telephone screening can simplify the hiring process a lot. Develop a telephone interview screening form. List the basic questions about experience, skills, coop background, minimum requirements and other items important in deciding whether someone should be sent an application or scheduled for a personal interview.

All applicants who are asked to submit a written application or to participate in a personal interview should also be provided a job description and a description of your coop's organization, operations, work environment (casual/formal) and goals. By doing this the prospective employees will get an idea of what they may be getting into.

In the interest of communication and fairness, it is very important to respond to all applicants. After reviewing a job application, communicate with the applicant: "We would like to interview you;" "The position is filled;" or "Review of your application tells us you are not the one for the job."

Likewise, upon completion of the interview process, all applicants interviewed should be told either they got the job or they didn't. The amount of explanation necessary will depend on the particulars of each situation. Keeping it simple and to the point has proven to be a good approach.

The Job Interview

The job interview process should not be haphazard and unorganized. Formal procedures will help the interview flow smoothly. The people doing the interview should be familiar with the job description. A three to five person interview panel usually works well. Too many interviewers tend to create a tense atmosphere for the applicant. A lot of note taking will also make your interviewee nervous. Administering tests is a major tension creator. Besides, test are not a good indicator of an applicant's qualifications.

Always begin a job interview by giving information instead of asking for it. Share some of the background and major goals of your coop and introduce the individual members of your interview committee. If the interviewer gives a little first, it tends to make the interviewee feel more at ease. One new employee of Peoples Warehouse in Ann Arbor, Michigan, said: "The most valuable part of the interview for me was the information the interviewers gave me about the warehouse. It equalized the interview so that it was a joint decision. When I was asked to take the job, I could say yes I would take the job. So it's very important for both sides to have as much information about each other as possible."

In the interest of keeping your job interviews lawful and nondiscriminatory, members of the interview committee should be familiar with the laws concerning fair employment practicies. Any inquiry made during an interview (or on an application form) should be both job related and a true business necessity. Avoid asking questions about such topics as age, race, religion, political beliefs, sexual preferences, arrest records, membership in community or social organizations and unrelated educational or work experiences. Questions dealing with these topics are often considered unlawful under federal and state laws and usually are not really job related.

Interviewers should know the questions they are going to ask. They should not be put in the position of being interviewed by the applicant. It helps to ask questions that require an explanation from the applicant, something more than a "yes" or "no" response. Acceptable questions might include: Why would you like to work for our coop? What were your duties on your last job? What kind of work do you enjoy most? Least? What does the word "cooperative" ("collective") mean to you? How would you describe yourself as a worker?

A good interviewer is a good listener. Listening to what applicants have to say and *how* they say it will provide a good basis for judging their qualifications and suitability for the job.

During the interview, if you have questions or doubts about an applicant's skills, experience or other job related subjects, do not hesitate to mention them. This will clarify matters for you by giving the applicant a chance to address them.

At the end of the interview, allow a comfortable time for the applicant to ask questions or to share any other information with you that would be helpful in making your decision. Summarize for the applicant the steps remaining before you will make a decision. Promise to let him know if he got the job.

After the interview, poll all committee members to see how they each feel about the applicant. Ask yourselves if you are looking forward to working with this individual.

It's a good idea to check an applicant's references when the applicant is a stranger. It is especially helpful to check with others who have experience working with him.

When it comes to making the final decision, sometimes the right person stands out among all the rest. The decision is easiest then. Usually, however, the choice is between a number of equally qualified people. In the latter situation, it is very important to choose the person who will best fit in with the other members of your coop and who you feel will best represent your coop.

Cooperatives usually have anywhere from a one to a six month probationary period for all new employees. At the end of this period, the employees are evaluated and either given permanent status, placed on extended probation or terminated.

The probationary period is the time to initiate employee education and training. It is necessary to educate new employees on cooperatives in general and your cooperative in particular. One person in the coop should be assigned responsibility to train the new member. Too often, someone is hired and put to work without any real instruction and without knowing who to ask for help.

Employee Evaluations

The most effective evaluations are those structured to give an employee positive feedback, encourage work improvement, strengthen interpersonal relationships and offer remedial action as an alternative to firing. Evaluations can be done by one's supervisors or by the entire membership or any designated individual. Evaluations should be both verbal and written. A copy should be kept in the employee's personnel file and another given to the employee. Evaluations should be read, under-stood and signed by both the evaluator and the member being evaluated. An employee is more secure when he knows where he stands.

Evaluations at regular intervals help to keep the workplace functioning smoothly. If one knows when he or she is to be evaluated there is less of a threat. The evaluation schedule may be used as a reference point by the employee for pacing his progress. Your coop might evaluate new employees after three months, after six months, at the end of their first year and then yearly thereafter.

Some people feel that evaluations should be based on job performance only and not on a member's personality. Others feel that personality, getting along with fellow workers, is at least as important as doing a good job.

Evaluations should be subjective as well as objective. The worker is not doing a good job. Why? Sometimes the circumstances underlying a poor evaluation are understandable.

Have a warning system built into your evaluation process so that the first time problems are discovered is not the time that the employee is fired. Give the employee a chance to improve. Come to an agreement with the employee that if he doesn't improve he will agree to leave.

Firings (Termination)

Sooner or later, most likely, your coop will be faced with the situation where an employee's behavior or non-performance on the job is cause for termination. It is a very serious emotional issue. What do you do? How do you do it? You should have a formal written system for dealing with this situation, including a grievance procedure which gives the employee some recourse. If both employer and employee understand the process, it is likely to result in fewer bad feelings.

Avoid the situation where one person is the heavy. It is better if the responsibility is assumed by the group.

Firing someone hurts everyone involved in the process, but it's better to deal with the issue rather than to let it drag on. The longer you wait the more painful the process becomes and the more damage done to the individual and to your coop as a whole.

Personnel Records

In addition to employee compensation records (gross earnings, taxes withheld, other deductions) an employer should maintain a personnel file for each employee. Employees' personnel files should be open to them and should contain the history of their employment with the coop. Included in their file should be their resume, their job application and job description(s), their address and phone number and who to contact in an emergency. It should also contain their written evaluations, disciplinary records, memos of commendation, and, in the case of employees no longer with you, why they left.

Job Sharing (Rotation)

Some worker coops traditionally operate with the goal of sharing all jobs. This way the members learn all aspects of their business; they are able to make better decisions. Rotating jobs is an equalizing process which allows the drudgery to be shared by all. Everybody has to take turns cleaning the toilet. In terms of efficiency, job rotation could be viewed as being less efficient than job specialization. But, in terms of "effective collectivism", it often works. Try to avoid re-inventing the wheel when you do practice job rotation. Once again, job descriptions are very helpful.

Not everybody will do each job equally well. People have different skills and different job preferences. Some coops have found that although philosophically they favor job rotation, in practice it wasn't necessary or practical. An example of this is the experience of a construction collective in southern California: "We went through that in our coop, particularly around bookkeeping. We initially practiced job rotation; we had evolved out of a political movement where everyone rotated. We decided that it wasn't important that everyone learn all the jobs. What was important was that the decision making was collective. We realized that if the decision making was collective, if someone specialized as the bookkeeper, the electrician or the architect, they had no more power than anyone else. In our coop that became an important distinction."

Another collective member, Peter Solomon of the San Francisco Mime Troupe, said, "Yeah, we decided also that equal voice doesn't mean equal skills. I mean, some people can't write inside those little lines."

Compensation (Pay Differentials)

Many coops have pay differentials. These may be based on seniority, need, skills or the distastefulness of the job being done. An example of a pay differential based on need is that used by the Wildflower Bakery Collective in Ann Arbor, Michigan. They give additional pay to those with dependent children. Arcata Cooperative, the second largest consumer cooperative in California, has about a 2 to 1 pay scale from top to bottom (general manager to cashier). All employees, however, receive the same fringe benefits.

Some coops, of course, give equal pay to all members regardless of need, skill, job requirement or seniority. There is a strong spirit of equality which permeates such coops. As long as every worker feels good about the equal pay arrangement, as long as none feel they deserve more than the next person, the system will work. Equal pay for all is most effective in coops which practice regular job rotation. Everyone is the president and everyone is the janitor, so everyone is entitled to the same wage.

More important by far than equal or unequal pay is a fair wage for all workers. At a recent Collective Conference we attended, a sentiment we heard over and over again was, "We are people striving to work together. We are not our own slaves. We cannot continue to collectively exploit ourselves because of our ideals. We must make a living wage."

Peter Solomon is a member of the San Francisco Mime Troupe, a collective theater company:

Until very recently we were completely collective in the sense that jobs rotated a lot. There were people who parlayed doing office work and acting work, or juggling office work with music. Those people found that they could be very happy indeed. If the bookkeeper wanted to go kick out the jams by going and playing the trumpet, it might not make him a better trumpet player but it did help to make him a healthier bookkeeper.

Basically, the company hired actors for their acting skill. We didn't ask people, "Can you type?" So we've had to train people into the office jobs. You might have had somebody with the job description Drummer/Bookkeeper. Preference has not usually been the criteria, it's obligation. You do have the situation where somebody doesn't like some project or for example, one who has a lot of trouble writing letters. We try not to force people into doing something, but still, a lot of work has to get done. So over the years it's involved drafting people for jobs. And you get "I can't do that," "Well somebody's got to, if you can't do that you gotta do this", "Well that's even worse". There was a period when the office manager was an officer of the day job, an "OD" job. It was rotating. There were other jobs that went along with running a theater company — cleaning the building, maintaining the equipment. And jobs were more or less formally assigned to people. People were allowed to choose but people were expected to put in their time, to help out, so that the company could continue to run. There were some slackers as everywhere, and some people who drove themselves crazy and worked themselves into a crisp as everywhere.

It was not an efficient system because there was not a lot of continuity or structure or form. The company would meet regularly depending on whether they were physically here or not. Touring is a large part of our income. This last year, six months of the year, people were on tour. But when the company was here and working there would be meetings of the company as a whole, usually once a week, to discuss whatever came up. Anything from "should we keep a cat?" — there was a strong anti-cat faction — to "what's our line politically about X?", a very heavy topic. So, that would involve the whole company. An agenda would be made up by writing down what we wanted to discuss. Not always, but usually, staff would have an agenda. We'd have a chairman, usually an appointed, rotating chairman; and somebody rotating to take notes — so the minutes varied in quality wildly as you can imagine. So, the people as a whole would decide, there were always minority positions, and around here, minority positions are fiercely held.

One of the things that happened or seemed to happen is that the office jobs were low level and when somebody new would come into the company they'd get stuck into the office. You, since you're new, work upstairs (upstairs office/downstairs studio). You come upstairs for a while, you can do rehearsals and workouts but basically your job is to be the booker for the first year or two. That has happened a couple of times. But as we grew, there were I think real dollar levels at which you begin to, you have to change. I think we hit that spot a couple of years ago. There had been very little training of individuals, not any formal procedures. There was a tendency for everybody as you termed it "to re-invent the wheel, over and over..." Bookers would quit to act and somebody new would come in and have to start all over again. It's not that we wouldn't help each other, it was just that there was no formal training, no formal rotation. It got crazy before, however, when you had somebody trying to book a tour, and would have to drop what they were doing at rehearsal, run upstairs to take a telephone call from New York about booking a tour and then run back downstairs and jump back into rehearsal. That was obviously not working.

People in the company decided they wanted a life that was a little more stable, they want to have a car, some way to get around, they want a nice place to live, some of them want to have children, stuff like that. There is a real desire to make a living wage and not to work so hard for that reason. Not to tour six months a year and play four months here, and so on. It's a real strong desire, and that translated into "We're going to hire a business manager.

If we run more efficiently, we'll have more income."

Now, one of the ideas is that the manager shouldn't be a person who wants to get into the company and act, but they should be somebody who likes to do the jobs of management.

So, last year, the company voted to hire a manager, at double salary. At that time people were making $100 a week. They voted to hire a manager at $200 a week, thinking that $200 a week was a good salary. There is that here: almost all of the people here haven't spent any amount of time working in the straight world. There was some very unrealistic thinking going on. $5 per hour is not the kind of salary that attracts high type managers.

We succeeded in hiring a manager who had experience in arts management, wanted the job etc., but he only lasted for 3 or 4 months. Because, of course, to come in and be a manager of a company who hasn't had a manager...What's a professional manager supposed to do when he says, "Here's what you have to do," to a company that's been surviving in its own way, but surviving for 10 years or so and they say, "But we don't do it that way." What's the manager supposed to do? It created incredible tension. It happened to the first manager, and the second manager who lasted only a few months. The job is a pain in the ass. The structure of the company is still collective. The manager whether higher paid or not, is still supposed to carry out the dictates of the collective meeting as a whole of which the manager is a part. We operate on the consensus basis of decision making. But the other leg of the argument is that in addition to making the office more efficient, this will allow the people who do acting and music to be able to spend all of their time developing their skills. So the parlay is that you get much more professional management in a much more professional theater. It certainly makes sense. It also means that I, and not I alone, am worried that people will become more divorced from the substance of what they are doing. If you have to spend some time every year or every two years or every three years actually doing publicity, actually doing booking, actually doing the books, then you have some sense of what the "stuff" of the business is. In your fingers practically. And you are less likely to scream when the publicity person doesn't quite do the job because you know it's impossible to quite do the job because you've tried it. You're less likely to scream at a bad booking because you know its inevitable, there is gonna be a wrong booking in almost every tour, there is gonna be one that doesn't work because you've done it. You're gonna be less likely to scream about the money because you know that every penny has got to be squeezed if you've had to squeeze the penny.

And if these things become separate, I fear that you have two strong groups that don't have much to do with each other except in meetings where one of them says we gotta do this and the other says we can't. I worry about that. I worry about class lines. There may be other problems with the coming changes and the attempt to generate more income. There may be real limits built in. I have no feeling that the company is going to change the kind of work it does. Which may be yet another contradiction. That even if you are really good, if your politics are anti-establishment, if your politics are critical, then there is a very real limit to the kind of money you are going to be able to make. There may be a real ceiling.

There is a great pleasure, a real joy in going out and doing your own work on your own terms when you know that nobody is taking any more than their share. That's wonderful and people are going to keep that. To be working with other people on common ideas, goals, you share in the control of it all. Looking forward to doing a task together, is one of the finest experiences I know of. To be able to carry that feeling of working together for yourselves in a collective way is one of the finest things.

Volunteers and the Law

Volunteer labor may have legal and tax complications both for the cooperative and the volunteers. The IRS and state taxing agencies have recently been ruling that volunteer labor is, one way or another, taxable and/or subject to certain employment regulations. This chapter covers these legal and tax issues.

Volunteers as Employees

Gordon Park Coop Foods in Milwaukee, Wisconsin is a large consumer coop with about 1,000 members and total annual sales of $700,000. The coop relies heavily on volunteer labor. Volunteers were offered a $1.50 discount on food for every hour worked at the coop.

The Internal Revenue Service audited Gordon Park and ruled that the volunteers' discounts were, in effect, employee wages subject to withholding, social security, unemployment tax and all federal employment regulations. The IRS ruled that the discounts were taxable to the volunteers as wages just like wages on any regular job.

As far as the IRS is concerned, a discount in exchange for labor is barter, and barter is taxable income. The law is very clear on the issue of barter; barter is definitely taxable. The law is not quite so clear about whether volunteers who earn discounts are or are not, if fact, employees. The IRS does not audit many coops, so the issue has not been worked out enough for anyone to make firm statements about this legality. Gordon Park's attorney appealed the IRS's decision through several layers of Internal Revenue Service bureaucracy and found the IRS not totally comfortable with its legal position and even a little embarrassed for picking on such a fine point of law.

Employees, by definition, work for "others". People who work for themselves are not employees. So, if a volunteer is a member of a food buying club, is the volunteer working for the club or working for herself? If a volunteer is a member of a cooperative, again, who is the volunteer working for?

In an unincorporated business, the owners are never employees of the business — that's the law. The owners can put as many or as few hours as they please and can take home *all* the store inventory — at a 10% discount or at a 100% discount — if they please. There is no tax consequence until someone other than the owners exchanges money or labor for goods.

A corporation is different than an unincorporated business in this regard. A corporation is a legal entity, legally separate from its owners and able to do business with its owners. The corporation you own can hire you as an employee the same as any other business or person might hire you. A corporation is in fact often described as a "legal person". So, when you work for pay — cash or food — for your incorporated coop, you are an employee. This is a point the IRS is making. It is not necessarily a valid point. As we said, the law does not address the issue clearly enough.

You will rarely find a coop which has taken the trouble to set up its volunteers as employees, set up a payroll system with withholding and all the government forms. Most coops would probably tell you they always ignored (or more likely, never knew about) this thorny law. And most have had no trouble from the IRS. True, they are not likely to get audited. But if they are audited and if the IRS decides that volunteers should have been set up as employees, the IRS can assess back taxes and penalties. That is exactly what happened to Gordon Park Coop. They had to come up with $2,000, though that was a reduction from an original assessment of $10,000. What's more, if your coop doesn't have the money to pay the taxes, the IRS can get the money from personal assets of the members. Corporate limited liability does not apply where back federal taxes are involved.

What do you do? If you are going to offer discounts to volunteers who work in your store, you should first get some professional advice. Is this a cut-and-dried employee situation? Is this a club or some unincorporated coop which clearly does not involve legal employment? Or, most likely, is this an untested and confusing area of law? You can also ask the local IRS office for a specific ruling on your situation. We suggest, however, that you talk to an attorney or an accountant before you talk to the IRS.

If the IRS does audit your coop and challenges your volunteers, you have several good arguments you can use that might satisfy the IRS:

1. The coop is not really a business. Its goal is not to make a profit. Its volunteers are its members who are merely buying food for themselves.

2. Neither the coop nor the volunteers consider themselves employer and employee. The volunteers are not required to work. When they do work, they can set their own hours.

3. Many coops specify a minimum number of hours to work in order to receive a discount. For example, if you work at least four hours, you get a 10% discount. If you work 8 or 30 hours, you still get the same 10% discount. This is not a normal employer-employee arrangement. Gordon Park Coop lost badly on this point. They gave volunteers a $1.50 discount for every hour worked; 100 hours of work paid better than four hours. $1.50 is a mighty low wage, but the IRS viewed it as a wage just the same. Your coop might also point out (if it is the case) that some members work and decline the discount.

Volunteers and Injuries

What happens if a volunteer is injured while working in your coop? Who is legally responsible? Who pays the medical bills? What insurance covers the volunteer?

If you have researched the previous chapter, "Volunteers As Employees", and have determined that your volunteers are in fact employees, then they must be covered by workers compensation insurance (often called simply "workers comp", and also discussed in the Insurance chapter). Most states require employers to purchase workers compensation insurance for all employees. Workers comp pays the medical bills if an employee is injured on the job. Workers comp is an expense the coop must bear; the insurance cannot be deducted from employees' paychecks. Failure to purchase workers compensation insurance is not only unfair to your employees, it is considered "gross negligence" on your part which means than not only your coop, but the members as well, can be sued.

If your volunteers are not legally employees, you still should have insurance on them. The best method is to either include all your volunteers on your workers compensation policy or obtain a special volunteer health and accident policy, which is available in many states. The Insurance chapter, under "Workers Compensation" also discusses this accident insurance and where to get it.

If a volunteer has personal health and accident insurance such as Blue Cross, don't assume you don't also have to insure the volunteer. Blue Cross cannot substitute for workers comp. If an injured volunteer is not covered by workers compensation or another policy purchased by the coop, his Blue Cross will probably pay the bills; but Blue Cross may turn around and sue the coop, claiming that the coop was legally bound to insure the volunteer.

Whether volunteers are employees or not, make sure they are insured. You may want to take a chance with the IRS; but don't take a chance with your workers.

Volunteers and Sales Tax

In 1981, the State of California threw a new monkeywrench into the already screwed up machinery of volunteers and the law. The State Board of Equalization (the sales tax people) audited the Cooperative Association of Sonoma County, a 900-member food coop. Each month at this coop, hundreds of volunteers put in four hours of labor in exchange for discounts on their food. The state sales tax people decided that the volunteers had paid for their purchases with labor, that the labor had a monetary value, and therefore the purchases made with volunteer labor are subject to sales tax. The state handed the Cooperative Association an unexpected bill for $12,000 in back taxes. A sales tax audit of the Co-Opportunity Consumers Cooperative of Santa Monica, California resulted in the same ruling.

The California decision to apply sales tax to purchases made (i.e. discounts received) with volunteer labor is an especially mean one because the dollar amount, over all, is very small compared to total sales tax revenues. Food is not taxed in California; taxable non-food items account for only 10%-20% of most coop's sales.

One way of avoiding the sales tax problem is to write up your sales and calculate sales tax before figuring the discount. Let's say, for example, a volunteer gets a 10% discount. The volunteer makes a purchase which includes $50 in non-taxable food and $10 in goods subject to a 6% sales tax (shelf prices before discount is applied). First calculate the sales tax — $.60 (6% of $10). Then apply the 10% discount to the purchase — $6 (10% of $60). The volunteer pays $54.60 ($60 less the $6 discount plus the $.60 sales tax). Needless to say, this elaborate calculation does complicate your bookkeeping and just may drive your check-out workers to drink.

Some coops simplify this procedure somewhat by calculating the entire sale and sales tax, at shelf prices, and then applying the discount to the total sale. For the above example, the coop would ring up a total sale of $60.60 ($50 non-taxable, $10 taxable, $.60 sales tax) and then take 10% off the $60.60. The volunteer pays $54.54 ($60.60 less $6.06). Now it's true the state sales tax people could say they've been shorted $.06, but we doubt they would be that picky.

The California sales tax assessments may stick or they may be overturned; they may be applied to other cooperatives in California and they may not; and, of course, what happens in California may never happen in another state. But still, like the IRS ruling about volunteers as employees, the sales tax ruling started with some government auditor who decided the letter of the law says *this* and tried to make it stick. You just never know what they'll throw at you next.

Income Taxes

"For purposes of subsections (a), (b), and (c), a partner who acquired all or part of his interest by a transfer with respect to which the election provided in section 754 is not in effect, and to whom a distribution of property (other than money) is made with respect to the transferred interest within 2 years after such transfer, may elect, under regulations prescribed by the Secretary, to treat as the adjusted partnership basis of such property the adjusted basis such property would have if the adjustment provided in section 743(b) were in effect with respect to the partnership property." — Internal Revenue Code.

Tax law is complex and constantly changing. Sole proprietorships, general partnerships, limited partnerships, profit corporations, Sub Chapter S corporations, non-profit corporations, cooperative corporations and all other legal business forms have different sets of income tax laws.

You should become familiar with the basics and the general rules of federal income tax law, but you should leave the tax returns to tax experts. A good tax accountant will almost always save you more money than she'll charge, not to mention ridding yourself of endless hours under pressure trying to understand the tax books — and here it is April 14. Our personal experience with tax clients who have tried to do their own returns is that they often fail to claim legitimate deductions and credits and they wind up paying more tax than necessary.

Here again we'd like to stress the importance of an accurate set of books. Tax accountants are not bookkeepers and they don't enjoy nor do they have the time to clean up or complete your ledgers. Give an accountant a complete, readable set of books and you'll have a friend who will devote his time to preparing your tax return and looking for tax savings. Give an accountant a sloppy, incomplete set of books, and you'll have a mad, possibly frustrated person who not only won't give you the best service he might but will charge you two or three times what he'd normally charge.

Don't be intimidated by the Internal Revenue Service or feel threatened by the possibility of an audit. Only 2% of all tax returns get audited and most of those are partial audits where the IRS wants to see receipts to prove this or that deduction. The IRS is primarily a money making operation. They go after returns which promise the most money for the least effort. The IRS is not usually interested in complex audits or in audits where little money is involved. The IRS does audit a random sample of tax returns every year, but the number is very small. Contrary to popular myth, the IRS is not interested in putting you in jail or repossessing your home; they only want your money.

Claim every expense you are entitled to. Talk to your accountant about questionable deductions, the "gray areas" of tax law are where honest people disagree. Even the professionals have trouble interpreting some tax laws, and sometimes the IRS will say yes and sometimes they'll say no. If the IRS audits you and disallows a deduction, you'll only owe the tax you would have owed in the first place plus interest. There usually isn't even a penalty if you pay up.

Tax accountants will accompany their clients to audits. If the IRS is challenging something the accountant did (as opposed to, say, a $3,000 entertainment expense you claimed) the accountant usually will not charge you for the time spent on the audit.

Coops have potential problems with the IRS which other, more conventional business structures do not have; and if your coop is audited, these problems should be of more concern to you than, say, proving that the numbers on your tax return are correct. The potential problems we are referring to involve the legal structure of your cooperative, how stock or memberships are issued and how surpluses or profits are distributed. The problems also involve who is and isn't an employee, particularly in the case of volunteers. These issues are covered in detail elsewhere in the book. These issues, when overlooked or when not clarified or written down right at the start of business, can cause you a whopping lot of trouble in an audit if the IRS decides that you didn't follow the correct procedures in setting up or operating your coop. For example, the IRS might claim that, as far as tax law goes, you are operating as a conventional for-profit corporation and you owe all these back taxes you thought you were exempt from paying.

Rarely is fraud or dishonesty involved. Rarely is a coop trying to slip something by the IRS. It is usually carelessness or ignorance: the coop didn't follow the rules of the game — and the IRS came along and changed the game on them. The members of the Gordon Park Coop in Illinois, which got hit with back taxes when the IRS ruled that its volunteers were in effect employees (see the chapter "Volunteers and the Law"), probably never imagined they were doing anything illegal. It was certainly unusual — and many would agree that it was a bit nasty — for the IRS to come down on the coop the way it did. But the barter laws have been on the books for many years; a good accountant should have recognized the volunteer-employees as a possible legal problem.

If you take some care in setting up your cooperative, if you get competent professional advice, if you file the forms and follow the procedures dictated by law, you are not likely to have problems with the IRS should you be audited. But even then, sorry to say, you never know for sure. Old laws which have been on the books for years are being reinterpreted by both the IRS and the courts all the time. Again, a good tax accountant or lawyer should be aware of current court cases and new IRS rulings and should be able at least to warn you about a new ruling or pending court decisions which may affect you.

Finding Professional Help — Accountants and Attorneys

The roles of accountants and attorneys often overlap, particularly in business situations. Both accountants and attorneys can help you set up your business, can explain the legal and tax pros and cons of different business structures and can draw up the papers for you. Some states require an attorney's signature on incorporation papers but most accountants can obtain an attorney's signature for you when needed. Most of the laws you need to know are tax and business laws, and accountants know these as well as (and often better than) attorneys. In most states, accountants and attorneys can prepare tax returns though this usually is the domain of the accountant.

When trying to find an accountant or an attorney, you have an unusual problem. Most accountants and attorneys are not familiar with cooperatives and the unique legal and tax regulations affecting cooperatives. Accountants and attorneys who specialize in small business are knowledgeable about conventional business structures: sole proprietorships, general partnerships and profit corporations; some but not all are knowledgeable about limited partnerships and non-profit corporations. So if you already have a conventional legal structure (such as a partnership or a profit corporation) and you know that the structure is right for you, any good business-oriented accountant or attorney should be knowledgeable enough to help you. But if you haven't yet set up your legal structure and you want help or advice about what type of legal structure to choose, you will need someone who knows coop law and who has first hand experience with coops. Such a person may not be easy to find.

If you need an accountant or an attorney knowledgeable about cooperatives, try to get a recommendation from other local coops. Who have they been using? If the legal structure of your venture is of a more conventional nature, ask small business owners you know to recommend someone.

Avoid referral panels set up by the local bar. Any lawyer can get on these panels. Stay away from storefront tax brokers, the ones who open shop every January and promptly disappear April 15. Most of the people who work for these chains have little experience and are usually familiar only with Mr. and Mrs. Nine-to-Five and their typical tax problems. These part time accountants are not trained in the tax areas where you need the most help. Don't feel you need to hire a certified public accountant (CPA). Most CPA's tend to specialize in big business, and they charge very high fees. Be more concerned with the person's experience than his or her title.

When you have an accountant's or an attorney's name, talk to the individual personally before you commit yourself. If he or she will not talk to you on the phone other in vague generalities, call someone else. Does the person seem familiar with your situation and your problems? Is she interested in cooperatiaves as a unique business form? Is she friendly and sympathetic? Most important, does she make sense to you? Beware of the accountant or attorney who talks Advanced Sandskrit or IRS code sections; accountants and attorneys should be able to answer your questions in understandable, conventional English. If you don't understand the advice you are getting, you've wasted your time and money.

If you are looking for an accountant, remember that tax season, late January through April 15, is an incredibly busy time for tax accountants. They are usually preparing tax returns from early morning until late at night. It is not the best time of year for a friendly chat.

You should be aware that accountants are not bookkeepers. Every accountant knows bookkeeping as well as any bookkeeper but the jobs are different, as is the pay. Bookkeepers post your books for you. Accountants analyze the books and prepare tax returns using the books. Accountants often will help you set up your books, but then they will expect you to get the books posted and balanced on your own. If you need to hire a bookkeeper, again your best bet is to ask other businesses and coops for recommendations.

Sometimes you can save money on lawyer's and accountant's fees by doing some of your own legal research. We include a legal research chapter in the Resource section at the end of the book.

The Community

"Community" refers to the neighborhood, the small town or the general area — a physical, geographical location usually with understood (if not legal) boundaries. "Community" also refers to people — the ones who know of your existence, the ones who support you and the ones who are otherwise affected by the existence of your coop. "Community" most certainly includes the owners of local businesses, who may view you benevolently or who may see you only as competition.

You will find it helpful to make contact with other coops, cooperatively-oriented organizations, local service organizations, etc. in the community. Besides getting and giving mutual support, you will find that shared information can be invaluable. Other cooperatives might be eager to tell their members and customers about your venture, very helpful to you if your business is a retail operation. More experienced coops can tell you about unique local problems such as city or county ordinances or even local business people or other individuals who you may want or have to deal with. All the business how-to books in the world are not half as useful as first hand experience. If you can find people who will share their experiences with you, you will be all the better for it. Most people love to talk about their work and they are often flattered that others seek their opinions.

Another important part of the community which should not be overlooked or ignored is the regular business community, the people they serve and others in the community not oriented towards coops. Coops often tend to isolate themselves from this part of the community, sometimes intentionally, sometimes not; and sometimes this community tends to isolate itself from coops. People who like the idea of worker cooperatives frequently have low opinions of regular businesses; regular businesses are often suspicious of worker coops. The grocery store owner does not like the food coop, and the food coop members think the grocery store owner just isn't doing things right. Sounds familiar, doesn't it? It is not a good situation.

Sometimes, friction comes directly from the regular business community. For example, we know personally of one small town food coop which is open only to members ($5 makes you a member) and sells some of the same food the local grocer sells but for less money. The coop, like many small food coops, has managed to stay "unofficial". The less generous people in the town call it "illegal". It pays no taxes, has no business license, files no government forms. The local grocer — who pays taxes, bought a business license and files more government forms than he cares to — sees the coop as "unfair competition".He's angry. He even got on the phone one day (or so it was reported) and called the health department and the county building inspector. "What about this damn coop?" Living in harmony with the members of your community is at least as important as buying food with the members of your coop. Share your ideas with the grocer and the local merchants' association or chamber of commerce or Elks club. It may sound hokey to you, but just that attempt to bridge the gap sometimes works wonders. The regular business people may not fall all over themselves with love and welcome, but they will respet you more for your effort to communicate and explain what you are doing. This communication is something every cooperative venture needs to develop but it becomes most important in small communities, pariticularly small rural towns where everyone knows everyone, and your business (whether you like it or not) is everyone's business.

You should also realize that coops are businesses too, and in their day to day operations they are very similar to conventional businesses. A friend in the regular business community will be as helpful to you as friends in the cooperative community.

W.W. Norton & Co., New York City, is an old and distinguished book publishing company founded in 1925 by Mr. and Mrs. Warder Norton. It is by no means a worker coop, but since 1952 the company has been set up so that the stock belongs to, and the profits go to the employees. Storer Lunt, former Norton Chairman, writes:

Warder more than once stated his view that the rewards of a publishing house should rightly go to the people who manage it. How to implement this concept, and at the same time have it accomodate the jungle of State and Federal laws, was the moot question...The concept was a subject of frequent thought and discussion between the principle stockholders, management and counsel. A binding instrument drawn in legal terms became increasingly necessary as the business kept growing.

The first Joint Agreement was dated October 15, 1952. Basically it confirmed both Warder's and Mrs. Norton's wish. The Joint Agreement placed the control of the company in the hands of those actively engaged in its management. It placed a ceiling on any single individual's share holdings so that it took three officers and/or directors to form a majority. It further included an understanding that any stockholder who for any reason severed his relations with the company should at once be bound to offer his or her stock holdings first to the remaining shareholders in proportion to their holdings; and if any shares remain, such shares must then be offered to the officers and directors not party to the Agreement, and lastly to the company. Fair and appropriate arrangements as to the value per share had been worked out and were incorporated in the agreement with the result that the purchase price was always reasonable and attractive.

In 1964, generous arrangements made possible the transfer of a substantial share of Mrs. Norton's holdings, thus reducing her voting interest. This block of stock was converted to non-voting shares and has from time to time been made available at the discretion of the directors to over eighty Norton employees. It is known as Class B stock and pays the same dividend as the voting shares. The voting shares at the same time became known as Class A stock. Everyone who has been with the firm for five years has a share in the business. The company is entirely owned by those actively engaged in the business.

Unique among book publishers, the Norton Joint Agreement realizes the control and the future continuity of the company. It completely protects the firm from outside intererence and it gives the management a free rein to devote its full energies to one of the most colorful and rewarding ways of life. Such is the firm of W.W. Norton and Company, Incorporated. Such is book publishing at its best.

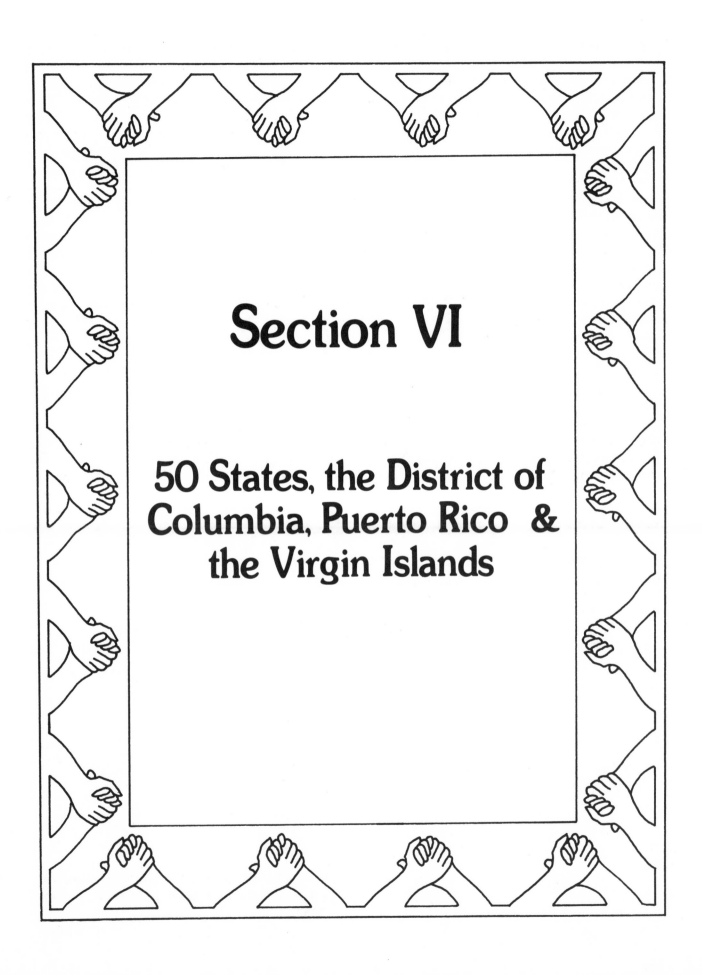

Section VI

50 States, the District of Columbia, Puerto Rico & the Virgin Islands

When we try to pick out anything by itself we find it hitched to everything else in the universe.

— John Muir

STATE BY STATE COOPERATIVE CORPORATION LAWS

The statutes for cooperative corporations vary widely from state to state. They tend to be archaic, poorly conceived, unsophisticated and focused on agricultural or consumer cooperatives. Some of the state laws date back 50 and 100 years. In some states, there are no coop laws at all except for large agricultural coops, rural electric coops and similar large undertakings. In these states, food coops can sometimes incorporate under agricultural coop laws but the procedure is usually difficult and not worth the effort. A few state cooperative laws require the members to be the ultimate consumers, which usually means that the coop statute is a consumer coop statute only and producer and worker coops may be excluded from incorporating as cooperatives. If your state is one of these, you will need to investigate the law further.

Unless otherwise noted, the state laws outlined below are general coop statutes and apply to consumer, producer and worker coops. But as we mention elsewhere in the book, some states may want to exclude worker coops from the general coop statutes on some technicality of the law, or a belief that a worker coop is just another business, or for political reasons. Worker cooperatives should consult a knowledgeable accountant or attorney.

The list below includes all 50 states, the District of Columbia, Puerto Rico and the Virgin Islands. The information should be used as a guideline only; additional research into your state's laws will still be necessary. Although most states do not regularly change coop statutes, what was current yesterday could be obsolete tomorrow.

Several different items are discussed for each state, such as corporate purpose, voting and membership requirements, required reserves, etc. If we make no mention of one or more of these items for your particular state, it is because we were unable to find any mention of them in the state's coop statute. Where coop laws do not address a particular issue, general corporation law will apply in most states. Usually, however, if something is not specifically disallowed by law, you can do it. For example, some states require that a certain percentage of the coop's business must be done with members. Other states don't even mention it in the statute. If your state does not specify how much business must be done with members, you can make your own rules.

All of these state coop laws are for cooperative corporations only. Basically, the laws define cooperative corporations, specify what kind of coop can be a cooperative corporation and set down the rules under which cooperative corporations operate.

The items we cover include:

Corporate purpose. Many states allow coops to operate any kind of business. The common terminology is "any legal purpose". Several states, however, restrict the kind of business a coop can conduct; we list those restrictions. A typical restriction is "agricultural, merchandising, merchantile, manufacturing and mechanical purposes only". Some state courts have interpreted "merchantile" to be limited to agricultural activities. "Merchandising", however, can usually be

135

stretched to include most coop activities. Again, you will need professional advice.

Profit or Non-Profit. A handful of states require coops to be incorporated as non-profit corporations. Coops in these states are both non-profit corporations and cooperative corporations, with the advantages of both. Other states may allow cooperative corporations to also be non-profits, but no mention is made in the coop statutes. As we discussed in the chapter on non-profit corporations, these coops will organize under state non-profit laws. The coops do not usually have to obtain federal tax exempt status.

Restriction of trade. Some states have specific trade limitations not imposed on regular businesses such as limiting the territory the coop may serve. If your state has trade restrictions, we mention that they exist but you will have to research the law yourself to determine exactly what the restrictions are.

Use of the word coop or cooperative is restricted by many states. States which do restrict the use usually allow only those coops which incorporate as cooperative corporations to use the word "coop"or"cooperative" in their name.

Annual reports are required by some states. These are usually general reports and are usually not elaborate financial statements. For most states, the reports must be filed with the secretary of state.

Memberships. Some states require that all members of your coop be individuals and some states allow organizations (such as corporations and other coops) to be members. Some states allow subscriptions — soliciting memberships where the future members pledge (i.e. promise) to purchase memberships or make partial payments on memberships. Most of these states require, however, that full payment be received before membership shares can be issued to the subscribers. A few states require that a certain percentage of the total membership shares available for sale be sold before the coop can commence operation. If your state has such a requirement, be careful when you write your articles of incorporation not to create too many shares. You want to be able to sell enough of them to meet your state's requirements.

Some states allow members to sell or transfer their memberships to others; some states restrict such sales. In your own bylaws, however, you may want to restrict such free transfer. If a state allows transfer from one member to another, your bylaws can override the state law. Some states also have laws allowing the coop to repurchase memberships from departing members. Some state laws spell out how and when a member can resign or be expelled or otherwise terminated.

One member, one vote. Some states require one member, one vote, some allow it, others say nothing. If your state says nothing, you may have a problem here. As mentioned above, where coop law does not exist, regular corporation law usually applies. Regular corporation law usually states that voting rights go with the shares, one vote per share. If you want your coop to be run on a one member, one vote basis and if different members own different numbers of shares, you may have a legal problem.

Amending articles and bylaws, merging or dissolving the coop. Many states specify that a vote of a certain percentage of the entire membership, or a certain percentage of the members voting, or a certain percentage of the directors is required to amend the articles or bylaws or to merge the coop or to dissolve the coop.

Reserves. Many states require that a certain percentage of the net savings (the profits) be retained by the coop in cash, and not distributed to members until a certain percentage of the total capital investment is reached. The capital investment is the total money raised from memberships. This money is usually spent as soon as it comes in, to pay the overhead, stock the store, etc. Some states feel that coops should have cash reserves as well, and thus this rule. The reserves, however, can come from the savings (surplus) of the business; you do not have to retain a percentage of the membership fees. Some states allow the reserves to be targeted for a specific use (expanding the building or a purchase of a large piece of equipment, for example). Some states allow, and some states require, a small percentage of the reserves to be used for educational purposes, which usually means literature or classes for members and prospective members explaining what a coop is and how it works. Some states allow the reserves to be used to lower prices.

Distributions. Most states allow distributions by patronage refunds; some states make this a requirement. Each state, however, has different rules defining who is eligible for patronage refunds, maximum and minimum amounts, taxability of the refunds, etc. We do not cover these rules; you will have to read your own state's regulations. Some states allow for forfeiture of patronage refunds: when a member doesn't claim a refund, the coop itself can keep it. Where cash dividends are paid, many states limit the maximum amount payable in any year to a percent of the investment. If, for example, your state limits the dividend to 6%, a member with a $100 investment can receive no more than $6 as a cash dividend (assuming, of course, that your coop decides to issue dividends — the percentages are maximums.)

Other. Some states require annual membership meetings. Some require that at least a certain percentage of the coop's business be done with members. Some require that a certain percentage of the "incorporators" (the original members) be state residents, which will be important to you if your coop is located close to a state border and you plan to draw members from more than one state or if your coop is incorporating in another state (discussed below). Some states allow and some restrict a coop's investment in other businesses or a coop's membership in organizations — and, of course, some states don't care. A few states have a specified lifetime for coops; after so many years the coop must either renew its charter or go out of business. Some states have other unusual coop laws and we discuss them.

For all state coop laws, it is important to distinguish between what is "required", what is "allowed" and what is not covered in the statute. Where a specific activity is required, such as a minimum cash reserve, you're stuck with it whether you like it or not. Where a specific activity is allowed, such as obtaining subscriptions for shares, you have the choice to adopt it or not. Your decision should be spelled out in your articles or bylaws. Often the state law will say that your articles or bylaws dictate how a certain activity is to be conducted. Where a particular activity is not mentioned in the law, general corporation law usually prevails, as we discussed above.

If you don't like your state's coop laws or if the laws exclude your kind of coop or if the laws simply don't exist, you may want to investigate the possibility of incorporating in another state. It is called "foreign incorporation". Most states allow in-state coops to incorporate in other states. Some states have more restrictions than others; some states make it difficult or undesirable for in-state coops to incorporate out of state. You will need some professional advice.

Not all states allow out-of-state coops ("foreign" coops) to incorporate in the state. Of those which do allow it, some states are more attractive than others. Incorporation by out-of-state coops is specifically allowed in Iowa, Maine, Maryland, New York, North Dakota, Rhode Island, South Dakota, Wisconsin, District of Columbia, New Mexico, Texas and the Virgin Islands. Some states require some or all of the incorporators to be state residents, which probably makes foreign incorporation difficult or impossible: Alaska, Arkansas, Colorado, Connecticut, Minnesota, New Jersey, North Carolina, South Carolina, Vermont and Puerto Rico. The remaining states probably allow foreign incorporation but no specific mention is to be found in the coop statute.

If you are considering out-of-state incorporation and if you are a consumer coop, you should investigate the District of Columbia. D.C.'s coop law is limited to consumer coops only but it is well structured, very detailed and based on an experimental model developed by coop supporters. It appears that the following states also have good coop laws: California, Washington, Kansas, Michigan (though a law requiring the coop to do at least 51% of its business with members may be too limiting) and Wisconsin.

Alabama

Alabama has no general coop statute. Alabama law provides only for agricultural, condomimium, motor vehicle carrier and electric cooperatives.

Alaska

Business activity is not restricted; coops may conduct business for any legal purpose. Use of the word cooperative or coop is restricted. Investment in other organizations is allowed. An annual report must be filed with the Department of Commerce and Economic Development, Anchorage, 99501.

Both individuals and organizations are allowed to be members of the coop. Shares are allowed to be subscribed but may not be issued until full payment is received. At least one incorporator must be a state resident. Members are allowed to transfer shares to other members. One member, one vote is allowed. A majority vote of all members is required to amend bylaws, amend articles or approve a merger. A 2/3 vote of the members voting is required to dissolve the coop. Patronage refunds are allowed.

The state income tax return is due April 15.

Arizona

Arizona has no general coop statute. Arizona law provides only for agricultural and electric cooperatives.

Arkansas

Business activity is restricted to "agricultural, dairy, merchandising, mining, manufacturing or mechanical purposes". State law gives the coop a 50 year life after which the coop must either renew its charter or go out of business. Investment in other organizations is limited to a maximum of 5% of the coop's accumulated reserves. An annual report must be filed with the Secretary of State, Little Rock, 72203.

Membership in the coop is restricted to individuals. Shares may not be issued until full payment is received. At least 20% of the incorporators must be state residents. At least 20% of the shares must be issued before the coop can commence operation. One member, one vote is required. Patronage refunds are allowed.

The state tax return is due May 15.

California

Business activity is not restricted; coops may conduct business for any legal purpose. Use of the word cooperative or coop is restricted. Inestment in other organizations and membership in other organizations is allowed.

Both individuals and organizations are allowed to be members of the coop. Shares are allowed to be subscribed but may not be issued until full payment is received. The statute specifies how a member may be terminated. The coop is allowed to repurchase shares from members. One member, one vote is required for members who are individuals and allowed for members who are organizations. A majority vote of all members is required to merge the coop with another.

General reserves are required: 10% of the net savings per year until at least 30% of the capital investment is reached. The law allows specific reserves. Savings are allowed to be used for educational purposes. Patronage refunds are allowed. The coop is allowed to keep unclaimed patronage refunds after one year. Dividends are limited to a maximum of 5%.

Coops are exempt from obtaining a stock permit as long as no member has invested more than $100 in shares or memberships. A permit is required if the coop solicits loans from over 25 people or if 10 or more people agree to loan money.

The State of California is very active in supporting and assisting cooperatives. The state provides technical assistance and publishes some excellent books and pamphlets. Write the Coop Development Program, Department of Consumer Affairs, 1020 N Street, Room 501, Sacramento, CA 95814.

Colorado

Coops may conduct business for any legal purpose except banking, but Colorado does impose some restriction of trade. Coops must be organized as non-profit corporations. Use of the word cooperative or coop is restricted. Investment in other coops only is allowed. An annual report must be filed with the Secretary of State, Denver, 80203. Coop memberships are exempt from security regulation.

Both individuals and organizations are allowed to be members of the coop. At least 51% of the incorporators must be state residents. At least 51% of the coop's business must be done with members. Shares are allowed to be subscribed but may not be issued until full payment is received. Transfer of membership shares between members is restricted. One member, one vote is required. A majority vote of all members is required to amend the articles. A 2/3 vote of all members is required to approve merger or dissolution.

General reserves are required: 10% of net savings per year until at least 20% of the capital investment is reached. Patronage refunds are allowed. Dividends are limited (percentage not specified in statute).

The state income tax return is due April 15.

Connecticut

Business activity is restricted to "any lawful merchandising, mechanical, manufacturing or agricultural business". An annual report must be filed with the Secretary of State, Hartford, 06115.

Membership in the coop is restricted to individuals. At least 51% of the incorporators must be state residents. At least 51% of the coop's business must be done with members. Shares may not be issued until full payment is received. Maximum value of total shares is $5,000. One member, one vote is required. The board of directors must vote to amend the articles or bylaws.

General reserves are required: 10% of net savings per year until at least 20% of the capital investment is reached.

The state income tax return is due April 1.

Delaware

Delaware has no general coop statute. Delaware law provides only for agricultural cooperatives.

District of Columbia

Coops may conduct business for any legal purpose, but this coop statute is for consumer coops only. In addition, D.C. imposes some restrictions on trade. Use of the word cooperative or coop is restricted. Investment in other organizations and membership in other organizations is allowed. An annual report must be filed with the Superintendent of Corporations, Washington D.C. 20001. An annual membership meeting is required.

Both individuals and organizations are allowed to be members of the coop. Shares are allowed to be subscribed but may not be issued until full payment is received. The statute specifies how a member may be terminated. The coop is allowed to repurchase shares from members. One member, vote is required for members who are individuals and allowed for members who are organizations. A 2/3 vote of the members voting is required to amend the articles. A majority vote of the members voting is required to amend the bylaws. A 2/3 vote of the entire membership is required to dissolve the coop.

General reserves are required: 10% of net savings per year until at least 50% of the capital investment is reached. The law allows the savings to be used for educational purposes and to lower prices. Patronage refunds are required. Dividends are limited to 6% (and in some cases 8%) and cannot be more than 50% of the net savings.

The District income tax return is due April 15.

Florida

Florida has no general coop statute. Florida law provides only for housing, banking, electrical, agricultural marketing, library and educational scholarship cooperatives.

Georgia

Georgia has no general coop statute. Georgia law provides only for agricultural marketing, electrical and educational service cooperatives.

Hawaii

Hawaii has no general coop statute. Hawaii law provides only for professional, housing, agricultural and fish marketing cooperatives.

Idaho

Idaho has no general coop statute. Idaho law provides only for agricultural, agricultural marketing, banking, forestry and electrical cooperatives.

Illinois

Business activity is not restricted; coops may conduct business for any legal purpose. By law, the coop is run by the board of directors. This provision may be unsuitable to your needs if you want the members to run the coop. Investment in other corporations is allowed; the investment is limited to no more than 25% of the coop's accumulated reserves. Membership in other organizations is allowed.

Membership in the coop is restricted to individuals. Shares are allowed to be subscribed but limited to no more than 5 shares per member. Share value must be between $5 and $100. The coop's bylaws or articles must specify how and when a member will be terminated. The coop is allowed to repurchase shares from members. One member, one vote is allowed. A 2/3 vote of the shares voting is required to amend the articles. Patronage refunds are allowed.

The state income tax return is due March 15.

Indiana

Indiana has no general coop statute. Indiana law provides only for agricultural and telephone cooperatives.

Iowa

Business activity is not restricted; coops may conduct business for any legal purpose. The coop must be set up as a non-profit corporation. Use of the word cooperative or coop is restricted. An annual report must be filed with the Secretary of State, Des Moines, 50319. An annual membership meeting must be held.

Both individuals and organizations are allowed to be members of the coop. Shares are allowed to be subscribed but may not be issued until full payment is received. The statute specifies how a member may be terminated. Transfer of shares between members is restricted. The coop is allowed to repurchase shares from members. One member, one vote is required for individuals. A 2/3 vote of the members voting is required to amend the articles, to merge or to dissolve the coop. A 3/4 vote of the directors is required to amend the bylaws but this vote can be repealed by a 3/4 vote of the members voting.

General reserves are required: 10% of the net profit per year or $1,000, whichever is greater, until at least 30% (but no more than 50%) of the capital investment is reached. The law allows for specific reserves. Savings are allowed to be used to lower prices. 1% to 5% of savings must be used for educational purposes. Patronage refunds are allowed. The coop is allowed to keep unclaimed patronage refunds after two years. Dividends are limited to a maximum of 8% (preferred stock only).

The state income tax return is due April 30. For farmer coops, the return is due September 15.

Kansas

Business activity is not restricted; coops may conduct business for any legal purpose. Use of the word cooperative or coop is restricted. Investment in other organizations is limited to coops and may not exceed 5%. An annual report must be filed with the Secretary of State, Topeka, 66625.

Membership in the coop is restricted to individuals. One member, one vote is required. A 3/4 vote of the entire membership is required to dissolve the coop.

The state income tax return is due October 15.

Kentucky

Kentucky has no general coop statute. Kentucky law provides only for electrical, agricultural, telephone and livestock production cooperatives.

Louisiana

Louisiana has no general coop statute. Louisiana law provides only for agricultural, agricultural marketing, electrical, banking, sea food and dairy cooperatives.

Maine

Business activity is not restricted; coops may conduct business for any legal purpose. Investment in other organizations is limited to cooperative corporations. Membership in other organizations is allowed. An annual membership meeting is required.

Both individuals and organizations are allowed to be members of the coop. Shares are allowed to be subscribed but may not be issued until full payment is received. The coop must register with the state as a dealer in securities. The statute specifies how a member may be terminated. Transfer of shares between members and repurchase of shares by the coop are both restricted. One member, one vote is required for members who are individuals and allowed for members who are organizations. A majority of the members voting is required to amend the bylaws. A 2/3 vote of the entire membership is required to dissolve the coop.

General reserves are required: 10% of net savings per year until at least 50% of the capital investment is reached. The statute allows reserves to be used to lower prices or for "the general welfare of the membership". The statute requires part of the reserves to be used for educational purposes (no percentage is specified). Patronage refunds are allowed. The coop is allowed to keep unclaimed patronage refunds. Dividends are limited to 6% and no more than 50% of the net savings.

The state tax return is due March 15.

Maryland

Business activity is restricted to "production of agricultural and fish products, selling or buying agents of those products, or purchasing or acquiring goods and services for the members." The coop is also subject to trade restrictions. The coop "may not deal in the products of non-members in excess of those of its members". The coop must be set up as a non-profit corporation. Use of the word cooperative or coop is restricted. Investment in other organizations is allowed. Membership in other organizations is limited to coops only.

Individuals and other coops are allowed to be members of the coop. Shares are allowed to be subscribed but may not be issued until full payment is received. The statute specifies how a member may be terminated. Transfer of shares between members and repurchase of shares by the coop are both restricted. One member, one vote is allowed. A 2/3 vote of the members voting is required to amend the articles or amend the bylaws. A 2/3 vote of the entire membership is required to dissolve the coop. At least 2 directors must be state residents.

The statute allows general reserves and allows savings to be used to lower prices. Patronage refunds are allowed. The coop is allowed to keep unclaimed patronage refunds after 3 years. Dividends are limited to a maximum of 12%.

The state income tax return is due April 15.

Massachusetts

Business activity is restricted to "agriculture, dairy or merchandising." The coop must be set up as a non-profit corporation and must be, in fact, operated "without profit". Use of the word cooperative or coop is restricted. An annual report must be filed with the Secretary of the Commonwealth, Boston, 02133. An annual membership

meeting must be held.

No member may hold more than 1/10 of the total shares; no member may hold more than $1,000 in shares. Minimum value per share must be $100. Transfer of shares between members is restricted. One member, one vote is required. A 3/4 vote of the members voting is required to amend the articles.

General reserves are required: 10% of the net savings per year until at least 30% of the capital investment is realized. No more than 5% of the reserves may be used for educational purposes. Patronage refunds are allowed "based on wages earned or products sold". Dividends are limited to a maximum of 7%.

The state income tax return is due March 15.

Michigan

Business activity is not restricted; coops may conduct business for any legal purpose. Use of the word cooperative or coop is restricted. Investment in other organizations and membership in other organizations is allowed.

Membership in the coop is restricted to individuals. At least 51% of the coop's business must be with members. Transfer of shares between members is restricted. The coop is allowed to repurchase shares from members. One member, one vote is required. A majority vote of the members voting is required to amend the articles. A majority vote of the entire membership is required to dissolve the coop.

General reserves must be at least 30% of the capital investment. Patronage refunds are allowed. Dividends are limited to a maximum of 8%.

The state income tax return (called a "single business tax") is due April 30.

Minnesota

Business activity is not restricted; coops may conduct business for any legal purpose. Use of the word cooperative or coop is restricted. Investment in other organizations and membership in other organizations is allowed. An annual membership meeting is required. State law gives the coop a 20 year life after which the coop must either renew its charter or go out of business.

Both individuals and organizations are allowed to be members of the coop. At least 51% of the incorporators must be state residents. Shares are allowed to be subscribed but may not be issued until full payment is received. At least 20% of the shares must be issued before the coop can commence operation. Maximum value of all stock may not exceed $100,000. The statute specifies how a member may be terminated. Transfer of shares between members is restricted. The coop is allowed to repurchase shares from members. One member, one vote is required for members who are individuals and allowed for members who are organizations. A majority vote of the members voting is required to amend the articles or bylaws. A 2/3 vote of the members voting is required to merge or dissolve the coop.

General reserves are required during the first two years only: 10% of the net savings per yer until at least 50% of the capital investment is reached. Specific reserves are allowed. Savings are allowed to be used to lower prices. No more than 5% of the savings can be used for educational purposes. Patronage refunds are allowed. Dividends are limited to a maximum of 8%.

The state income tax return is due March 15. For farmer coops, the return is due September 15.

Mississippi

Mississippi has no general coop statutes. Mississippi law provides only for agricultural marketing and credit, aquatic, electric and insurance cooperatives.

Missouri

Business activity is limited to agricultural coops and to consumer coops only. Use of the word cooperative and coop is restricted. An annual report must be filed with the Secretary of State, Jefferson City, 65105.

Membership in the coop is restricted to individuals. One member, one vote is required. A majority of the entire membership is required to amend the articles or the bylaws. An 80% vote is required to dissolve the coop.

General reserves are required: 10% of the net savings per year until at least 50% of the capital investment is reached. Patronage refunds are allowed. Dividends are limited to a maximum of 10%.

The state income tax return is due April 15.

Montana

"Cooperative corporations may be developed for the purposes of trade and industry, for the purpose of consumption, borrowing or lending, or for industrial purposes." Use of the word cooperative or coop is restricted. State law gives the coop a 40 year life after which the coop must renew its charter or go out of business. An annual membership meeting is required.

Membership in the coop is restricted to individuals. At lest 10 shares must be subscribed prior to formation. Termination of membership is allowed for "nonpayment of stock". Transfer of shares between members is restricted. The coop is allowed to repurchase shares from members. Minimum share value is $10; maximum share value is $5,000. One member, one vote is required. A 2/3 vote of the entire membership and a 2/3 vote of the directors is required to amend the articles. A majority vote of the entire membership and a 2/3 vote of the directors is required to amend the bylaws. A majority vote of the entire membership is required to merge or dissolve the coop.

General reserves are required: 5% of the net savings per year until at least 30% of the capital investment is reached. No more than 5% of the savings can be used for educational purposes. Patronage refunds are allowed. Dividends are limited to a maximum of 6%. If no dividend is paid within 5 years "it may be grounds for dissolving the corporation".

The state income tax return is due May 15.

Nebraska

Coops may conduct business for any legal purpose but coops are subject to trade restrictions. Investment in other organizations and membership in other organizations are allowed. An annual report must be filed with the Secretary of State, Lincoln, 68509. An annual membership meeting is required.

Only individuals are allowed to be members of the coop. Transfer of shares between members is restricted. The coop is allowed to repurchase shares from members. One member, one vote is allowed.

General reserves are allowed. Patronage refunds are allowed. Dividends are limited to a maximum of 6%.

The state income tax return is due March 15.

Nevada

Business activity is not restricted; coops may conduct business for any legal purpose. Coops must be set up as non-profit corporations. State law gives the coop a 50 year life after which the coop must renew its charter or go out of business.

Membership in the coop is restricted to individuals. At least 51% of the coop's business must be done with members. Transfer of shares between members is restricted. One member, one vote is required. A 2/3 vote of the entire membership is required to amend the bylaws, merge or dissolve the coop. Dividends are limited to a maximum of 8%.

Nevada has no state income tax.

New Hampshire

New Hampshire has no general coop statute. New Hampshire law provides only for agricultural and bank cooperatives.

New Jersey

Business activity is restricted to "merchandising, mining, manufacturing or trading in goods, wares or chattels". The coop may invest in other organizations but may own no more than 1/3 of the assets of another organization. An annual report must be filed with the Secretary of State, Trenton, 08625. The Commissioner of Labor has the right to require an audit.

Only individuals are allowed to be members of the coop. All incorporators must be state residents. Shares are allowed to be subscribed. The bylaws govern all membership rights.

General reserves are allowed: 5% of the net profit per year until 30% of the capital investment is reached. The bylaws govern distribution of profits.

For those of you interested in researching New Jersey's coop laws, the statutes (which we couldn't locate at first) are found in the workers compensation section of New Jersey law; we have no idea why.

The state income tax return is due April 15.

New Mexico

Coops may conduct business for any legal purpose but coops are subject to trade restrictions. Use of the word cooperative or coop is restricted. Investment in other organizations and membership in other organizations is allowed. An annual report must be filed with the Secretary of State, Santa Fe, 87503. An annual membership meeting must be held.

Both individuals and organizations are allowed to be members of the coop. Shares are allowed to be subscribed but may not be issued until full payment is received. The statute specifies how a member may be terminated. Members are allowed to transfer shares to other members. The coop is allowed to repurchase shares from members. One member, one vote is required for members who are individuals and allowed for members who are organizations. A 2/3 vote of the members voting is required to amend the articles.

General reserves are required: 10% of the net savings per year until at least 50% of the capital investment is reached. Savings are allowed to be used for educational purposes. Patronage refunds are allowed. The coop is allowed to keep unclaimed patronage refunds. Dividends are limited to no more than 6%.

The state income tax return is due March 15.

New York

Business activity is not restricted; coops may conduct business for any legal purpose. Coops must be organized as non-profit corporations. The coop is allowed to invest in other coops only. Membership is allowed in other organizations. An annual report must be filed with the Secretary of State, Albany, 12225.

Both individuals and organizations are allowed to be members of the coop. Shares are allowed to be subscribed but full payment must be received before shares may be issued. The statute specifies how a member may be terminated. Members are allowed to transfer shares to other members. One member, one vote is required for members who are individuals. A 2/3 vote of the members voting is required to amend the articles or the bylaws or to dissolve the coop.

General reserves are allowed. Patronage refunds are allowed. Dividends are limited to no more than 12%.

The state income tax return is due March 15.

North Carolina

Business activity is restricted to "agricultural, housing, horticultural, forestry, dairy, merchandising, mining, manufacturing, telephone or electric purposes." Use of the word cooperative or coop is restricted. Investment in other organizations is allowed. An annual report must be filed with the Department of Agriculture, Raleigh, 27600.

Membership in the coop is restricted to individuals. Shares are allowed to be subscribed but may not be issued until full payment is received. All incorporators must be state residents. At least 50% of the shares must be sold before the coop can commence operation. The statute specifies how a member may be terminated. A majority vote of the members voting is required to amend the articles.

General reserves are required: 10% of the net savings per year until at least 30% of the capital investment is reached. At least 2% of the savings must be used for educational purposes. Patronage refunds are allowed. Dividends are limited to no more than 6%.

The state income tax return is due March 15. For farmer coops, the return is due September 15.

North Dakota

Coops may conduct business for any legal purpose but coops are subject to trade restrictions. Use of the word cooperative or coop is restricted. An annual membership meeting is required.

Both individuals and organizations are allowed to be members of the coop. Shares are allowed to be subscribed. One member, one vote is required for members who are individuals and allowed for members who are organizations. A 2/3 vote of the members voting is required to amend the articles. A majority vote of the members voting is required to amend the bylaws or merge the coop with another. A 3/4 vote of the members voting is required to dissolve the coop.

General reserves are allowed. Specific reserves are allowed. 1% to 5% of the savings must be used for educational purposes. The savings is allowed to be used to lower prices. Patronage refunds are allowed. The coop is allowed to keep unclaimed

patronage refunds after 6 years.

The state income tax return is due April 15. For farmer coops, the return is due September 15.

Ohio

Business activity is not restricted; coops may conduct business for any legal purpose. Coops must be set up as non-profit corporations. Membership in the coop is restricted to individuals. Patronage refunds are allowed.

The state income tax return is due March 31.

Oklahoma

Business activity is restricted to "agriculture, dairy, livestock, irrigation. horticultural, mercantile, mining, manufacturing, merchandising or industrial business operation." Use of the word cooperative or coop is restricted.

Membership in the coop is restricted to individuals. Shares are allowed to be subscribed. At least 20% of the shares must be sold before the coop can commence operation. The value of shares any member may own is limited to 10% and $3,000. One member, one vote is required. A 2/3 vote of the members voting is required to amend the articles.

General reserves are required: 10% of the net savings per year until at least 50% of the capital investment is reached. No more than 5% of the savings is allowed to be used for educational purposes. Patronage refunds are allowed.

The state income tax return is due April 15.

Oregon

Coops may conduct business for any legal purpose but coops are subject to trade restrictions. Use of the word cooperative or coop is restricted. An annual report must be filed with the Corporation Commissioner, Salem, 97310. An annual membership meeting is required.

Membership in the coop is restricted to individuals. Shares are allowed to be subscribed. At least 51% of the coop's business must be done with members. The statute specifies how a member may be terminated. Transfer of shares between members is restricted. The coop is allowed to repurchase shares from members. One member, one vote is allowed. A 2/3 vote of the members voting is required to amend the bylaws. Patronage refunds are allowed. Dividends are restricted (no percentage specified).

The state income tax return is due April 15.

Pennsylvania

Pennsylvania has no general coop statutes. Pennsylvania law provides only for agricultural, insurance, bank and electrical cooperatives. Other forms of production may be included under agriculture.

Puerto Rico

Coops may conduct business for any legal purpose but the members of the coop must be the ultimate consumers. It appears that this statute may be for consumer coops only. The coop must be set up as a non-profit corporation. Use of the word cooperative or coop is restricted. An annual report must be filed with the secretary of state. An annual membership meeting must be held.

Both individuals and organizations are allowed to be members of the coop. Shares are allowed to be subscribed but full payment must be received before shares are issued. All incorporators must be residents of Puerto Rico. The statute specifies how a member may be terminated. A 2/3 vote of the members voting is required to dissolve the coop. Transfer of shares between members is restricted.

General reserves are allowed. 1/10 of 1% of net savings must be spent for educational purposes. Patronage refunds are allowed. The coop is allowed to keep unclaimed patronage refunds after 2 years.

Rhode Island

Coops may conduct business for any legal purpose but coops are subject to trade restrictions. Use of the word cooperative or coop is restricted. Investment in other organizations and membership in other organizations is allowed. An annual report must be filed with the Secretary of State, Providence, 02903. An annual audit is required.

Both individuals and organizations are allowed to be members of the coop. Full payment for shares is required before the shares can be issued. The statute specifies how a member may be terminated. Transfer of shares between members is

restricted. The coop is allowed to repurchase shares from members. One member, one vote is required for members who are individuals and allowed for members who are organizations. A 2/3 vote of the members voting is required to amend the articles.

General reserves are required: 10% of the net savings per year until at least 50% of the capital investment is reached. Savings are allowed to be used for educational purposes. Patronage refunds are allowed. The coop is allowed to keep unclaimed patronage refunds. Dividends are restricted to no more than 8% of the membership fees or 6% of the capital shares.

The state income tax return is due March 15.

South Carolina

Business activity is restricted to "agricultural, dairy, merchandising, mining, manufacturing and mechanical purposes." Use of the word cooperative or coop is restricted. Investment in other organizations is restricted to coops only and may not exceed 25% of the accumulated reserves. An annual report must be filed with the Department of Agriculture, Columbia, 29200.

Membership in the coop is restricted to individuals. All incorporators must be state residents. Shares are allowed to be suscribed. At least 50% of the shares must be sold before the coop can commence operation. One member, one vote is required.

General reserves are required: 10% of the net savings per year until at least 20% of the capital investment is reached. Specific reserves are allowed. Up to 5% of the net savings is allowed to be spent for educational purposes. Patronage refunds are allowed. Dividends are limited to no more than 6%.

The state income tax return is due March 15.

South Dakota

The coop may conduct business for any legal purpose except banking and insurance. Use of the word cooperative or coop is restricted. Investment in other organizations and membership in other organizations is allowed. An annual report must be filed with the Secretary of State, Pierre, 57501. An annual membership meeting is required.

Both individuals and organizations are allowed to be members of the coop. At least three individuals must be incorporators and at least one of them must be a state resident. A registered agent must be used to incorporate the coop. Full payment must be received before shares can be issued. Transfer of shares between members is restricted. The coop is allowed to repurchase shares from members. One member, one vote is required for members who are individuals and allowed for members who are organizations. A 2/3 vote of the members voting is required to amend the articles or merge the coop with another. A majority vote of the members voting is required to amend the bylaws. A 3/4 vote of the members voting is required to dissolve the coop.

General and specific reserves are allowed. 1% to 5% of the savings must be used for educational purposes. Savings are allowed to be used to reduce prices. Patronage refunds are allowed.

South Dakota has no state income tax.

Tennessee

Tennessee has no general coop statutes. Tennessee law provides only for agricultural, electric, telephone and sheep producers cooperatives.

Texas

Business activity is not restricted; coops may conduct business for any legal purpose. The coop must be set up as a non-profit corporation. Use of the word cooperative or coop is restricted. Coops are allowed to invest in other organizations and become members in other organizations. An annual report must be filed with the Secretary of State, Austin, 78711. An annual membership meeting is required.

Both individuals and organizations are allowed to be members of the coop. Shares are allowed to be subscribed but full payment must be received before shares can be issued. The statute specifies how a member may be terminated. Transfer of shares between members is allowed. The coop is allowed to repurchase shares from members. One member, one vote is required for members who are individuals and allowed for members who are organizations. A 2/3 vote of the entire membership is required to amend the articles or dissolve the coop. A majority vote of the entire membership is required to amend the bylaws.

Savings are allowed to be used for educational purposes or to lower prices. Patronage refunds are allowed. Dividends are restricted (no percentage specified).

Texas has no state income tax.

Utah

Business activity is not restricted; coops may conduct business for any legal purpose. Coops must be set up as non-profit corporations. An annual membership meeting is required.

Membership in the coop is restricted to individuals. One member, one vote is allowed. A majority vote of the members voting is required to amend the articles.

The state income tax return is due April 15.

Vermont

Coops may conduct business for any legal purpose but coops are subject to trade restrictions. Members of the coop must be the ultimate consumers. It appears that this statute may be for consumer coops only. The coop must be set up as a nonprofit corporation. Use of the word cooperative or coop is restricted. Investment in other organizations and membership in other organizations are allowed. An annual report must be filed with the Secretary of State, Montpelier, 05602. An annual membership meeting must be held.

Both individuals and organizations are allowed to be members of the coop. Shares are allowed to be subscribed but full payment must be received before shares may be issued. At least 51% of the incorporators must be state residents. One member, one vote is required. A 2/3 vote of the members voting and a 2/3 vote of the directors is required to amend the articles. A majority vote of the entire membership is required to amend the bylaws. A 2/3 vote of the members voting is required to merge the coop with another.

General reserves are required: 10% of the net savings per year until at least 50% of the capital investment is reached. Patronage refunds are allowed. Dividends are restricted to no more than 6%.

The state income tax return is due March 15.

Virginia

Business activity is restricted to "agricultural, fishing, dairy, merchantile, merchandising, brokerage, manufacturing and mechanical purposes." Use of the word cooperative or coop is restricted. Investment in other organizations is limited to no more than 25% of the accumulated reserves.

Membership in the coop is restricted to individuals. Shares are allowed to be subscribes. A 2/3 vote of the members voting is required to amend the articles or the bylaws.

General reserves are required: 10% of the net savings per year until at least 30% of the capital investment is reached. Up to 5% of the savings is allowed to be used for educational purposes. Patronage refunds are allowed. Dividends are restricted to no more than 8%.

The state income tax return is due April 15.

Virgin Islands

Coops can conduct business for any legal purpose. Members of the coop must be the ultimate consumers. It appears that this statute may be for consumer coops only. The coop must be set up as a nonprofit corporation. Use of the word cooperative or coop is restricted. Investment in other organizations is limited to coops only and may not exceed 25% of the accumulated reserves. Membership in other orgnizations is allowed. An annual report must be filed with the secretary of state.

Both individuals and organizations are allowed to be members of the coop. Full payment must be received before shares can be issued. Transfer of shares between members is restricted. The coop is allowed to repurchase shares from members. One member, one vote is required for members who are individuals and allowed for members who are organizations.

General reserves are required: 10% of the net savings per year until at least 30% of the capital investment is reached. Savings are allowed to be used for educational purposes. Patronage refunds are allowed. Dividends are limited to no more than 5%.

Washington

Business activity is not restricted; coops may conduct business for any legal purpose. Investment is allowed in other coops only. Membership in other organizations is allowed. An annual report must be filed with the Secretary of State, Olympia, 98501.

Membership in the coop is restricted to individuals. Shares are allowed to be subscribed. At least 25% of the share must be sold before the coop can commence operation. The coop is allowed to repurchase shares from members. A majority vote of the entire membership is required to amend the articles.

General reserves are allowed. Patronage refunds are allowed. After one year, the coop is allowed to keep unclaimed patronage refunds.

Washington has no state income tax.

West Virginia

West Virginia has no general coop statute. West Virginia law provides only for agricultural, banking and housing cooperatives.

Wisconsin

Business activity is not restricted; coops may conduct business for any legal purpose. Use of the word cooperative or coop is restricted. An annual report must be filed with the Secretary of State, Madison, 53702. An annual membership meeting must be held.

Membership in the coop is restricted to individuals. Shares are allowed to be subscribed. One member, one vote is required. A 2/3 vote of the members voting is required to amend the articles and bylaws, to merge or to dissolve the coop.

General and specific reserves are allowed. Up to 5% of the savings is allowed to be used for educational purposes. Patronage refunds are allowed. The coop is allowed to keep unclaimed patronage refunds after six years. Dividends are limited to no more than 6%.

The state income tax return is due March 15.

Wyoming

Wyoming has no general coop statute. Wyoming law provides only for agricultural marketing cooperatives.

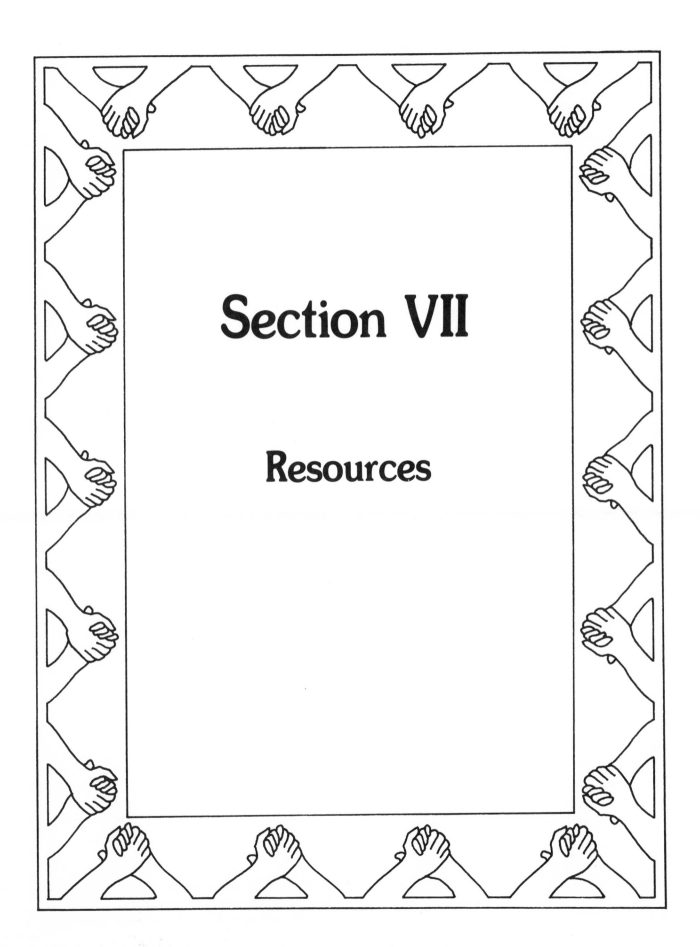

Section VII

Resources

Starting a food coop is not unlike attending an orgy. Neither requires any experience.
— William Ronco, author of **Food Coops**

RESOURCES

This is an encyclopedia/catalog/bibilography of useful books, pamphlets (many of them free), periodicals, government agencies, organizations, supplies and miscellaneous tidbits. We have included publishers' addresses but left off prices — they change too fast.

Publishers take books out of print without any warning. A book which is no longer available from the publisher may be in your local library. You might also try writing the author, care of the publisher, and ask where you can obtain a copy of the book; the author may have a couple hundred copies sitting in the garage.

We have read and evaluated as many publications as we could. But we have not seen all of the publications and have not dealt with all the organizations we list. We have reviewed those we've seen and we recommend those we like; the rest we just list for your information.

History and General Information

Dozens of books have been written on international and U.S. cooperative history. Most, however, are either very old and long out of print or published in other countries. Fine old books such as *The History of Co-Operation* by George Jacob Holyoake, published in 1906 in London by T. Fisher Unwin, *Introduction to the Cooperative Movement* by Andrew J. Kress, published in 1941 by Harper and Brothers, and *History of Cooperation* in the U.S. by H.B. Adams, published in 1888 by Johns Hopkins University Press might be in your library. We list a few recent publications below.

History of Work Cooperation in America: *Cooperatives, Cooperative Movements, Collectivity and Communalism from Early America to the Present* by John Curl (1980, published by Homeward Press, PO Box 2307, Berkeley, CA 94702). 58 pages, 1775 through 1980, with emphasis on the earliest days.

"The first Americans to practice collectivity, cooperation and communalism were of course Indian. Families typically included a number of related adults in the same household, sharing a common store of provisions and tools; groups of families were organized into larger cooperative units, and the collection of these made up the tribe. The concept of individual private property in land was unknown, and tools were commonly shared within the communal group."

"Contemporary labor unions have organized and supported food coops, housing complexes, credit unions and various service coops, but virtually no worker industrial cooperatives. Their attitude is mainly the long-standing AFL-CIO policy of opposing any clouding of the line between employer and employee, accepting basic employer-control of the workplace in exchange for contracts (and, for many bureaucrats, safe jobs in union hierarchies). They hold that any clouding of employee-management lines confuses their own role as bargaining agent and weakens the union, and they point to the many profit-sharing schemes that employers have offered their workers over the past century, which were geared to accomplish exactly that confusion and weakening of the unions."

American Cooperative Enterprise, Volume I, 1620-1920; Volume II, 1920-1945 by Joseph Knapp (Vol. I, 1969; Vol. II, 1973; published by Interstate Printers, 19 North Jackson Street, Danville, IL 61832). The focus of these volumes is on producer coops.

Co-ops, Communes & Collectives: Experiments in Social Change in the 1960's and 1970's. Edited by John Case and Rosemary C.R. Taylor. Published in 1979 by Panthenon Books, 201 East 50th Street, New York, NY 10022. This 311 page book is a well-researched collection of 11 essays (several are reprints of magazine articles) about community-oriented alternative organizations. Included are six case studies of actual 1960's enterprises: free health clinics, free schools, underground newspapers and radio, food coops, communal living situations and people's law. These are followed by five general articles about the coop movement and its multitudinous problems.

"It is not surprising that many of the new institutions failed, or that those still in existence have been forced into compromises. Nor is it surprising that their problems should be similar: that what plagues a food coop in Santa Barbara will also plague a free clinic in Chicago. The demands of democracy, for example, can conflict with getting the work done: you can't spend endless hours in meetings and still teach your students or get your newspaper out on time. Job sharing, job rotation, and egalitarian work relationships sometimes lead to ineffectiveness or inefficiency. Immediate practical goals — making the organization work, raising funds, and so forth — frequently conflict with the objectives of political reform. Most alternative organizations have found themselves caught in dilemmas like these every day, and have developed strategies to cope with them."

Democracy in the Workplace: Readings on the Implementation of Self-Management in America by the Ithica Work Group (1978, published by Strongforce, 2121 Decatur Place N.W., Washington D.C. 20008.)

Democracy At Work: A Guide to Workplace Ownership, Participation & Self-Management Experiments in the United States & Europe by Daniel Zwerdling (1978, published by Association for Self-Management, 1414 Spring Road N.W., Washington D.C. 20010). 191 pages, mostly case histories of large worker-controlled businesses.

Cooperatives At The Crossroads: The Potential For A Major New Economic And Social Role by Michael Schaaf (1977, published by Exploratory Project for Economic Alternatives, 2000 P Street N.W., Washington D.C. 20036). 145 pages discussing the origin and development of cooperatives, the coop movement today, some case histories and hopes for the future.

The U.S. Department of Agriculture publishes dozens of books and pamphlets on all aspects of cooperatives. The main emphasis is on farm coops but many of the publications are applicable to all types of coops. Most are free. Some of their titles:

How to Start a Cooperative; What Are Cooperatives?; Is There a Co-op in Your Future?; Guides to Cooperative Bookkeeping; Cooperative Development in Rural Areas; Cooperative Approach to Crafts. For a complete list, write the Agriculture Cooperative Service, Department of Agriculture, Washington D.C., 20250 and ask for a copy of **Farmer Cooperative Publications** (Cooperative Information Report #4).

A Guide to Cooperative Alternatives by Paul Freundlich, Chris Collins and Mikki Wenig (1979, published by Community Publications Cooperative, PO Box 426, Louisa, VA 23093) is an excellent resource directory. 182 pages of organizations, publications, funding sources, communities, networks and the like.

No Bosses Here: A Manual on Working Collectively (1976, published by Vocations for Social Change, 107 South Street, Boston MA 02111). 103 pages on starting and operating worker coops.

Food Coops

Food Co-ops for Small Groups by Tony Vellela. (1975, Workman Publishing, 231 East 51st Street, New York, NY 10022).

This is a fine book for people with zero experience who want to start a small food coop. It's very well written, thoughtful, non-technical and totally useful.

Part One, "First Steps", discusses getting together the first members, finding out what you want and need and what you should and shouldn't do at the start. The book includes a long section on the art and science of bulk food purchasing. Several sections cover day-to-day operations: how to handle distribution, how to share the work, different ways to handle food orders and money. The last section is about evaluating your coop and dealing with (and surviving) growing pains. There are several useful appendices.

"A small group of people who can work together to create and run a food coop must have a few things in common. They should all be willing to share responsibilities; they should have a preference for some of the same foods; they should be part of a similar economic situation. For these reasons, I recommend starting your group with people you already know."

"In the early period, I advise keeping the foods ordered at one time to no more than ten or twelve items. This increases the probability of garnering a wholesale quantity for each item, and also makes the learning of the whole coop process far less complicated for everyone. In the beginning, members must learn how to put theory (your group's agreed-upon money/-buying/work system) into actual practice (actually receiving food and paying money). Once this process is learned, new items can be added with little complication."

Food Co-ops: An Alternative to Shopping in Supermarkets by William Ronco (1974, Beacon Press, 25 Beacon Street, Boston MA 02108).

188 Pages of useful general information, much of it based on interviews with people in many different food coops. While *Food Co-ops for Small Groups* deals more with step-by-step instructions, this book deals more with people and how they work together. The two books are almost companions.

"All organizations, even loosely structured ones like food coops, are governed by forces that move them away from informality and decentralized power structures towards bureaucracy, patterned behavior, and centralization of authority...Creeping oligarchy may occur in food coops when volunteers don't show up for their designated work and some members take on added responsibilities. As "regulars" emerge, they take on more work, more responsibility, and more authority. Their experience and involvement gives them power..."

Nonprofit Food Stores: A Resource Manual, edited by William Ronco (1978, published by Strongforce, 2121 Decatur Place, N.W., Washington D.C. 20008). Case histories of four food coops. 65 pages.

The Food Co-op Handbook by the Co-op Handbook Collective (1976, published by Houghton-Mifflin, 1 Beacon Street. Boston MA 02107). 382 pages.

Consumer Food Cooperatives, edited by Ron Cotterill (1982, published by Interstate Printers, 19 North Jackson Street, Danville IL 61832).

CLUSA and **NASCO** (listed under "Organizations") both publish extensive literature on food cooperatives. **Associated Cooperatives Resource Center** (PO Box 4006, Richmond, CA 94804) publishes and distributes books and pamphlets about consumer coops; much of it is specific to California but still useful in other states. Write for their free catalogs.

Housing Coops

The National Association of Housing Cooperatives, 1012 14th Street N.W., Washington D.C. 20005, is a membership organization of housing coops and regional associations. Provides technical assistance and general information, publishes booklets, a monthly newsletter (**The Cooperative Housing Bulletin**) and a bibliography of books and pamphlets on cooperative housing.

Of The People, By The People, For The People: Cooperative Housing For Rural America by Jaime R. Bordenave (1979, published by the Rural Community Assisstance Corporation, 1900 K Street, #202, Sacramento CA 95814). 157 pages. Comprehensive and well written.

If your housing coop involves people living together communally, you might be interested in reading **Shared Houses, Shared Lives: The New Extended Families and How They Work** by Eric Ramey (1979, published by J.P. Tarcher, 9110 Sunset Boulevard, Los Angeles CA 90069).

Management Manual For Cooperative Houses by Max Kummerow is an 18 page pamphlet published by NASCO, Box 7293, Ann Arbor MI 48107.

Model Documents for Housing Cooperatives: A Primer for the Members of the Board of Directors in Housing Co-operatives, edited by Frank O. Myles (published by National Economic Development Law Project, 2150 Shattuck Avenue, Berkeley CA 94704). Model sale agreement, occupancy agreement, bylaws, articles, and membership application as well as other miscellaneous legal necessities.

Condominiums, Cooperative Apartments, and Homeowners Associations (publication 588) is free from any IRS office.

Neighborhoods: A Self-Help Sampler (1979, U.S. Department of Housing and Urban Development; for sale by the Superintendent of Documents, U.S. Government Printing Office, Washington D.C. 20402). 160 pages of case histories of organizing neighborhoods, rehabilitating housing and forming housing coops. Includes a good resource list.

Organizations

North American Students of Cooperation (NASCO), Box 7293, Ann Arbor MI 48107; 96 Gerard Street East, Toronto, Ontario, Canada M5B1G7. NASCO, founded in 1971, is a national organization of individuals and cooperatives providing information, training and technical assistance in all areas of cooperatives with special emphasis on consumer coops. NASCO publishes numerous booklets. Many of the books listed in this "Resource" section are also available from NASCO.

Cooperative League of the USA (CLUSA), 1828 L Street N.W., Washington D.C. 20036. CULSA is primarily a professional trade federation of large consumer coops, though membership is also open to individuals. Like NASCO, CLUSA sells its own publications and is an excellent source of other publishers' books and pamphlets.

Center for Community Economic Development, 639 Massachusetts Avenue, Cambridge MA 02139. Provides research and publications to cooperatives and other community-based economic development organizations.

Community Ownership Organizing Project, 349 62nd Street, Oakland CA 94618. Provides technical assistance and research on economic development projects with special emphasis on community and worker-owned enterprises.

Industrial Cooperative Association, 249 Elm Street, Somerville MA 02144. Assists in the creation and development of worker owned and controlled businesses, particularly in low-income communities. ICA also publishes literature on the subject of worker coops.

Association for Self-Management, 1414 Spring Road N.W., Washington D.C. 20010. A loose network of individuals and local chapters, they publish a newsletter and books and provide information on worker self management.

Exploratory Project on Economic Alternatives, 2000 P Street N.W., Washington D.C. 20036. Provides information and publications about consumer, producer and worker coops.

League for Economic Democracy, PO Box 1858, San Pedro CA 90733. Publishes a newsletter about worker self management.

Project Work, 490 Riverside Drive, New York, NY 10027. Information and advice for worker self-managed businesses in New York City.

Strongforce, 2121 Decatur Place N.W., Washington D.C. 20008. Technical assistance for worker coops in the D.C. area. They also publish a series of booklets and provide information to coops outside the area.

Workers Self Management Group, American Friends Service Community, 48 Inman Street, Cambridge MA 02139. Offers workshops, conferences and technical assistance to worker self-managed businesses in New England.

Movement For A New Society, 4722 Baltimore Avenue, Philadelphia PA 19143. A network of small groups "working nonviolently for fundamental social change" of which cooperatives are an integral part.

Vocations For Social Change, 107 South Street, Boston MA 02111. Publishes and distributes literature, operates workshops and maintains an extensive resource library.

New Ways to Work, 457 Kingsley Avenue, Palo Alto CA 94301. A non-profit work resource center offering support and technical assistance with emphasis on cooperative ownership, democratic management and self employment.

National Economic Development Law Center, 2150 Shattuck Avenue #300, Berkeley CA 94704. Information and resources.

Consumer Cooperative Alliance, 1828 L Street N.W., Washington D.C. 20036; and 7404 Woodward Avenue, Detroit MI 48202. A member controlled non-profit organization serving the U.S. and Canada. Offers education and training institutes.

Schools

New School For Democratic Management, 589 Howard Street, San Francisco CA 94105, (415) 543-7973.

The New School for Democratic Management was established in San Francisco in 1976. The school has two programs: the first provides basic business instruction designed specifically for smaller organizations, including coops, neighborhood clinics, senior citizens' organizations, CDC's, social service agencies and other such community-oriented enterprises. The second program focuses on building employee and union participation in the management of large, traditional organizations.

The Co-operative College of Canada, 141 105th Street W., Saskatoon, Sask., S7N 1N3.

Established in 1955 as an educational and training center for cooperative organizations. The school has an extensive mail lending library.

Magazines and Periodicals

Communities: Journal of Cooperative Living, Route 4, Box 246, Louisa VA 23093.

Working Papers For A New Society, 123 Mt. Auburn Street, Cambridge MA 01238.

Co-op Magazine, PO Box 7293, Ann Arbor MI 48107. This excellent magazine, published by NASCO, recently ceased publication but back issues are available.

In Business, PO Box 323, Emmaus PA 18049. This is primarily a small business magazine, a very good one, and occasionally runs articles about coops.

Cooperative News Service, 1828 L Street N.W., Washington D.C. 20036. Published by CLUSA.

Dollars & Sense, 324 Somerville Avenue, Somerville MA 02143. Focuses on analyzing the U.S. economy.

Self Management, 1414 Spring Road N.W., Washington D.C. 20010.

Volunteers

Volunteers National Center For Citizens Involvement, 1540 30th Street, Boulder, Colorado, sells books and provides information about volunteers.

Volunteer Handbook is available from U.S. Department of the Interior, Heritage Conservation & Recreation Service, Washington D.C.

Recruiting Low-Income Volunteers is available from National Center for Voluntary Action, 1785 Massachusetts Avenue N.W., Washington D.C.

Grants and Loans

Grants and loans are available from federal, state and local government agencies, from foundations, from non-profit organizations, from churches and charities, from large corporations. Organizations and literature abound which tell you how and where to obtain grants and loans.

Catalog of Federal Domestic Assistance, available from the Superintendent of Documents, U.S. Government Printing Office, Washington D.C. 20402, is a massive volume listing over 1,000 federal programs. It is published annually.

The Foundation Directory, published annually by Columbia University Press, 136 South Broadway, Irvington NY 10533, is the king of guides to foundation grants. It lists over 3,000 of the most important foundations in the country. Columbia University Press also publishes an annual **Foundation Grants Index** which lists 20,000 grants given in the U.S., which foundations are giving how much, for what and to whom. Over 500 pages.

The National Directory of Corporate Charity by Sam Sternberg, published by The Regional Young Adult Project, 944 Market Street, San Francisco CA 94102, lists corporations which give grants, how much they give, what their policies are, and who to write for information and grant applications.

Cultural Directory II: Federal Funds and Services for the Arts and Humanities, produced by the Federal Council on the Arts and Humanities, published (1980) by Smithsonian Institution Press, 1111 North Capitol Street, Washington D.C. 20560. Identifies more than 300 programs which support the arts and humanities, including information on grants and loans.

National Directory of Grants and Aid to Individuals in the Arts, published by Washington International Arts Letter, PO Box 9005, Washington D.C. 20035. Lists over 2,000 grants and other awards.

Funding Sources for Cultural Facilities lists 156 public and private sources of grants for arts facilities. Free from the Design Arts Program, National Endowment for the Arts, 2401 E Street N.W., Washington D.C. 20506.

Resource Guide for Rural Development, and **Private Funding for Rural Programs** list sources of grant money. Both are free from the National Rural Center, 1828 L Street N.W., Washington D.C. 20036.

The Cultural Directory, published by American Council for the Arts, 570 7th Avenue, New York NY 10018, is a guide to 250 federal programs which give grants to arts-related organizations.

Foundation News, a magazine published by the Council on Foundations Inc., 1828 L Street N.W., Washington D.C. 20036, reports on foundation activities.

Grantmanship Center, 1031 South Grand Avenue, Los Angeles CA 90015, offers information and training in the areas of fund raising and publishes **The Grantmanship Center News**.

The Foundation Center maintains four regional comprehensive libraries of information on foundations and other grant giving organizations. The four main libraries are open to the public and are located at 888 7th Avenue, New York, NY 10106; 1001 Connecticut Avenue N.W., Washington D.C. 20036; Kent H. Smith Library, 739 National City Bank Building, 629 Euclid, Cleveland OH 44114; 312 Sutter Street, San Francisco CA 94108.

"How to get a grant" is the subject of many books. Here are a few, in no particular order:

Getting Grants by Craig W. Smith and Eric W. Skjei (1981, published by Colophon, Harper & Row, 10 East 53rd Street, New York, NY 10022).

The Grants Game by Lawrence Lee (1981, published by Harbor Publishing, 1668 Lombard Street, San Francisco CA 94123).

The Bread Game published by Gilde Foundation, 330 Ellis Street, San Francisco CA 94102.

The Art of Winning Corporate Grants, The Art of Winning Foundation Grants, The Art of Winning Government Grants (three volumes) by Howard Hillman (published by Vanguard Press, 424 Madison Avenue, New York NY 10017).

Grants For The Arts by Virginia L. White (1980, published by Plenum Publishing, 227 West 17th Street, New York NY 10011).

Fund Raising: The Guide to Raising Money from Private Sources by Thomas Broce (1979, published by University of Oklahoma Press, 1005 Asp Avenue, Norman OK 73019).

The Grants Planner (1979, published by Public Management Institute, 333 Hayes Street, San Francisco CA 94102).

The Grass Roots Fundraising Book by Joan Flanagan (1977, published by The Youth Project, 1555 Connecticut Avenue, Washington D.C. 20036).

A Guide to Fundraising and Proposal Writing by Joan Kennedy (1975, published by Independent Community Consultants, Box 141, Hampton AR 71744).

The Seven Laws of Money, by Michael Phillips; Word Wheel/Random House, 1974. (Random House, 201 E. 50th Street, New York, NY 10022).

This book is an "underground" classic, unique in its ideas and its approach to finances. If money is a problem to you, if finances have got you down, *Seven Laws of Money* may just be the spark to pick you up.

"The First Law: Do It! Money Will Come When You Are Doing the Right Thing...The essential argument, plea, advice here is that if an idea is good enough, and the people involved want it badly enough, they'll begin to put their own personal energy and time into it, and the idea will soon be its own reward. Money itself cannot accomplish their goal; only the people themselves can accomplish it."

Six more laws: Money Has Its Own Rules; Money Is a Dream; Money Is a Nightmare; You Can Never Really Give Away Money; You Can Never Really Receive Money As a Gift; There Are Worlds Without Money.

"There are logical fallacies in all the Seven Laws. They cannot be arrived at by a 'logical' process. The Seven Laws deal with a part of man that is outside the realm of the typical body of Western thought."

Michael is not joking. The laws work. Bankers don't know everything.

Management and General Business

Good management is as important to a cooperative as it is to any other type of business. Good management is vital to the success of your coop. Just about every study made on small business failures blames over 90% of those failures on poor management.

We've seen dozens of books on business management, ranging in price from less than $2 to over $30. We found almost all of them are good. Price is no indication of quality.

The U.S. Small Business Administration publishes dozens of books and pamphlets that are about small business management. SBA publications are consistently among the best. Some are free; the ones for sale are inexpensive. For a complete list of SBA publications contact a local SBA office or write the Small Business Administration, P.O. Box 15434, Fort Worth, Texas 76119. Ask for forms SBA-115A and SBA-115B.

The Bank of America publishes a series of pamphlets called **The Small Business Reporter.** Several of them deal with various aspects of small business management. They are brief, well written and inexpensive. For a complete list, write the Bank of America, Department 3120, P.O. Box 37000, San Francisco, California 94137.

Financial Management in Co-operative Enterprises by A. Eric Rasmussen (1975, Co-operative College of Canada, Saskatoon, Saskatchewan, Canada S7N 1N3).

Any book about financial management is going to be slow reading and a little dry; this 180-page book is no exception. The tax laws are Canadian but the basic information is useful to coops in the United States as well. The book covers balance sheets, operating statements, cash flow, rate of return, raising capital and the cost of capital, budgeting, break even analysis, asset management and financial analysis. Financial management for coops is not much different than for conventional businesses, so any good book, on financial management will be useful to a coop. Still it is nice to find one with a cooperative slant.

"Investment projects in a cooperative may not always be valued in relation to their monetary return. It is often argued that cooperatives have as their main mission the accomplishment of objectives that are not directly measurable in dollars and cents; and, therefore, financial planning becomes secondary to planning in the social and service areas of a cooperative. It is true that a cooperative would not normally have as its prime objective the 'maximization of profit', but the efficient use of capital in a cooperative is mandatory if the cooperative is to compete with other types of business in achieving its objectives. It takes money to meet a payroll whether the business has as its prime objective the maximization of profit or the providing of goods and services at cost."

Cooperative Business Enterprise by Martin A. Abrahamsen (1976, McGraw Hill, 1221 Avenue of the Americas, New York City 10020).

This is a 490-page college textbook, one of the only textbooks about cooperatives ever published in the United States. The book defines coops, traces their history and evolution (both in the U.S. and overseas), discusses state and federal laws and taxation, covers in general and specific detail coop organization, membership, management, and financing. The book's main emphasis, however, is on agricultural coops.

"Cooperatives do not operate in isolation. They are part of the economic and social fabric of their community. Therefore, an evaluation of the general local economic and social conditions that have a bearing on the desirability of organizing a community cooperative should be the starting point of exploring cooperative opportunities...People considering the organization of a medical cooperative, for example, would want information on the present status of available medical services in the community, on what additional services are needed, and on the most realistic way to obtain such services. As to the last point, it might well be asked: is a cooperative the answer?

Small Time Operator: How to Start Your Own Small Business, Keep Your Books, Pay Your Taxes & Stay Out of Trouble, by Bernard Kamoroff (revised annually, Bell Springs Publishing, P.O. Box 640, Laytonville California 95454).

Small Time Operator is by Bernard Kamoroff, one of the authors of *We Own It*. The book includes chapters on the market, location, financing, licenses and permits, insurance, business name, bookkeeping, bank accounts, cash accounting versus accrual, credit sales, petty cash, calculators, financial management, hiring help, partnerships, incorporating, federal and state-by-state taxes, retirement deductions, operating losses, the IRS, balance sheets, filing, and 43 pages of blank ledgers and worksheets with step by step instructions for filling them out. Several chapters from *Small Time Operator* were exerpted in *We Own It*.

"Your choice of location will be one of the most important decisions you will make when going into business, so consider it carefully. Most people want to locate in their own neighborhood, but is it a good business area? How many people shop in your neighborhood? Is there adequate parking? Is there already a similar business in the area?

"Before you rent a storefront, find out why it's vacant in the first place. Try to locate the former tenant and ask him why he moved. Talk to other shopkeepers in the area and learn as much as you can about the area and its shoppers. A nearby supermarket or discount store is usually a plus because it will draw a lot of people to your area. Be wary if there are several unoccupied buildings for rent. Besides being a general sign of a poor business area, vacant buildings make poor neighbors — shoppers tend to stay away from them and from you. Spend a full day or two observing the area; a steady stream of pedestrians passing by your door is the biggest single help a little store can get.

"Before you sign a rental agreement, be sure the building is right for you. Is it large enough, or is it perhaps too large? Will it require extensive remodeling? Can you afford it? Can you get a suitable lease? Have the store examined by the local building inspector, and if you plan to serve food, by the health inspector. You don't want to learn after you've moved in that you must spend $300 to bring the toilet up to code."

Tax Choices in Organizing a Business, by the editorial staff of Commerce Clearing House, 4025 West Peterson Avenue, Chicago, Illinois 60646.

This 184-page book explains the different legal forms a business can take and the tax advantages and disadvantages of each, in much greater detail than we cover in *We Own It*. The book also discusses the tax consequences when money is withdrawn from a business and when part or all of a business is sold or liquidated. This is a law book and the information is at times quite technical, but it is not difficult to understand. Though the book does not deal specifically with cooperatives, the information is very useful. Commerce Clearing House is a highly respected publisher of legal and tax books.

"Taxpayers who decide to incorporate a going business should weigh the advantages and disadvantages of retaining some business assets individually or through a partnership. Retention of particular assets might preserve the benefits of particular depreciation methods, avoid problems that sometimes arise from a change of accounting method, or, under some circumstances, prevent acceleration of installment income. Accounts receivable and goodwill merit special consideration. From a corporation's point of view, renting a building or equipment may be preferable to direct ownership."

"Current distributions of partnership property are not always nontaxable events. If a distribution includes money, a partner realizes gain to the extent that the money exceeds the recipient's basis in his or her partnership interest. And the general rule that neither a partner nor partnership realizes gain or loss on distributions of partnership property other than money is subject to an exception for uneven distributions of unrealized receivables and substantially appreciated inventory items."

Honest Business by Michael Phillips and Salli Rasberry (1981, Random House, 201 East 50th Street, New York City 10022).

"Business should be fun...going slow is fundamental to business...being honest is a superior way to do business...being open about business is important, beneficial and necessary...too much capital is like too much food, it makes people lethargic...love of business is vital: you *have* to love business to put up with the trials it brings you."

Michael (who wrote *The Seven Laws Of Money*) and Salli don't just throw out these gems; they back them up with solid reasoning and real life examples. We agree with most everything they have to say, and we recommend this book highly.

Doing Your Own Legal Research

Legal advice is expensive. Lawyers charge high fees to pass on the legal information they have researched, studied and assimilated. For cooperatives, who often need more legal advice than conventional small businesses and who often can least afford it, lawyers' fees are even higher than usual because most lawyers are not immediately familiar with federal and state coop laws and must take the time to research them. You are paying for time spent in a law library, pouring over documents in search of the right law or, too often with state laws, trying to determine if a state law even exists.

If you have the time and inclination, you can do your own legal research. Law schools and county, state and federal courthouses usually have extensive law libraries which are open to the public. Public and university libraries and city courthouses also have basic if not complete sets of law books. Law firms (if you are friends with a lawyer who will let you sit there and read) have their own libraries of legal books; the larger the firm, the bigger the library.

Peter Jan Honigsberg, one of the authors of *We Own It*, wrote **Gilbert's Legal Research** (1979, Harcourt Brace Jovanovich, 757 Third Avenue, New York City 10017). This 143 page book explains how to use a law library; where to find a case, statute or regulation; how to read and understand a case. The book defines legal terminology. It explains how to analyze the law once you have found it.

"Codes group together or "codify" the laws dealing with a specific subject. The laws on obtaining unemployment insurance would be in one section of the codes, the laws on setting up non-profit corporations in another section. Of course some laws will apply to more than one subject and so you will need to check in more than one place for a complete survey of the law affecting your problem.

"The federal laws are codified in a government published edition known as *United States Code*. Most people, however, use the commercially annotated editions, *United States Code Annotated* and *United States Code Service*. The annotated editions publish citations to cases which have interpreted or applied a particular act. This is important because one cannot always tell just by reading a statute precisely what it means or to whom it applies. One word or phrase can easily conjure up a wealth of possibilities...By checking to see how the statute has been interpreted through court decisions, you will be able to gauge the actual intent of the statute and sense how it would apply to your situation."

Another good book is **Legal Research: How to Find and Understand the Law** by Stephen Elias (1982, Nolo Press, 950 Parker Street, Berkeley, California 94710).

Employees

If you plan to hire employees or if you will be legal employees of your coop (if your coop is a corporation) you should obtain the following free government publications:

Circular E — Employer's Tax Guide (publication 15) from any IRS office.

All About OSHA, and **OSHA Handbook for Small Businesses**, from Occupational Safety and Health Administration, Department of Labor, Washington D.C. 20210.

Handy Reference Guide to the Fair Labor Standards Act (which is primarily about minimum wage), from the Department of Labor, Washington D.C. 20210.

Your state probably publishes a state guide for employers similar to the IRS's *Circular E*. Contact your state department of employment.

Partnerships

A comprehensive book specifically about partnerships is **The Partnership Book** by Denis Clifford and Ralph Warner (1981. National edition published by Addison-Wesley, Reading MA 01867. California edition, which is almost the exact same book, published by Nolo Press, 950 Parker Street, Berkeley CA 94710). Clifford and Warner are attorneys, partners (not in the same business) and experienced authors, and they have included in their 290 page book just about everything there is to know about partnerships. The book covers partnership agreements in great detail.

"A partnership cannot legally hold itself out to be a corporation. This means that you can't use Inc., Ltd., Corporation, Incorporated or Foundation after your name. However, terms that don't directly apply that you are incorporated, such as Company (Co.), Associates, Affiliates, Group and Organization are normally okay. As far as titles the partners take for themselves go, you are legally free to let your imagination run loose. You can call yourselves partners, managing partners, or Dukes or Barons for that matter. Denis's law firm has but three partners, all of whom are 'senior partners."

"A partner can loan, lease or rent property to the partnership. Loaning (etc.) property to a partnership can be particularly appropriate where one partner possesses an item that the partnership wants to use, for example, a valuable set of antique restaurant furniture, but does not want to donate it to the partnership and it's too expensive for the partnership to buy."

"Outgoing partners remain personally liable for all debts of the partnership incurred up to the time they leave. An incoming partner may or may not assume personal responsibility for those debts. Either way, this doesn't release the leaving partner from potential liability to existing creditors. If all the partners (including the new one) are broke, creditors of the old partnership can still come after the departed partner."

Tax Information on Partnerships (publication 541) is free from any IRS office.

Non-Profit Corporations

The California Non-Profit Corporation Handbook, by attorney Anthony Mancuso (1982, Nolo Press, 950 Parker Street, Berkeley, California 94710).

This is a comprehensive, well written 282-page book which we recommend highly to any coop interested in becoming a non-profit corporation. It covers, in great detail, all aspects of forming a non-profit corporation and includes step by step instructions for obtaining a federal tax exemption under IRS Code section 501(c)(3), sample articles and sample bylaws. This handbook is written primarily for Californians and includes the complete California law, but the federal information (a subustantial part of the book) is valid in all 50 states.

"This public charity category is most appropriate for groups which will rely primarily on grants from state, federal or local government agencies, or contributions from the general public for sources of support for their non-profit organization. Generally, an orgainization is a publicly supported one if it normally receives a substantial part of its support from a government unit *or* from the general public (e.g. *publicly* or *privately funded* museums, libraries, community centers to promote the arts). However, when you look at specific IRS requirements related to this support test, you will see that it can be difficult for some tax-exempt groups to meet. Why? Because, as we'll see, the "public support" definition often doesn't include sources of funds which many non-profit groups must rely on. The requirements of the "public support" support test are that: *Alternative A* — The organization must "normally" (the word has a special meaning which we discuss later in this section) receive at least 1/3 of its total support from government units, from contributions made directly or indirectly by the general public, or from a combination of these sources; **or** *Alternative B* — The organization must receive at least 1/10 of its support from the above mentioned sources *and* meet an "attraction of public support" requirement…"

A Financial & Accounting Guide for Nonprofit Organizations by Malvern J. Gross Jr. and William Warshauer Jr., partners in the accounting firm of Price Waterhouse (published by John Wiley & Sons, 605 Third Avenue, New York NY 10016). Written for both accountants and non-accountants.

Managing Non-Profit Organizations by Diane Borst and Patrick J. Montana (1977); and **Marketing in Nonprofit Organizations** by Patrick J. Montana (1978). Both published by AMACOM, 135 West 50th Street, New York NY 10020. Both of the 300-plus page books are aimed at larger organizations.

Internal Revenue Service Exempt Organizations Handbook (available from the IRS, Attention TX: D:F:RR, 1111 Constitution Avenue N.W., Washington D.C. 20224). This is the basic non-profit manual used by IRS agents and now available to the public through the Freedom of Information Act.

Three free tax publications available from any IRS office are **How to Apply for and Retain Exempt Status for Your Organization** (publication 557), **Tax**

Information for Private Foundations and Foundation Managers (publication 578), and **Tax on Unrelated Business Income of Exempt Organizations** (publication 598).

Arts Administration, a guide on setting up a non-profit arts organization is published by Lawyers for the Creative Arts, 111 North Wabash, Chicago. IL 60602.

Non-Profit Corporations, Organizations and Associations by Howard L. Oleck (1974, published by Prentice Hall, Englewood Cliffs NJ 07632). This is a comprehensive legal text, not designed for casual reading.

A book about insurance for non-profits, by Mary Lai, is available from the Consortium for Human Services, P.O. Box 1183, San Jose California 95108.

And Maybe You Can Be A Resource For Us

We have done our best to give you useful, accurate and up to date information about every aspect of cooperatives, both legal and personal, which we have been able to learn from our research, from talking to others and from our own first hand experience. Is there something important to you which we have not covered? Is there a new coop law in your state or some obscure federal regulation we failed to mention? Has your coop run into a problem we don't discuss in the book? If you will write us, care of Bell Springs Publishing, P.O. Box 640, Laytonville, California 95454, we will try to include it in a future edition of the book.

Thank you. We wish you success and happiness.

we thank you

The cooperation, help and encouragement we've received from so many people in researching and preparing *We Own It* has been the most rewarding part of our work.

David Thompson of the Coop Bank wrote the history chapter for us, provided information for the chapter on the Coop Bank, shared his extensive book and photo library and provided help and encouragement throughout the project.

Ann Evans, Coop Specialist with the California Department of Consumer Affairs, gave generously of her time, provided technical assistance and encouragement and, way back when, produced an excellent coop seminar which brought together many of the people who assisted in this project.

James Cunningham, a Seattle attorney, researched and organized the state-by-state laws and patiently explained the details to us.

Tony Mancuso, attorney and author of the excellent Nolo Press series of California corporation books, helped tremendously with the entire corporation section.

Andy Blasky and Sam Sternberg, early collaborators, helped get the book off the ground. Paul J. Paul, an independent insurance agent, and Mary Lai, a Berkeley California insurance broker specializing in non-profits, helped with the insurance chapter. Barry Waldman, an attorney, researched the government agencies for the chapter on financing. Janet Bramson and William Nelson of the SBA provided information about SBA loans. Vera Graves of the U.S. Department of Labor provided information about minimum wage laws. Carl Hedman of the University of Wisconsin explained the trials and tribulations of the Gordon Park Coop to us.

Special thanks to the people who gave so generously of their time and knowledge, and allowed us to interview them: Steve Hargraves and Terry Nemeth of Bookpeople; Bart Brodsky and Janet Geis of Open Education Exchange; Christopher Hale of Christopher Crooked Stitch Collective; Peter Solomon of the San Francisco Mime Troupe; Sahag Avedisian of the Cheeseboard Collective; Seph of the Country Mouse; Douglas Uranek (via letter) of the Good Day Market. Jerry Goldstein, publisher of *In Business* magazine, allowed us to reprint the interview with Peter Barnes of the Solar Center. James Mairs of W.W. Norton kindly provided the story of that company.

Special thanks also to the Homestead Exchange, the Swallow, Bookpeople and Mendocino Distribution Cooperative for allowing us to reprint their articles and bylaws.

Thanks to CLUSA, NASCO, the California Department of Consumer Affairs, the National Association of Housing Cooperatives, the National Consumer Cooperative Bank, Nolo Press and the other organizations, publishers, authors, magazines and newspapers whose publications were a great resource and from whom we borrowed a sentence here and a paragraph there.

Photos were provided by David Thompson, Jane Scherr, *In Business* magazine, Bart Brodsky, New York Times/Richard Faverty (South Bend Lathe), and the authors.

The cover illustration is by Eric Jungerman. The text illustrations are by Kitty Emerson. Book production by our good friends at the distributors — many thanks.

Peter would like to offer special thanks to the Swallow. Mr. Bear dedicates this book to Sharon, who took care of the Pose and kept the rest of the world going while the book was taking shape; she as much as anyone is responsible for the existence of *We Own It*.

INDEX

The companion to We Own It

Small Time Operator

How to Start Your Own Small Business, Keep Your Books, Pay Your Taxes & Stay Out of Trouble.

by Bernard Kamoroff C.P.A.

One of the most popular small business books of all time — over 100,000 copies sold — **Small Time Operator** is a step-by step guide to starting and successfully operating any small business.

Includes complete information about business location, bank loans, venture capital, business name, bank accounts, cash accounting versus accrual, bounced checks, extending credit, petty cash, calculators, financial analysis, cash flow, inventory control, LIFO versus FIFO, outside contractors and employees, calendar year versus fiscal year, tax calendar, deductible and non-deductible expenses, investment credit, self employment tax, retirement deductions, estimated taxes, tax losses, excise taxes, state-by-state tax laws, and more. The book includes a full year's set of ledgers and complete, simple bookkeeping instructions.

What the reviewers have to say about **Small Time Operator:**

"An extremely refreshing guide to starting and operating your own small business."
   — National Society of Public Accountants

"The best of the genre. A remarkable step by step manual that is a delight to read."
   —**Library Journal**, New York

"Particularly good on the basics of getting started."
   — American Library Association

"Mr. Kamoroff has done an amazing and praiseworthy job. No doubt about it: this is THE book to have if you want to become an entrepreneur."   — **Mother Earth News**

"The most successful book of its kind ever printed." — **Nolo News**

Small Time Operator is an 8½" x 11", 192 page paperback. Available at your local bookstore or direct from Bell Springs Publishing. To order the book, use the coupon on the opposite side of this page.

BELL SPRINGS PUBLISHING
P.O. Box 640, Laytonville, California 95454   W1

Please send me:

_____ copies of *We Own It* (paperback) @ $9.00 each

_____ copies of *Small Time Operator* (paperback) @ $8.95 each

Add $1.00 shipping to all orders. California residents add 6% sales tax.

Enclosed is my check or money order for $_____

Name _____

Address _____

City _____ State _____ Zip _____

BELL SPRINGS PUBLISHING
P.O. Box 640, Laytonville, California 95454   W1

Please send me:

_____ copies of *We Own It* (paperback) @ $9.00 each

_____ copies of *Small Time Operator* (paperback) @ $8.95 each

Add $1.00 shipping to all orders. California residents add 6% sales tax.

Enclosed is my check or money order for $_____

Name _____

Address _____

City _____ State _____ Zip _____